THE SPIRITUAL ODYSSEY
OF FREDA BEDI
ENGLAND, INDIA, BURMA, SIKKIM,
AND BEYOND

Edited by Nancy Simmons
Cover photo courtesy of the Bedi Family Archives
Design and layout: Kasia Skura

© 2018 Shang Shung Foundation
Published by Shang Shung Publications,
an imprint of the Shang Shung Foundation
Merigar
58031 Arcidosso (GR)
http://shop.shangshungfoundation.com

ISBN: 978-88-7834-160-9

THE SPIRITUAL ODYSSEY OF FREDA BEDI

ENGLAND, INDIA, BURMA, SIKKIM, AND BEYOND

Norma Levine

SHANG SHUNG PUBLICATIONS

CONTENTS

CHAPTER ONE A Conscious Death 11

CHAPTER TWO Girl from the North Country 31

CHAPTER THREE A Passage to India 69

CHAPTER FOUR Breakthrough in Burma 105

CHAPTER FIVE The Tibetans 133

CHAPTER SIX Meeting the Guru 169

CHAPTER SEVEN Freda Bedi In Her Own Words 199

CHAPTER EIGHT When The Iron Bird Flies 215

CHAPTER NINE Karmapa and the Gelongma 255

CHAPTER TEN Transmission of Dharma 289

Acknowledgments 317

Dharma Chakra Centre
Seat of H. H. The Gyalwa Karmapa
P.O. Rumtek - 737 135
East Sikkim, India

The XIIth Goshri Gyaltsabpa

Densa Palchen Chosling
Seat of H. E. The Goshri Gyaltsabpa
P.O. Ralang - 737 139
South Sikkim, India

Freda Bedi was one of the most important female disciples of the 16th Gyalwang Karmapa. Her life was one of dedication to the wellbeing of others, whether through politics, social work or religion. After taking part in the Indian independence movement and playing a prominent role in other social and political activities, she entered the path of Buddhism.

Freda Bedi was ordained as a Buddhist nun by the 16th Karmapa, who became her root guru. She received many teachings from the 16th Karmapa, and completed the retreats of Amitabha Buddha, Vajrayogini and many other practices at Rumtek. Under the 16th Karmapa's instruction, she taught English and comparative religion to the young tulkus at Rumtek. She also supported them in other ways, such as finding sponsors to provide financial support for their education and activities. I was one of those tulkus who benefited from her generous support.

She was one of the main figures who introduced Tibetan Buddhism to the West by introducing new Buddhist terminologies, establishing dharma centres, and supporting many prominent Rinpoches of Tibetan Buddhism.

Freda Bedi's life is an example of devotion to the dharma and commitment to social service. I am therefore very happy that Miss Norma Levine has written a book about her. I am sure that readers will learn many valuable lessons from her life.

The 12th Goshir Gyaltsabpa
Palchen Chosling Monastery

26-4-2017

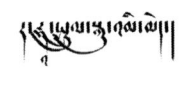

MARPA HOUSE
RECTORY LANE
ASHDON
ESSEX CB10 2HN

The Venerable Lama Chime Rinpoche

I recently read Norma Levine's book detailing the life of Freda Bedi. It was both incredibly fascinating and poignant. It contained many rich details about Freda's life, both from her time in England and India many of which I was not aware of previously.

I feel like I know so much of her former life now and before I only knew her as the Principal of the school in Dalhousie, which I attended. I remember her very fondly from my time there, having benefited from her generous support and the education and activities she helped provide to young tulkus.

I remember all the wonderful international volunteers who came to teach us there, too many to name, but they include one Tony Attenborough who I met in the early 1960's who I am still in touch with today. So life-long friends were created under her watch as well. Many others and I no doubt feel she played a very special part in our lives.

Freda was, in my humble opinion, a fantastic Buddhist and a very holy woman. As one of the influential people who helped to bring Tibetan Buddhism to the West she worked tirelessly to teach and find sponsors for the Tibetans to help them survive outside Tibet. Her kindness was without bounds.

She was also a devout disciple of the 16th Karmapa and as such she received many teachings, took retreats and was a shining example of the virtues of a Buddhist life.
I would say she embodied the very spirit of our teachings. I have the utmost respect for her and what she achieved during her lifetime.

I am very pleased that Miss Norma Levine, a respected journalist, has taken the time to chronicle Freda's life, so that its many lessons can be passed on through generations and help to keep the Tibetan story alive.

CHAPTER ONE
A Conscious Death

I met Freda Bedi not in her life but in her death. From the little I knew at the start, I imagined her an English memsahib, a vestige of the British Raj, a great organizer, a doer of good deeds, an Oxford-educated aristocrat. In photographs, she was to be seen always standing behind her guru, the great Sixteenth Karmapa, her large deep-set eyes glowing with tender devotion, her gaze showing no trace of a history that could have been any other. I saw her simply as a nun in maroon robes although on closer inspection, her face showed she had drunk deeply

His Holiness the Sixteenth Karmapa at Karme Choling 1974. Top row: far left, Sister Palmo; second from the right, John Gorman; far right Karl Springer. Original slide 1974, KCL Foundation *Courtesy of Shambhala Archives*

of a potent spiritual elixir. Nonetheless I thought of her only as a quiet presence in the eclectic entourage of monks, spiritual seekers, and hippies of the '60s who surrounded the Sixteenth Karmapa. Her death in 1977 had been barely noted in Buddhist circles.

But when her attendant Anila Pema Zangmo described the manner of her death, I had to reconsider my first impressions. Zangmo described her death as manifesting signs that indicated Freda Bedi had reached a high level of realization. Implausible as it seemed, Freda, the daughter of a watchmaker from Derbyshire, might have been a bodhisattva, a remarkable incarnation. Why had I never heard this? Such things seldom pass unnoticed in the Buddhist world where news of a conscious death usually travels far. As I delved deeper, I was intrigued by the mythic dimension of her life's journey and its conclusion amid signs of the miraculous.

◆ ◆ ◆

Anila Pema Zangmo was an unusually confident Tibetan nun. She had every reason to feel blessed by the Buddha in the spring of 1980 when I first met her at Sherabling, the monastic seat of Tai Situ Rinpoche where I lived for five years. The monastery spread like a fan on three ridges high in the Dhauladhar Mountain Range of the Kangra Valley, thirteen kilometers from where Freda Bedi had built a simple retreat house in the village of Andretta.

Pema Zangmo had been the lifelong attendant of the first Western woman to be ordained as a nun in the Vajrayana or Tibetan Buddhist tradition. After Freda's death in 1977, she had continued to develop Tilokpur, her nunnery, located on a site above the cave of Tilopa, an enlightened Indian master who had meditated there a thousand years before. Now here was Ani Zangmo, strong enough at the age of forty to manage the construction of a nuns' retreat center in a pine forest on the western slope of Sherabling.

CHAPTER ONE ❖ A Conscious Death

Pema Zangmo's karma had borne fruit of an unusual kind for a village girl from a simple family. Only the most fortunate see with their own eyes the fruition of a spiritual path or bear witness to the signs of attainment, as she claimed to have beheld.

Born to a Buddhist family in a remote village in Himachal Pradesh, at the age of twenty-five she paid homage to the lineage of enlightened masters in a year's retreat, completing 110,000 arduous full-length prostrations in one month at a back-breaking rate of 4,000 per day. Fortune led her, following a lama's advice, to Dalhousie in 1963, where Freda Bedi had started the Young Lamas' Home School and was helping Tibetan refugees. Although Ani Zangmo was not a refugee, her faith in the Buddha Dharma brought her into close contact with an especially courageous woman at the forefront of her time.

Freda Bedi was the first English woman to voluntarily enter prison as a freedom fighter under Mohandas Gandhi for Indian

His Holiness the Sixteenth Karmapa and Sister Palmo   *Courtesy of Shambhala Archives*

independence. She became a close friend of Nehru, the first Prime Minister and his only daughter Indira and was appointed Social Welfare Advisor as the Tibetans flooded the borders of India escaping from the Chinese in 1959.

On meeting the Sixteenth Karmapa, the renowned hierarch of the Karma Kagyu tradition, Freda embraced Tibetan Buddhism and became the Karmapa's chela or heart disciple.

In 1966 at the age of fifty-five she shifted her focus from worldly achievements and family life to take ordination as a Buddhist nun. The Karmapa gave her the name Karma Khechog Palmo but like all the Tibetans, he called her by the more familiar but respectful Mummy-la. In the same year he ordained Pema Zangmo on his visit to Freda Bedi's school for young lamas in Dalhousie. Ani Pema Zangmo was twenty-six.

Outwardly, Freda Bedi and Pema Zangmo seemed at opposite ends of the social and physical spectrum. Freda's aristocratic demeanor did not reveal the fact that her parents were simple English country folk nor that her Oxford education, significant as it was, resulted in a graduation with only a third class degree. She was elegant, fair, delicate but strong-minded; Anila Zangmo was robust, determined, and earthy in manner. What they both embodied with singular certainty was an intensity of faith and devotion to the spiritual path. And they shared a guru, the Karmapa.

Pema Zangmo became Sister Palmo's attendant, serving her with devotion day and night, both on her numerous retreats and outside of them. "Karmapa said to me, 'Look after Mummy. Looking after me and looking after Mummy are the same.'" On March 26, 1977, the night before the World Buddhist Conference was to begin, she attended Mummy-la on the last day of her life in their room at the Oberoi Hotel in Delhi. The miraculous signs she witnessed at Sister Palmo's passing marked Pema Zangmo's life forever, for one thing inspiring her

CHAPTER ONE ✤ A Conscious Death

to reach out to Westerners at Sherabling in contrast to the attitude of the suspicious elderly Tibetan monks.

I arrived at Sherabling two years after Freda's death. You had to be strong to survive there. In winter leopards came down from the mountains and snatched small dogs and calves. The summer heat brought out the reptile population. Gigantic lizards like small dinosaurs emerged from behind the thin exhausted trees to sun themselves on the rocks. Long thick muscular snakes slithered hastily out of sight at the sound of approaching footsteps. At night jackals prowled the forests, shrieking their relentless grief. The water supply dried up and we all suffered from dysentery. No cars, no paved roads, no phones, no taxis, no clean water, no ATM's, no taps, no flush toilets, no culinary variety. Under these primitive conditions six Westerners were building retreat houses.

The sloping site I chose for my construction was at the furthest end of the same hillside as Pema Zangmo's retreat hut, about a five-minute sprint on the topmost ridge. She walked unusually fast and came through the woods to arrive breathless at dusk after a full day in the bazaar procuring a consignment of black-market cement.

Barely had we exchanged greetings before she mentioned what was uppermost on her mind. In broken English she related the highlights of Freda's amazing story that emerged in bursts with every phrase an exclamation. "Mummy-la! Mummy-la! Holy Mother!" she intoned excitedly as if to invoke her presence. "She is very high incarnation. Karmapa said she is bodhisattva, White Tara emanation. All the lamas call her Mummy. She is like the sun shining. Everywhere is Dharma. People are all the same. She is real bodhisattva. Everything she gives away."

Anila hurriedly blurted out the story of a remarkable death. "When she die, her body get smaller and smaller and there are rainbows. I see it with my own eyes. Her death is very famous." I listened with surprise. No one else seemed to be aware of what Anila was telling me, that this Western woman who had led a full, active life, had shown signs of enlightenment at her death. Miraculous signs in after-death meditation shown by great lamas are made known immediately to inspire their disciples. Thus there was something about Anila's account that I felt did not quite ring true. My suspicion was confirmed when I asked Tai Situ Rinpoche about it; he was disinclined to commit himself as if the subject were taboo.

Sporadically over a few years at Sherabling and decades later at our meeting in Delhi, more fragments of Mummy-la's story, as narrated by Pema Zangmo, came to light. "The night she died," Anila continued, "I said 'Karmapa is far away.' She said, 'Not far away. He is always with me.' She said we needed the record of Karmapa chanting Lama Chenno, "Calling the Lama." We played the Lama Chenno tape of Jamgon Kongtrul and Karmapa. She said, 'My guru is always with me, not far away.'"

"That night she did Mahakala protector puja. I made some bread, she ate, and then we talked. She gave me some advice. She said, 'Tomorrow go to find some Lama.' She put her clothes away nicely. She was wearing her normal ani robes, no zen. She went into meditation. I didn't sleep properly. I heard her breathing heavily. When I went into her room she was sitting in meditation, but she was gone, still in meditation."

"Do you think she did Phowa," I asked, "transferred her consciousness?" If a highly advanced yogini practices Phowa at the time of death, the consciousness leaves the body through the crown chakra and she is liberated from karmic rebirth. Anila replied with certainty, "She was good at Phowa. Mummy-la did Phowa for a sponsor's husband who had died."

She continued,

CHAPTER ONE ✤ A CONSCIOUS DEATH

If person dies in hotel, people go to police station. Police came. They said, 'O Mahatma give me blessing.' They came and wanted to take her out but I didn't let them touch her. In the morning her children Kabir and Ranga went to their Uncle Binder's house (where the body had been moved). There she became smaller and smaller and rainbows coming. We keep her body three days. Her children put cold ice around her body. Ranga and Kabir called Karmapa. He told them what to do. 'Take her to Rumtek,' he said. Ranga said he didn't want to. Then we took her to the Oberoi farm for cremation. Many Buddhists came from different schools. Theravadin lamas took pictures of her body but they didn't come out.

One day at Sherabling, Anila gave me the true version of what she had actually witnessed written on a few small sheets of notebook paper. Later, in 1983 a greatly elaborated version was composed and published in an obscure Buddhist newsletter. A prayer was added and the broken English smoothed into coherent sentences. Clearly, someone other than Pema Zangmo had written it. The complete version was titled "The Last Days of Sister Palmo." It contained the same details that Pema Zangmo had imparted in our conversations, but included a retrospective view of events three months prior that were interpreted to indicate a premonition of death.

In early 1977 Sister Palmo consulted with the Karmapa before he left on his second tour of the West, and after completing a month-long retreat, she took a special initiation from Situ Rinpoche offering him in return a booklet with a hand-sewn cover. After another month-long retreat she left for Calcutta to write her life story at Ranga's house. "I have to do it now," she told Anila, "because I don't have time." She went with Anila to Bodhgaya where she meditated under the Bodhi tree every day for fifteen days, gave presents to the poor, and made offerings. At Sarnath she lit butter lamps and gave to the poor. She gave and gave: "I will make everyone happy. I live to make everyone happy, to make everyone shine."

She insisted on going to Rumtek, the monastery of the Sixteenth Karmapa, for one week to celebrate the New Year. There she continued giving: sweaters and money to the monks and gifts to the workers building her new retreat house. She pleaded with Anila to take a nun to help her after getting back to Rumtek and when Anila asked "Why, where are you going?" she replied, "You don't know. I know." She sorted out Anila's handbag, telling her what to keep and what to discard and predicted, "You'll miss Mummy." They went then to Bombay to be with her daughter Guli who was in hospital waiting for the delivery of her baby. Guli asked her mother to pray for a girl and a baby girl was born who apparently looked just like her grandmother.

Several decades after hearing Pema Zangmo's story, a serendipitous meeting with Freda's eldest son Ranga rekindled my interest and I began to piece together scraps of knowledge about her last days. I contacted a few of the witnesses I knew were present at the time of the World Buddhist Peace Conference in 1977. Kiran Lama, manager of the Daijokyo Temple Guesthouse in Bodhgaya was one; and Goodie Oberoi, wife of Biki Oberoi, owner of a five star hotel chain in the Delhi branch of which Freda had died, was another. Some fragments of Pema Zangmo's story began to find their place in the tapestry of that last day and a few did not.

As preparations for the World Buddhist Conference were underway at Vigyan Bhavan, Kiran Lama, a delegate from Calcutta, seeing "a tall, shaggy-haired, hippie type" in front of us, inquired: "Sir, who are you representing? Which country?" "None," he replied, "I am Freda Bedi's son, Kabir." We were so excited. He was the talk of the town in those days, a famous, successful movie star, what we would now call a celebrity. "My mother died last night," he announced very simply

CHAPTER ONE ❖ A CONSCIOUS DEATH

and left. Later on I conveyed this to the General Secretary of the Mahabodhi Society of India."

Goodie Oberoi, at the news of her best friend's death, had returned that day from Kashmir. Freda had introduced her to the Sixteenth Karmapa who became her guru. The love between the two women was like that of mother and daughter with Freda protecting and guiding her through the ups and downs of a turbulent marriage. "She was an absolute saint. She took care of everybody," said Goodie whose labyrinthine suite of white rooms with mirrored walls was next to Room 146 where Freda had passed away. Whenever Freda came to Delhi she would stay there and enjoy the comforts of a five star hotel.

Goodie recalled,

> She looked like she was in deep sleep. She was sitting in meditation when she died. When I came the day after, Anila had made her lie down with her hands crossed over her breast. She wasn't sick or anything. She died just like that in her meditation. She did the Phowa and liquid came out of her crown chakra. His Holiness said she was an emanation of White Tara.

The cremation took place at Goodie's farmhouse in South Delhi.

❖ ❖ ❖

The Karmapa was in the Yukon on his second world tour with his heart son Jamgon Kongtrul Rinpoche and two attendants. The sun was shining brightly in a clear sky on March 25, a full twelve hours behind Indian Standard Time, when they were told the news.

Dr Bob Clendenning, a devoted student, observed,

> Karmapa was in a car outside. Jamgon Kongtrul was standing beside me. Phuntsok, his attendant, came running out in a state

of shock, 'Sister Palmo has died.' All the monks and Jamgon Kongtrul were extremely upset. 'Oh no, Mommy-la,' said Jamgon Kongtrul, grief-stricken. His Holiness looked over at him and didn't miss a beat. '*Mitakpa*,' he said loudly, 'impermanence.' He was expressionless, no emotion evident. In his presence I felt there was nowhere else to go and nothing to be done. Everything is perfect as it is.

Rager Ossel, a Dutch disciple, remembered differently.

I was in a private room with His Holiness when his personal attendant came in and told him that Sister Palmo had died. His Holiness started to ask many questions about position and signs.

Achi Tsepel, the translator for Karmapa on that tour, recalled that His Holiness was not grief-stricken but rather pleased when he heard the signs indicating she was in *samadhi*. Ceremonies were conducted both at Rumtek Monastery in Sikkim, the seat of the Karmapa, and in Canada at the house of a wealthy sponsor Hanne Strong in Calgary.

Finally I found, tucked away in an issue of an obscure Dharma newsletter from 1983, a simple statement from Tai Situ Rinpoche saying that Freda Bedi was the first Western woman to attain enlightenment. It seemed a scant acknowledgment.

A few years after Sister Palmo's final meditation, the Sixteenth Karmapa became ill with cancer. He died in a hospital in Zion, Illinois on November 5, 1981 surrounded by his heart sons and doctors who witnessed the miraculous signs of his enlightenment. He remained in after-death meditation for three days, his body supple, with warmth around the heart. Tai Situ Rinpoche, his heart son, noted the perspiration on his brow, a sign that the meditation had been completed.

CHAPTER ONE ✦ A CONSCIOUS DEATH

The whole Buddhist world was ablaze with awe and wonder. Almost immediately after his passing, the Kagyu lineage went into a dark age. A controversy raged over the two candidates for the title of the Seventeenth Karmapa. The nine-hundred-year-old lineage of the Karmapas split. An invisible wall arose and no one from either side dared climb it.

Painting of Kabir Bedi by Umi Bedi, Ranga's wife *Courtesy of the Bedi family*

In the chaos and confusion of the conflict, Pema Zangmo left the nunnery at Sherabling and crossed over the invisible wall. As the main witness to Sister Palmo's final meditation, she left a blank page in the book. The history of Freda Bedi's key role in the transition of the Tibetan Buddhist lineage to the West had never been truly acknowledged. That was how it appeared to me when I met Ranga and Kabir, her sons.

In 2015, thirty-five years after I was first intrigued by the story of Freda's death, the unfathomable play of karmic coincidence brought me to the door of her eldest son Ranga Bedi in Bangalore. I thought I was just stopping by at his invitation on my way to Goa. A tall, dignified gentleman, later confessing to an implausible eighty years of age, opened the door onto a spacious, light room artfully decorated in warm hues with bold paintings.

One of them was of Ranga's famous Bollywood film star brother Kabir as a ten-year-old boy when he took novice monk's vows in Burma for a month. Ranga, the eldest of Freda's three children, had established a more conventional life as manager of a tea plantation in Assam.

Ranga and his radiant wife welcomed me as if we were old friends. It was clear they were the guardians of something intangible but precious. They escorted me graciously to the family shrine in a small room on the upper floor.

On the central inner panel of the intricately carved wooden edifice was a photo of Guru Nanak, founder of the Sikh religion, with his long thick white beard; a crucifix of Jesus was hanging next to it; and beside it in a niche of its own was a regal photo of the Sixteenth Karmapa, the Dharma King. Beneath it were placed two clay stupas containing Freda's ashes and a bronze statue of the Tibetan deity, Padmapani. At the top of the shrine was a statue of the Four-Armed Chenrezig, buddha of compassion, underneath which were images of the Buddha, Tara, and Guru Rinpoche. The lowest shelf had Freda's

CHAPTER ONE ❖ A Conscious Death

Ranga Bedi family shrine *Courtesy of the Bedi Family Archives*

Ranga Bedi family shrine *Courtesy of the Bedi Family Archives*

bells, a gold-embossed prayer wheel, butter lamps, a bronze gong, and vases adorned with peacock feathers, all untouched as if waiting for the right moment to come back to life.

On another table were pechas, the horizontally long Tibetan scriptural texts in their traditional form wrapped in faded cotton, containing Buddhist meditations. The texts were placed on either side of a framed tribute picturing three Indian women, hands clasped at the heart in prayer. Written in red ink and signed by Indira Gandhi, the tribute read:

To Sister Palmo

In this International Women's Year,
the Women of India recall your service to India
and present this to you as a token of their gratitude.

CHAPTER ONE ❖ A CONSCIOUS DEATH

The Holy Koran, Ranga Bedi family shrine *Courtesy of the Bedi Family Archives*

Inscription in the Koran reads "To Oggee, my better Self, on Gandhi Jayanti, '48, Bedi,"
Ranga Bedi family shrine *Courtesy of the Bedi Family Archives*

On a small table was a large black book wrapped in red containing the Koran. The shrine showed all the faiths as respected equally: Christian, Buddhist, Moslem, Sikh, and was above all a memorial to the humanitarian service Freda bestowed on her beloved Mother India.

The next morning after a non-Indian breakfast of sprouts and watermelon juice, Ranga spoke at length about his mother's last days:

> She came to Delhi for the World Buddhist Conference a few days before it started, staying at the Oberoi, thanks to Goodie Oberoi. Russian monks were there for the first time. The evening before the inauguration of the conference, she called a meeting of the Tibetan friendship group (the secretary, the treasurer, and two or three members who were in Delhi) at about five pm. At the meeting she passed on signing powers for all checks to a member of the group and completely divested herself of the financial responsibilities of the group. The meeting concluded about seven pm. She had her light meal and went to bed.
>
> Ani Pema Zangmo was in the same room. Hearing her hiccup a few times, she put on the light. She found Mummy sitting up in bed cross-legged and gave her some water to drink. Then Freda closed her eyes and passed away in the sitting position. She remained in the sitting position. After Goodie had been informed, the doctors arrived. They were there twenty minutes after she had died, so they saw that she was in the sitting position. Anila wasn't the sole witness to that but she was the only one who witnessed the exact moment of her death. Pema had fought them off saying she was in samadhi, "Don't touch her." Pema would not allow them to inject anything into her body to preserve it, no embalming fluid or anything else.
>
> Kabir and I received the news in the middle of the night and arrived in Delhi the next morning by about ten am. I came

CHAPTER ONE ✤ A Conscious Death

from Calcutta, Kabir from Bombay, and we arrived at the same time. He went straight from the airport to our Uncle Binder's house in Nizamuddin where her body had been transferred that morning. A stream of monks came to pay their respects. Mrs. Gandhi and her two sons were present. She was lying in one room on the floor. The expression on her face was totally serene as though she were asleep on her back.

It was March 27 and Delhi was quite warm, thirty-five or thirty-six degrees. We put slabs of ice around her body. His Holiness the Karmapa was contacted in Canada and he said, 'Take her body to Rumtek.' Already more than thirty hours had passed. Kabir and I looked at each other and said, 'By the time we get a booking, change flights in Siliguri....take her up the hill.... We agreed it wasn't possible to wait that long with changing flights and so forth. We didn't want to see her in rigor mortis and decided we would go through with the funeral the following morning. Goodie had said she would be cremated at the farm and made all the arrangements.

That evening a Rinpoche from the Ladakh Buddha Vihara came with a few monks and said you cannot cremate her in under three days. We were shocked and kept her body in Nizamuddin. We had decided not to take her to Rumtek because of rigor mortis and then we thought rigor mortis will set in here. The funeral occurred at the farm on the fourth day after her passing.

The World Buddhist Conference was supposed to start at nine am and it was postponed until two pm because of her funeral. All the delegates from the Conference came. Monks from Cambodia, Vietnam, Burma, and Mongolia. Buses were arranged to travel to Goodie's farm. Over a thousand people were at the farm in an area bigger than a football field.

> There was no rigor mortis and on the fourth day when the van arrived to take her to the funeral site, and we had to pick her up off the floor, her neck was totally loose, her arms were supple, there was no stiffness anywhere and not a trace of rigor mortis. She was so supple that we had to support her head with a pillow, and even on the funeral pyre the body was floppy. She was put on the wood fire and when the pyre was lit, she had white sweat on her brow which also was white. Goodie had a stupa built there which was open on all sides with various things placed inside. Our family kept some of the ashes.
>
> Had we followed His Holiness the Karmapa's instructions, we would have taken the body to Rumtek in accordance with his wishes. He knew the body would not get rigor mortis. If only we had known….

Freda Bedi's family had no preconceived ideas about what they had witnessed at her death. Without knowing it, Ranga had seen all the signs of *tukdam* or after-death meditation: the body was supple on the fourth day after her passing and white sweat appeared on her brow, a sign that the meditation was over.

As for the special signs that only Anila reported, such as rainbows and the body becoming smaller, both Ranga and Kabir agreed she had exaggerated.

> We knew Anila from the time she became Mummy's attendant. She could make up a story and sway either way. It used to annoy Mummy intensely, especially her political bickering. She seemed to have it in her genes. She even came up with the proposal that there was a reincarnation of Mummy [said Ranga with disbelief]. As far as the family is concerned, we would need endorsement from the highest in the realm to accept her incarnation,

CHAPTER ONE ❖ A Conscious Death

preferably both His Holiness the Dalai Lama and His Holiness. the Seventeenth Karmapa Ugyen Trinley Dorje.

Kabir added,

I heard the story of what Pema Zangmo said. I think religious mythmaking is a source of much of that. It is possible that certain manifestations occurred given who she was, but the extent that Pema Zangmo made out – ash, rainbows – I think there's some exaggeration. I saw a golden glow through the room, real gold. I saw it as well when my son Siddartha died. It was more intense with Mummy's passing. The room was dark, afternoon in an east-facing room. It was like gold lit up. The body seemed soft but cool.

Not to take away anything from Mummy's elevated state of spirituality, something did happen, but my sense is that Pema Zangmo is embroidering more than what occurred. Nobody will ever know. All we know is that a truly great spiritual being passed on.

When you talk of enlightenment as a state of realization, I cannot imagine what that means. In the immensity of it all what I can relate to is that an enlightened person would radiate a certain kind of energy, think in a certain way. Those aspects I saw in my mother. She became a very aware, radiant person. In these terms of what I imagine an enlightened person is, yes, that is what she was.

It was a beautiful cremation. Buddhist prayers were said, the monks were all there. I brought some of the ashes to Rumtek.

"We never treated her differently than as a mother," said Ranga in conclusion.

We didn't think there was anything special about her. When she became a nun we felt it was a novelty, particularly in my case. The family was brought up in such a manner that it was accepted. She would spend time with us in Assam; she went to Kabir and his wife in Bombay. When Guli was having a baby in Bombay, she was sitting outside the delivery room praying for the life of her infant granddaughter, waiting seventeen days for the baby to arrive because the umbilical cord was wrapped three times around her head, and only then she went to the World Buddhist Conference. She was a mother all the way through.

Thirty-five years after I first heard the story from Pema Zangmo, I saw that although she had exaggerated the details, she had told the truth in essence. The politics of reincarnation, so common in Tibetan Buddhism, had played its mythmaking part. All the major Hindi and English newspapers in India had carried her obituary.

Who was this lady who tread so lightly yet left an indelible footprint, obscured but not erased? The myths surrounding her death point to the epic journey of her life. Freda Bedi, Mommy-la, Sister Palmo, Gelongma Palmo, the stages that marked her life, propelled her onto a daunting ancient esoteric path whose goal was enlightenment.

Before I left his home, Ranga told me, "If you want to write a book about Mummy, the ball is in your court."

CHAPTER TWO
Girl from the North Country

Sometimes I wonder, for all the control I seem to have on the way my life shapes itself, if there is any such thing as "me" at all or if it was not blown away on the winds of Fate long ago.

The great divide between England's green and pleasant land and the dark satanic mills of the Industrial Revolution conjured in Blake's Jerusalem is a crooked line that traverses England from Bristol in the southeast to just below Hull in the northwest. Everything below that line is the south while above it, euphemistically called the North, are the major cities of Liverpool, Leeds, Birmingham, Nottingham, Manchester, Derby, and Newcastle. In broad terms, it is – with generous pockets of middle class prosperity and rural affluence – a demarcation between Britain's industrial heartland and the political establishment's wealth and influence centered in London and the so-called Home Counties surrounding it.

Derby where Freda Bedi was born is considered the North although its exact location is East Midlands. The heartland of the Industrial Revolution, it also held a special place in the history of the Labour movement as one of two seats gained in the general election of 1900 by the newly formed Labour Party. The first water-powered silk and cotton mills were created there during the Industrial Revolution. Later it was the birthplace of the Midlands Railway and became famous for the manufacture of Rolls Royce engines.

There was a romantic and cultural side to Derby, not only industrial mills, railways, and transport. In the mid-eighteenth century, the young pretender Bonnie Prince Charlie marched from Scotland with six thousand troops and took up residence in the town center at Exeter

Freda and her brother Jack *Courtesy of the Bedi Family Archives*

House on his way south to contest the British Crown. In the same period Charles Darwin's grandfather established the Derby Philosophical Society. It was also the birthplace of Florence Nightingale and in the twentieth century of the actor Alan Bates. To the north, Derbyshire stretches into the Peak District with gaunt granite ice age rocks, stark stone walls, close-cropped grass, and grazing sheep. It has a mysterious almost mystical quality unlike the pastoral landscape of southern England.

CHAPTER TWO ❖ Girl from the North Country

Francis Houlston   *Courtesy of the Bedi Family Archives*

Freda's Derby birthplace, Monk and Forman Streets   *(photo by the author)*

Wade House, Derby   *(photo by the author)*

It was snowing on February 5, 1911, the day Freda Houlston was born to parents Frank and Nellie. The location, Monk Street near Friary Lane, was a sign of the destiny that was to mark her entire life. The birth was so painless that the midwife commented that Nellie should have all the children in the world, such was her gift for childbirth.

CHAPTER TWO ❖ GIRL FROM THE NORTH COUNTRY

Brother Jack was born eighteen months later; both children had the Houlston's Nordic beauty. The family name was a derivation of Holstein – tall, blue-eyed ancestors from Denmark and Germany on the paternal side enlivened with a touch of French blood flowing through the maternal grandfather, adding zest to somber northern bones.

Her father Francis was a teetotaller, having vowed never to drink a drop of alcohol even if his life depended on it.

By no stretch of the imagination could the featureless two-storey brick box construction she was born in be mistaken for a cosy middle-class dwelling. The family was what was known as respectable working class. Francis Houlston, like his father before him, was a skilled watchmaker and jeweller, and the family lived above his workshop which occupied the ground floor.

From the street the building looks cramped and utilitarian as though assembled with no time for adornment while a clock whistled out the final seconds. A sign with a palm tree now proclaims it somewhat grandly a sun lounge or tanning salon, but the surrounding area has all the marks of an unemployed underclass. Wind whips empty plastic bags into the air in the car park across the road. A red-eyed youth reels unsteadily on the pavement as he targets me for spare change. His girlfriend pulls out a paper showing a hospital appointment and asks for bus fare. I know it is a ruse to get blind drunk but I empty my purse in honor of Freda's birthplace and to pay for my release.

Sometime around Jack's birth, the family moved to Littleover, at that time a separate village connected to Derby by a tramline, where Freda's maternal grandmother Hannah lived. It was a move up the social ladder. Hannah's husband, Grandfather Walker, a successful coal contractor in the Peak District, provided whatever signs of middle-class prosperity the family then showed.

Derby now encompasses Littleover but the area retains its village character with The White Swan, a well-established pub, an eleventh-century church called Saint Peter's, and tree-lined streets of semidetached houses, all with door knockers, neat gardens, clean recycling bins, and paved walkways.

Wade House on Wade Street where the Houlston family lived is a pleasant Victorian two-storey red brick dwelling with sitting room and kitchen on one floor and above it two bedrooms and a bathroom.

Freda's trunk of childhood memories retains an image of a dove grey and lilac carpet in the drawing room, copper plate engravings on the walls, a wireless radio contraption activated by a crystal 'cat's whisker,' a tea service, and exquisite Sheraton furniture inherited from her grandfather. Nonetheless, daily life was preindustrial with no household appliances: butter and eggs cooled in a larder, the grate in the fireplace baked the bread, toast came directly from the fire; water was heated over the fire, and clothes were washed in a copper pot. And they walked happily to the tram or bus.

Through the years, the house has retained a modest, comfortable anonymity, conforming to the requirements of lower middle-class respectability. The small garden in the back still has the laburnum and lilac trees that Freda coaxed into full bloom.

> We used to wait every year for the lilac tree to blossom outside the kitchen door with its exquisite perfume and chanted the old rhyme of "Laburnam's a lady and lilac's her lover." At the other end of the garden was a laburnam. Sure enough the lilac had faded, waiting so long for the laburnam to let down her golden hair.

At the age of eleven when her recovery from a serious bout of diphtheria faltered, the doctor recommended she move to a tent in the garden under the laburnam.

CHAPTER TWO ❖ GIRL FROM THE NORTH COUNTRY

As soon as I neared the laburnam with the pear tree showering its white blossoms over the wall I was on the way to recovery.

Beyond the village lay open meadows and country lanes where children could wander freely. Freda and her beloved brother Jack, innocent as Rackham's fairy children, wandered "over the hedges and the fields and meadows on the outskirts of Littleover, down The Hollow; and on the Mickleover side, collecting mushrooms and blackberries, which my mother turned into blackberry and apple jam; making daisy chains and wandering into the blue bell woods in those magic days of spring in England." Country butter in huge earthen bowls tasted on freshly baked bread was a childhood treat.

One late afternoon in 1916 Freda's childhood world went BOOM. "That's a bomb," said her mother, "and it must have fallen on Derby station." The sound rattled the cups as she was pouring tea in the tastefully furnished drawing room of Wade House. German zeppelins had bombed the town, killing five people.

Her father had been called up to serve in the Sherwood Foresters at the outbreak of war. While Nellie tended the shop in Derby, Grandmother Hannah cared lovingly for the children. Her exquisitely embroidered moire apron with forget-me-nots and roses left a lasting impression on Freda, her favorite grandchild. A few months before the end of the war on April 14, 1918 when Freda had just turned seven, Francis Houlston died of wounds suffered in the Battle of the Marne. He was buried in a nearby military cemetery in the north of France. Just before her Oxford years, Freda would visit his grave covered in climbing roses and catmint.

Freda cherished the memory of a deeply religious man whom she had barely known. "Father is something like a concept for me, very sacred. His death shadowed my whole childhood. The memorial service

World War One gravestone at St Peter's Church in Littleover *(photo by the author)*

CHAPTER TWO ✢ GIRL FROM THE NORTH COUNTRY

on Poppy Day November 11 used to open the wound again and I almost fainted when the service was held."

His name is carved on a headstone in the cemetery at Saint Peter's Church in Littleover, alongside those of thirty-seven of the town's young men.

Up to that time her mother Nellie had been a devout Christian, but from the moment she heard news of her husband's death in France, she renounced belief in a just God. In the depression that followed the loss of her beloved, her faith vanished and she never went to church again. "If God can take away a person as saintly as my husband, there is no God," she reasoned. The memory of "mother's breakdown" would remain with Freda forever.

Nellie became a liberal atheist, "not one of these religious people," Ranga commented. "They did religion when it was required as on Christmas day, like any normal person."

Although Nellie ceased to have genuine religious feelings, she conformed to the conventional attitude that her children should be raised in a good Christian way and sent them to church and Sunday School.

Her father's death had an equally profound effect on Freda's life. The word father became an abstraction and with a mother who had rejected the Christian Church, she was free to choose her belief system. "While Mummy always had great respect for the Church and what it stood for culturally and historically, she was searching all her life," said Kabir.

What she was searching for was a direct experience of God, "the sense of awe in the face of the divine." She found it when she took Holy Communion at the age of fourteen, but direct experience was not what the Church wanted to cultivate in sensitive young girls: fetes, meetings, services, but not spirituality. The minister warned her mother to keep an eye on her daughter.

Freda, however, went her own way, developing a strong spiritual life as a child. Every day before going to school she would enter the ancient stone chapel of St Peter's, kneel in front of the altar, and sit in silence for an hour.

Then she would emerge and go to school "just like any other perfectly normal kid," said Ranga. She found the mystical side of the Old

Nellie Houlston   *Courtesy of the Bedi Family Archives*

CHAPTER TWO ✤ Girl from the North Country

Chapel in St Peter's Church, Littleover   *(photo by the author)*

Testament particularly compelling. After confirmation in the Church of England she avidly read Cardinal Newman and the lives of the founders of the Anglo-Catholic movement and the lives of saints such as St Teresa.

> I found that all these saints had sought reality, the truth, and were not satisfied until they reached a direct intuition of the light, the life in the cosmos. The life story of St Teresa and the book of St John of the Cross were the books that influenced me.

Her hour of silent meditation nurtured her. "This busy life of a school girl going to school and studying for examinations used to trouble me a lot," she commented years later. "I felt I needed peace." She never told anybody about the subterranean life that was growing inside her while sitting quietly every day. Meditation was not a word in common use nor was there even a glimmer of Buddhism, but the seeds were already present and growth happened naturally. It was "... the childhood of a Christian child brought up in a Christian family."

Two years after her husband's death in the war, Nellie married Frank Swan, the youngest of ten who lived at the end of Wade Avenue in a Georgian house with three elderly spinster sisters. Freda remembered him as a kindly man, interested in attending the hunt, churchyard walks, and country pubs, but he was more like another child than a father figure. Life carried on more comfortably after the death of Grandmother Hannah provided an inheritance and they moved to Echoes, a newly built house on Chain Lane in Littleover with an inglenook fireplace, polished wood floors, and large windows opening onto the golf course where Nellie could indulge her passion for golf.

From there Freda could cycle or take the Keddleston tram to Parkfield Cedars, a girls' grammar school, named after the stately twin cedar trees that guarded the entrance to an architect-designed villa set in a six-acre garden. It was the best secondary school in the area, an elegant early nineteenth century house with a magnificent, intricately carved wooden staircase with its half-landing dominated by a huge stained glass window and an imposing carved stone and tile fireplace in the main reception room. Derby council bought it in 1917 and converted it into a successful girls' grammar school that continued until 1965 when it burned to the ground leaving only the twin cedars standing.

Freda loved the school. Every morning the head mistress, an austere Scotswoman, read from the Psalms and the Prophets with the light from the stained glass windows falling on her white hair, a painting of Botticelli's Annunciation behind her. Miss Glass, her French teacher, took a keen interest in improving her knowledge of French literature by lending books and bringing her to a high standard of fluency in the language. "All I learned in French which led me to Oxford was due to her." She had a photographic memory and excelled in her studies, becoming head prefect. Her family's class status climbed a few notches reaching the safety net of the educated middle class.

CHAPTER TWO ✤ Girl from the North Country

The chance for a bright young woman from the North without wealth or family connections to attend Oxford in the 1920s was statistically slight. Only a few girls from grammar schools were admitted to the most renowned universities. Oxford in the '20s and '30s was the preserve of the privately educated sons of the elite. However, there were four women's colleges, among them St Hugh's College established in 1886 by Elizabeth Wordsworth, great niece of the poet, initially for impoverished clergymen's daughters. Competition was keen. There were over one hundred applications for forty places each year. It was no easy task for a girl to win a place especially if she had no financial resources. The scholarships were £30 a year and the college fees were £50 a term.

A Quaker school friend Elsie Ludlow asked Freda to sit the preliminary exams with her for moral support. Three hundred girls were competing for twelve places that year. One day a letter arrived with an Oxford postmark addressed to Freda. She read it, barely able to absorb its contents, and put it into her pocket. Sitting near the door on the tram to school, she kept the letter tucked away safely while her teacher Miss Glass was seated at the back.

At the Park Cedars stop she took it out and showed it to her. Miss Glass's voice shook with emotion. It was a bursary for Oxford. Freda was the first girl from Parkfield Cedars to be accepted. Then something more unbelievable happened. She passed two further examinations and received both secondary and state scholarships, sufficient for an allowance of £33 a term pocket money. Her sojourn with a pen friend in northern France where she studied for a term at a lycée, had improved her French immeasurably and she romped through the entrance exam to Oxford. The railways paid her train fare, her mother, her clothes bill. Carrying her bicycle, she changed trains at Birmingham to the tiny Victorian line to Oxford. "Within weeks of my arrival in September 1929, I had been drawn into the life of St Hugh's." Her

St Hugh's College, Oxford, 2016   *(photo by the author)*

childhood was over. In retrospect, everything had been a preparation for admission to the hallowed walls of the ancient, most revered university in Christendom.

◆ ◆ ◆

St. Hugh's College is not one of "the dreaming spires of Oxford," the exquisite medieval stone cloisters with arches and delicately swirling lattice windows such as Magdalen, Christ, or Balliol for which the University is renowned.

It is an extended but well-proportioned late nineteenth century red brick manor house set in a remarkably spacious, superbly designed fourteen-acre garden outside the hub of the historical colleges.

The College became inexorably linked to the suffragette movement of the early part of the century when the militant activist Emily Wilding Davison, a St Hugh's graduate, was killed under the hooves of King George V's horse while staging a protest at the Derby. A framed poster from The Suffragette, dated Friday June 13, 1913, which hangs in the College library, imaginatively captures her heroic moment, in

CHAPTER TWO ❖ GIRL FROM THE NORTH COUNTRY

striking contrast to the strong solemn faces of the college's founding mothers displayed nearby.

Poster celebrating Emily Wilding Davison, St Hugh's College   *(photo by the author)*

THE SPIRITUAL ODYSSEY OF FREDA BEDI

Portrait of Aung San Suu Kyi, St Hugh's College, Oxford *(photo by the author)*

CHAPTER TWO ❖ GIRL FROM THE NORTH COUNTRY

It shows Davison with arms uplifted in a flurry of feathery wings rising in rapturous flight like a swan in pre-Raphaelite pose. The inscription in a band around her head reads:
Love that Overcometh
In Honour and in Loving Reverent Memory
of
Emily Wilding Davison
She died for women.
"Greater Love hath no man than that he lay down his life for his friends." Miss Davison who made a protest at the Derby against the denial of votes to women was knocked down by the King's horse and suffered terrible injuries of which she died on Tuesday, June 5th, 1913.

Davison was pinning a rosette on the King's horse when it reared and trampled her. Because she was a militant feminist, her accidental death turned her into a martyr in the fight for women's rights. The swan was the College emblem linked to St. Hugh of the Middle Ages, patron saint of swans, displayed in a sculpture on the stairwell outside the library with his hand resting on a swan.

Today the most celebrated St Hugh's graduate is Nobel Prize winner Aung San Suu Kyi who graduated with a PPE – Politics, Philosophy and Economics degree, in the '60s. An impressive, vibrant portrait of her dressed in a burnished red and gold sari, with a dangling red flower touching her chin, strikes the eye immediately in the entrance hall of the College. She is the epitome of self-sacrifice for one's country and her portrait bears no inscription.

"Suddenly locked doors opened," said Freda after her entrance to Oxford, "and I understood something about different religions and ways of thought. For a country girl, going to Oxford was a revelation. Her spiritual life changed when she realized that Christianity was not the final answer. She was now awakening to some of the leading thinkers and political movements of her time.

Freda Houlston as a schoolgirl   *Courtesy of the Bedi Family Archives*

CHAPTER TWO ✤ Girl from the North Country

During her three years at Oxford she had the opportunity to see and hear Mohandas Gandhi at the Oxford Union, H.G. Wells at the Communist October Club, and Arthur Koestler at the Labour Club. The flamboyant Rabindranath Tagore, India's ageing poet/guru gave the Hibbert Lectures in 1930. Albert Einstein spoke twice on the theory of relativity, once in German (which few understood but listened spellbound anyway) and once in English. C.S. Lewis lectured on medieval literature. "Fascinating" wrote a contemporary of Freda's, "a brilliant lecturer." There were lectures on Anglo-Saxon by Professor Tolkien and Rachmaninoff conducted concerts.

> It was a quiet little student who came up to St Hugh's College and wore the long exhibitioners' gowns to lectures. I joined every society, the League of Nations, the Ornithological Club and the YMCA, the Anthropological Club. I listened to Bach in College chapels. I went to Holy Communion. I went to Manchester College. I listened to Tagore and Dr Radha Krishna's magnificent lectures on eastern philosophy.

After the first year Freda realized that her initial choice of a degree in French which she spoke fluently would make her eligible for nothing more than a career teaching or lecturing.

> I passionately did not want to go back into the world of childhood that being a teacher meant. My eyes were on journalism, writing and interpreting that incredible international adult world that poured into magazines and newspapers.

She conjured working her way up from a cub reporter on the Derby Telegraph to Fleet Street. With the potent mixture of romance, spirituality, and ambition for an international life that was bubbling inside her, she switched to Modern Greats - Politics, Philosophy and Economics, a newly designed course, more relevant to her current ambitions. It marked another fateful turn in her life.

Her decision was influenced by Barbara Betts, later to become Barbara Castle, Labor Cabinet Minister, who was one of her close circle of lifelong friends, together with Olive Shapley who would go on to originate BBC Radio 4 Women's Hour and Olive Chandler, "a quiet little grey dove with very short hair who became a pillar of the Civil Service." She was Freda's good conscience who guided her when she became overly excited and gave her true friendship.

Nick Salt, Olive Shapley's son, remembers how his mother "talked to us when we were children about the time she went to Oxford in 1929 and met with Freda Houlston and Barbara Betts and how the three of them became close friends. What brought them together in Oxford was that they were, unlike the wealthy girls, from middle-class homes. Actually, my mother called herself lower middle-class."

Freda was unique in her own way, said Olive Shapley.

> She was strikingly beautiful and was sometimes referred to by other undergraduates as 'the Mona Lisa.' She was a romantic and an Anglo-Catholic and very interested in religion; I can remember her reading the lives of the saints and the mystics. By contrast Barbara was unmoved by religion and my own interest in it rapidly became replaced by politics. During the first walk that the three of us took together in the University parks, we were passing some poplars and Freda said, "How lovely they are without their leaves. The boughs look like the hair of some Botticelli angel." Barbara stopped dead in her tracks, looked at her and said, "My God, what a damnably silly thing to say. I hope you're not going to go on like this all the time."

CHAPTER TWO ✤ GIRL FROM THE NORTH COUNTRY

As different as they seemed, Freda admired Betts' political resolve, what she called "the sturdy atmosphere of the early pioneers of the labor movement." With roots firmly in the soil of the respectable working class of the north of England, Betts was as recognizable to her as family.

Barbara Castle's memoirs include a telling picture of Freda during the Oxford years. Having described the hilarious scrapes she had with Olive who was a natural rebel against the petty restrictions of college life, she turned her attention to Freda, the third member of the group.

> She was a dark, strikingly attractive girl who came from a modest middle-class family of whose conventional values Mrs Thatcher would have approved. She was not as light-hearted as Olive and I were, alternating between bursts of gaiety and moods of deep and almost somber seriousness.

For most undergraduates in the '30s Oxford was packed with exhilarating exploration but it was also leisurely. On Sunday evenings in May, singing in Magdalen Cloisters ushered in "almost a moment of holiness" wrote one undergraduate. The wisteria and magnolia were in bloom. Almost everyone cycled, even middle-aged and elderly ladies who cleverly managed open umbrellas and laden bicycle baskets with an air of complete imperturbability. It was a time for tasting everything and committing to nothing, from the radical October Club to the Conservative Club with dinner jackets and boutonniers. They attended debates in the Union where women were admitted only as guests, and evenings of films offered by the Maglis, the Indian society. They despaired that terms were too short for everything they wanted to see and hear: "We realized that nothing like these three years would ever come again."

Outside the bubble of University life, the entire decade was tumultuous. It was the era of the Spanish Civil War and the Great Depression. In the mid-1930s the Hunger Marchers from Jarrow in the north passed through Oxford on their three-hundred-mile protest march to Westminster. The students washed their feet and fed them. The College ran an annual Christmas party for children from the Oxford slums. Some students experienced their first contact en masse with the children of the poor and were shocked to see how the chronically underfed fell on the food with both hands and stuffed it into their pockets. When the children felt hot water running from the taps they stripped to the waist and washed themselves with joy and energy, using masses of hot water and soap.

The political situation was threatening with standoffs between supporters of Oswald Moseley and his British Union of Fascists and anti-Fascists. In these early days lectures on the rise of Nazism in Germany were heard by crowded audiences. The threat of war was hanging over the nation. The German Club included people who had escaped from Hitler and many believed war was bound to happen in the not too distant future. "We couldn't tell which of the nations would be aligned or who in that room would be talking to each other and who not," wrote one member of the Club.

At the famous King versus Country debate held at the Union, hooligans interrupted the young Socialist Michael Foot who was debating pro-country, and he looked on in helpless amazement while hefty young men burst into the chamber and tore out what they considered offending pages from the minute book.

Given the challenges of the time, St Hugh's College welcomed its undergraduates by allowing them to live there for all three years and to decorate their rooms to their own liking. Three buckets of coal per week at six pence each were allocated to heat the cozy coal fireplaces. Freda had a room of her own.

CHAPTER TWO ❖ Girl from the North Country

"What does one do at the University except talk," she commented. From nine o'clock to midnight Freda and her friends would gather over cups of cocoa and discuss everything from Socialism and Karl Marx to the family and birth control, taking time to delve into the intricate sense perceptions of Proust and explore the raw sexuality of D.H. Lawrence. Lady Chatterley's Lover had just been published and its explosive description of sexual love between the upper-class Constance and her gardener lover, a Derbyshire man who spoke the local dialect with his Lady, would be censored for thirty years in Britain. Like interracial marriage, sexual relationship between the classes was unheard of.

While Oxonions were leading a privileged intellectual life, the children in the slums of Derby were walking barefoot in the winter, so desperate was their poverty.

Our enjoyment of Oxford was a crown of roses through the years. The walks in parks, the crocuses, the delightful visits to Christchurch on May mornings, Shakespeare's A Midsummer Night's Dream accompanied by OUDS in the dew-filled meadows with the first fireflies of the evening. All the special things that Oxford means to so many people for us had an underlying theme, an underlying sense of guilt in face of the reality of economic conditions as they were. It is almost impossible for people to understand in these relatively prosperous post-World War II days, the kind of life that people did live at that time. The right was sharply divided from the left. It wanted things to go on as they were.

The idealism of our generation was the idealism of helping the underprivileged. If the labour club to which I belonged together with Barbara Castle, Tony Greenwood, Michael Foot, and others had any meaning it was a meaning of showing that we cared if people didn't have enough food and we did care if hunger marchers went from Reading to London. We cared if there were children in the slums with no shoes and the children hadn't good enough food.

Politics and spirituality suddenly merged when she encountered a fellow PPE student with whom she had a dramatic meeting of minds. She found her soulmate, as Castle described him. "She used to come with us occasionally to meetings of the Majlis, the mock parliament where Indian undergraduates launched themselves into rowdy and often disorderly debates." There she encountered the man who would radically change the course of her life. His name was Pyare Lal Bedi. He was a "quiet and rather stolid Sikh," reported Castle.

Their first meeting, marked by synchronicity, was outside a large lecture hall where both had come twenty minutes early. "Good morning," said Freda thinking to show openness toward the young Indian man reading a newspaper. "Good morning," he replied cursorily and returned to his newspaper. Later he remembered the beautiful, well-mannered young lady and realized he had been somewhat curt. He extended a written invitation to his room for tea. She was surprised but delighted and came with a chaperone. When the invitations continued, they dispensed with a chaperone and met alone for vegetarian lunches. Under Gandhi's influence Bedi had become a vegetarian six months before.

They soon formed a deep spiritual and political connection. Baba Pyare Lal Bedi was a direct descendant of Guru Nanak, founder of the Sikhs, a noble warrior caste, known and admired for their strength. He could trace his ancestry to Guru Nanak on the paternal side and on the maternal side his family were prime ministers of Kapurthala, a small state that forms a triangle with Amritsar and Jullundur. The Maharajahs of Kapurthala who were reputedly colorful characters had built a palace on the pattern of Versailles. At that point in his student life, Bedi was a Marxist and his Marxist creed moulded Freda's caring nature.

They befriended a leftist group of artists and intellectuals like Vidya Shankar who would become the right-hand man of Sardar Patel, the founding father of the Republic of India, and included the great political minds of that generation: Professor Lipsom, Professor Harlow, the famous Professor Harold Laski who came from the London School of Economics to teach a special student seminar on Karl Marx, and Professor Keir Hardie, the renowned constitutionalist. Her tutor at St Hugh's was Miss Headlam Morley, "a wonderful lively mind," who was to become professor of international relations. "Of pre-eminence, there was Professor Alfred Zimmern and his French wife who were the center of a whole group of international thinkers."

> It meant that we got Marxism not as political propaganda but in a deep way. We studied Hegel and the German philosophers. Our efforts to get literate in German, to speak and understand it were practical because we wanted to read Hegel in German. There were great people in communications, like Lakshman, the first director of Indian radio, and the journalist Frank Moraes were among our close friends. It was a very interesting generation. Somehow all this turmoil of the Indian freedom movement and the students who were dedicated to it, all these people entered my life in a natural way. I began to feel for India even while I was in Oxford.

Freda was swept off her feet by Bedi's political ideals, his Indian origins, and the gentle strength of his masculinity. Throughout his life Pyare Lal Bedi had the kind of charisma that attracts women. Freda bared her soul and showed him a drawing she had made when she was seven years old. He identified the unknown figure to be a buddha and

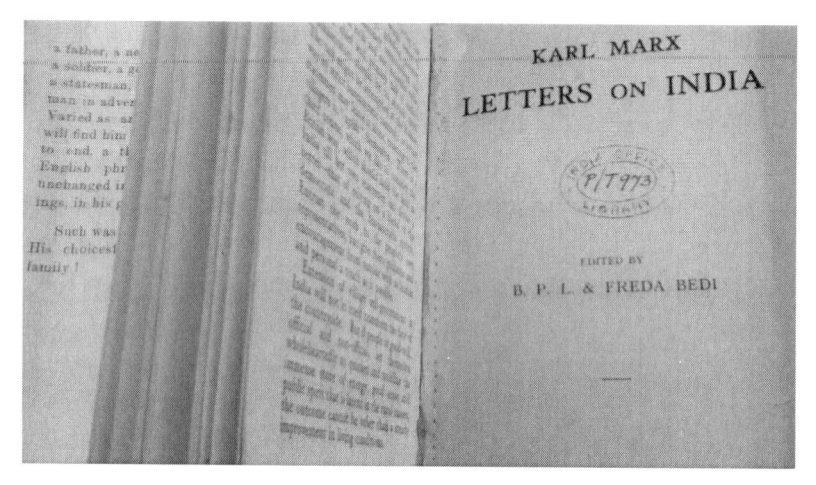

Karl Marx, Letters on India, edited by B.P.L and Freda Bedi, Contemporary India Publication, 1936 *Courtesy of the British Library, London (photo by the author)*

recognized that the woman he adored had Buddhist past lives. She recognized her soul mate.

Said Kabir Bedi,

They were both inherently spiritual people from the start; that's what attracted them to each other. They both had a very compassionate, caring sensibility.

They decided to work together and started compiling and editing for publication Karl Marx's series of letters that he had written as the London correspondent of the New York Daily Tribune.

It would not be published until December 19, 1936 after they had left Oxford but it was a worthy project that had anchored their developing relationship.

Their relationship catalyzed a crisis. Freda and her friends took pride in flouting conventions. "They climbed out of the College at night, went walking by the river – things you were not supposed to do. All three of them were breaking rules and getting away with it," said Nick Salt.

Freda paid a heavy price. For all its admirable stance on women's rights, the College was Victorian with curfews, chaperones, and a fierce principal Miss Gwyer who exuded the impression that intellect and sex did not mix. Brothers were allowed to come to tea but of course the rule was stretched. Miss Gwyer, a dowager/countess figure, had the good sense to lace her irony with a generous dollop of wit while keeping the close watch of a boarding school headmistress on her girls. She admonished one resident, "Really Miss, I am inclined to think that if all the men you invite to tea were your brothers then your father must have been a rabbit."

When Freda went openly to Bedi's room in Hertford to work on the book with him, she was reported as if it were "a heinous offence," as Castle put it. The interracial relationship of two Oxford students was unprecedented. The result was that she was rusticated, that is, suspended for the remainder of the academic year as a punishment.

From her parents' home in Derby on the edge of fields two minutes from the golf course, Freda chatted like a schoolgirl ingénue with not a care in the world, setting down the minutiae of country life to Olive Chandler, with whom she continued to correspond for decades, about garden seeds ("Ever heard of godetia?"), walking the dog, the wonder of a fox coven, and the art of ploughing the fields. She blithely but solemnly announced, "I hereby warn you I am not likely to develop into a golf fiend these next fifty years." Toward the end of her suspension, she was "livid because I gained a pound and a half last week" and excited at the prospect of going up to London to buy an evening gown. Returning to St Hugh's, she continued to see Bedi, disregarding the rules. Even more shocking to the authorities, they became lovers.

While Barbara Betts was campaigning for sex education with a book called Planned Parenthood complete with explicit diagrams and invited a sex expert to talk at the Labour Club, Freda was making her discoveries in the time-honored way, by direct experience. However, her clandestine relationship weighed heavily on her mind and the pressure of their illicit affair made the lovers decide to marry which exacerbated the situation. Family, friends, and College authorities all had violent reactions to an interracial marriage.

Nick Salt heard about the uproar from his mother:

> I remember Olive saying that Freda decided to marry her boyfriend. Her College, her family and friends all tried to dissuade her. My mother and Barbara were completely backing Freda. According to my mother Freda had a breakdown and ended in a psychiatric hospital, the Warneford, in Oxford. Olive and Barbara went to the College authorities to plead Freda's case and they said this was a genuine thing, what right did they have to oppose it.

Freda's breakdown meant that she lost more time at St Hugh's. By Christmas 1932, six months before her marriage to Bedi, she had recovered enough to write to "Olive Cherub" that she was "getting along swimmingly" and was making herself a purple woolen frock with pearl grey collar and cuffs. "I've had a glorious chameleon bag for Christmas, also a grey neck scarf in that new chewed suede material, and Jack (her brother) has given me a shattering pair of grey silk kayser stockings. So I thought I might as well complete the picture." The only clue that she was about to make an imminent departure with Bedi for Berlin was her asking Olive in a postscript if she had a German picture calendar for 1933.

CHAPTER TWO ✥ GIRL FROM THE NORTH COUNTRY

Bedi's marriage proposal set the tone of their lifelong relationship. He admitted, "I have nothing to offer you, I am just a follower of Gandhi and you may have to wait outside jail walls. I have nothing to offer you except my love and this companionship." "Whatever it is," she replied, "let's share it together."

Freda broke the news to her mother of her decision to marry her secret lover while she was washing the pots in the kitchen. She reconstructed the scene many years later. She had a dental appointment just before the traumatic moment of telling her mother but she was so bottled up inside, the anaesthetic had no effect. The dentist could not remove her tooth.

Mother was very quiet. She said, 'I trust you and your judgment and I know you wouldn't marry a bad man. Do as you wish. I am only sorry you are leaving England.' Air travel was almost unknown. People went to the East and didn't come back for many years. I didn't return to England for fourteen years till the eve of Indian independence, so she was not wrong. That was because the whole of the Great War period came inbetween and there was no moving back and forth.

Whether she had blocked the truth with this statement or whether she simply decided to gloss over the tensions cannot be known. However, her decision to embrace an interracial marriage caused a deep rift within the family.

Said Kabir,

She talked fondly of her mother but there was tension between my father and her mother and my father wasn't happy about that, so his relation with her mother was always a little distant. It was a very controversial thing to do, (he agreed). A lot of people

B.P.L. and Freda Bedi, wedding photo, June 1933 *Courtesy of the Bedi Family Archives*

Freda Houlston, seated front row sixth from left, Oxford graduation class, BA Honors PPE 3rd class, 1933

wanted to beat up my father but he was a hammer thrower so nobody could mess with a man like that.

The day of their marriage in June 1933 it rained. "Don't worry," said her husband. "Rain is auspicious for an Indian bride." A wrinkled newspaper cutting shows a smiling, thick-moustached man in a dark suit holding an umbrella over the white-capped head of his young

CHAPTER TWO ❖ Girl from the North Country

bride who holds a small bouquet in her white-gloved hands. It was to be the last time Freda would wear English dress. From the moment she married she discarded Western clothing and began to wear either a sari or salwar and shirt.

The Oxford Registry Office was, said Freda, "an incredibly drab place, dark and pokey." The officiating registrar looked sour and pointedly refused to shake hands.

> Our marriage was very simple. After finishing school we called my mother and stepfather from Derby and my husband called his cousin, Kuldeep Bedi, to take part as witnesses in the Oxford registry office. After we had a breakfast party. We went back to BPL's home in North Oxford and we stayed there for a short time.

Freda's parents attended the marriage although they opposed it. Olive Shapley was the only friend from St Hugh's College.

Together with their marriage vows they pledged to fight for Indian independence and to make it their one and only aim. "There is no good or satisfaction in amassing money and possessions," Freda declared in a letter to Olive, "when people with any independent political opinions are liable at any minute to be either imprisoned or have their goods confiscated."

All three bright grammar school friends graduated with a third class degree, not with the coveted mark of great distinction, a first. Freda's tutorials showed that she studied hard, had a facility for clear thought, expressed herself well, and was strongly inclined toward political philosophy, but that she lacked background and needed to broaden her reading. Her essays were well-prepared but her views were "apt to be commonplace." One tutor remarked that she was not a "born philosopher." Another said, "Her essays have been real attempts to express her own views and although she still finds it difficult

ST. HUGH'S COLLEGE.

REPORT ON MISS Houlston

Trinity TERM, 1932

Miss Houlston has read widely and covered a large amount of ground in Political Organization. Her essays are always stimulating and intelligent but she sometimes allows her interest in the wider aspects of a question to lead her into too much generalization. She has got well ahead with her work this year and would I think benefit greatly from the more detailed study of a more specialized subject.

Please return to Miss A. Hatterni — Morly for
THE PRINCIPAL, St. Hugh's College.

Freda's University report   *Courtesy of Amanda Ingram, archivist, St Hugh's College, Oxford*

CHAPTER TWO ❖ GIRL FROM THE NORTH COUNTRY

ST. HUGH'S COLLEGE.

REPORT ON MISS Houlston

Hilary TERM, 1931

Up to the last fortnight of term, when her health broke down, Miss Houlston had done quite good work. Her essays were carefully prepared and clearly put, and she has a certain quickness of mind and power of argument, though there is at present little distinction about her work, and it promises a Second-class only.

D.C.Kei

Please return to Miss Rowe for
THE PRINCIPAL, St. Hugh's College.

(continued) Freda's University report *Courtesy of Amanda Ingram, archivist, St Hugh's College, Oxford*

to be critical, the fault is generally her own temerity. She should try to develop her own powers of discussion."

Miss Headlam Morley whom she admired for her wonderful lively mind was her principal tutor. In 1932 in one of her reports she wrote that, "her essays are always stimulating and intelligent but she sometimes allows her interest in the wider aspects of a question to lead her into too much generalization. She has got well ahead with her work this year and would, I think, benefit greatly from a more detailed study of a specialized subject."

Oxford was the making of her. The bright, thoroughly English schoolgirl acquired an extra layer to her personality. She earned her first outside the educational system as a rebel. She may have failed to be awarded even a second-class degree, but she did learn about racial bigotry. She experienced what it was like to stand alone, to disregard conventional views, and to follow her own path.

Freda's deeply romantic spirit found fulfilment with Pyare Lal Bedi in an archetypal union of soul mates. By overcoming all the obstacles that a revered establishment like Oxford could conjure, the couple triumphed over social prejudice and became deeply bonded. She then followed her tall dark man on a journey into the unknown in foreign lands.

> I have lived those classic words of Ruth, "Your people shall be my people" and we have added, "God is the same the world over: he is your God and my God.

Their first stop was Berlin where Bedi had secured a research post at the university. They took a circuitous route through France, Belgium, Germany, Czechoslovakia, and Austria and called it a honeymoon in the company of a friend from Kenya who had a car and wanted to journey through Europe. By the time they arrived in Berlin,

CHAPTER TWO ❖ GIRL FROM THE NORTH COUNTRY

Freda holding three-month-old Ranga on the veranda of their Berlin house, 1934

Freda was pregnant and they rented a charming cottage with a garden on the Potsdam side. She took lessons in Hindi from a professor at Berlin University together with two elderly ladies, one from the German aristocracy and the other the wife of a Nazi. "Both charming women," said Freda. "Politics never entered into it. We were just learning Hindi and something of Indian philosophy. Those twelve lessons I had in Hindi were the basis of my knowledge and I found them immensely useful when I came to India."

With no experience of babies and no relations to help, Freda relied on the parcels of beautiful baby clothes and saris sent by her mother-in-law, "a great matriarch and extraordinary woman" who also sent delicacies for her son. An eight-kilo parcel of dried dal cakes arrived which Bedi sampled in front of the customs to prove its contents.

Freda had a natural childbirth in a nursing home in Berlin that advocated minimal anaesthetic and no exercise. After a four-hour labor, "a delighted young father and mother were presented with Ranga[1] who seemed to me the most beautiful baby in all the world, a healthy child, with astoundingly beautiful eyelashes and rosy cheeks. We took a photo when he was six weeks old."

As long as political events did not affect their identity as leftists, they continued to live a normal daily life, shopping at Alexanderplatz for fruit and vegetables. When they offered their landlady Jaffa oranges, "she said, 'I don't eat Jewish oranges,' so I found out she was a Nazi." Freda added, somewhat naively, that this contretemps did not interfere in their daily life: "We didn't come up against anything like this, although the student houses were being dominated by Nazi representatives."

On August 1 Bedi put down the newspaper abruptly and told Freda that Hitler had just been made president of Germany. The Nazis had already begun to harass Indian students at the university. She started packing immediately for the train journey to Switzerland. They reached Geneva the next day where a friend gave them a flat to caretake for the summer.

Carrying the infant Ranga in her arms, the fair-skinned, blue-eyed girl from the North Country and her strong, dark protector set out for Bombay in September 1934, leaving the unimaginable horrors of Nazism in Europe and embracing Gandhi's noble Independence

---

1 He was named after Ranga Swami Iyengar, editor of the Hindu Madras, who had supported their controversial interracial student marriage.

CHAPTER TWO ✤ Girl from the North Country

movement against British imperialism. The voice of an English girl from the educated elite who claimed she loved her country but hated colonialism would ring loud and clear.

Freda would not set foot in Europe for another fourteen years when she would return to England with their second son Kabir in her arms. From the moment they arrived in India, their political activism nourished them emotionally. Although there was food on the table, they always hovered on the poverty line. The war had closed the seas, making travel by ship impossible.

Whether Freda passed at Oxford with a first or third class degree made no difference in the life she was destined to lead. In a country where accents define status and career, she spoke the Queen's English. Her once broad North Country accent now reverberated as the perfect cut glass enunciation of the British upper class. Her vowels had lengthened and her delivery was crisply pitched. She arrived in India with the label "Oxford-educated" and possessed the self-confidence of the establishment elite. It was enough to open all the doors that needed opening for the rest of her varied, unconventional life, those of the British establishment, the Indian bureaucracy, and the Tibetan spiritual aristocracy.

She walked into a foreign land with no fixed identity. Her life choices had been blown away by the winds of fate. She could be Ruth who adopted her husband's people, Constance Chatterley who broke through sexual barriers, or Emily Wilding Davison who sacrificed herself for a noble cause.

For Freda, the nobility of self-sacrifice rang true. It was not the end but the beginning of the path less-travelled. Along the way she used for the greater good all the contacts available to an Oxford graduate.

CHAPTER THREE
A Passage to India

When I left England, I carried one gown of the West with me, because I was already wearing the sari. It was my wedding dress. It lay in my luggage for six months, a glory of white leafy lace, until one day I missed it. It had been stolen.

A family photograph stained yellow with age shows a young, delightfully smiling girl in a sari with a gangly baby of four months in her arms, two men flanking her and a well-built attractive man with a pronounced moustache standing slightly apart.

On board ship to Bombay, India, 1934 with Chinese friends from Oxford   *Courtesy of the Bedi Family Archives*

They are on deck next to an inflatable lifesaver imprinted with the name of the shipping line, Verde Trieste. "The journey by boat was horrifying," said Freda. Their cabin was cramped, the beds uncomfortable. Each night she entered a nightmare world in the ship's kitchens looking for milk for her infant son. "Millions" of cockroaches came crawling out of the walls at her approach.

After three weeks at sea, they reached Bombay and saw as they came to land, the Gateway of India, a monumental arch towering eighty-five feet into the blue sky, constructed for the visit of King George V and Queen Mary in 1911 and completed in 1924. It was designed to glorify the British Raj and create an imperial entry for the viceroys' landings in India.

Their entry was anything but glorious. The Bedis' reputation as political radicals had preceded them and they were singled out by

"Gateway of India," 2016   *(photo by the author)*

CHAPTER THREE ❖ A PASSAGE TO INDIA

customs officials who conducted a thorough body search, even removing Ranga's diaper to see if messages had been hidden there. It was a hot sticky day and the search took a long time. Ranga began to wail and Freda longed for a good bed and a nice room.

With over one thousand miles to the Bedi family home, two days had passed before they had finally completed the train journey to Kapurthala in the Punjab. The homecoming that awaited them was imprinted so indelibly on Freda's memory that she recounted it decades later to His Holiness Sakya Trizin, head of the esteemed Tibetan Sakya School of Buddhism and family friend.

She was welcomed into the extended family presided over by her widowed mother-in-law of cousins, sisters, grandfather, uncles, and aunts in a traditional ritual, staged like a set piece of classical theater. They bathed her in waves of gratitude and love as if a long lost child were returning to her ancestral home. The most unusual thing about it was the way she fitted in.

It was late at night when they arrived and Freda's spirits were down. She felt ill and her white sari was stained from nursing Ranga. Even that was auspicious she later discovered, because it relieved the sisters who were terrified of meeting her. When she appeared wearing a dingy white sari, their fears disappeared.

They walked through a crowded bazaar and entering a doorway, climbed a flight of dark narrow stairs into a large room filled with light and decorated with elaborate scrolls and sculptures.

At the head of the stairs an affectionate aunt almost smothered us in jasmine garlands, a heap of piercing fragrance around our necks. My husband's mother, short but very dignified, came to meet us wearing the tunic, veil, and baggy trousers that the Punjab woman wears. He touched her feet with the traditional greeting of respect, and I copied him, feeling a little awkward, but all my shyness disappeared when she smiled at us both with tears in her eyes, and embraced us and the child as if she could not hold us close enough. An old servant Panditji who had brought up

Bedi family: uncle, father, and grandfather *Courtesy of the Bedi Family Archives*

CHAPTER THREE ❖ A Passage to India

my husband and his brother took Ranga in his arms who was crying, having been awakened by the unaccustomed noise late at night. He was carried by Panditji to a cradle in the bedroom and rocked to sleep.

The room was full of people and I felt quite dazed. A drum was being played somewhere in the background, and someone was singing. We were taken to the center of the room and sat down on a carpet in front of my mother-in-law. She placed a long scarlet muslin scarf over my shoulders, spreading the ends out on the floor in front of me, and various relatives and intimate friends of the family put on the cloth sugar baskets and rupees the usual offerings to a new bride. Blessings were given, and finally the sugar and rupees were tied up in bundles in the red cloth. We were quite unprepared for such a ceremonial welcome, and neither of us had given a thought to it.

As part of the ceremony they performed a dignified puja. The state band played trumpets outside the windows of the family haveli. All the delicacies had been cooked for her – pullao, curds made with vegetables, and sweets. Her sisters-in-law presented her with a silk cream-colored Punjabi dress embroidered in gold with a purple head covering. The grandfather, a venerable retired Chief Justice, gave her the traditional eleven rupees, the offering made when young brides are introduced in the house.

He was a grand old man, a pious figure of great dignity sitting cross-legged in spotless white cotton clothes. We were then taken up to the living room and welcomed very warmly by all the aunts and uncles and cousins of the family. The other visitors had melted away as we left the pillared room, but I could still hear the drum somewhere outside. Actually it never stopped until six in the morning. I could not speak to my husband's mother or to any of the women (the men, young and old, could all speak English) but there was unmistakable happiness in their eyes, and, strange though the whole surroundings were, I was moved by this coming "home." I was sure that even the most orthodox bride could not have been more sweetly and sympathetically received.

From the time her mother-in-law accepted her as her own daughter, "a very happy family life began," said Bedi. "It became an extremely united family."

Never once was I made to feel a stranger or an 'untouchable.' We all ate together, and I was taken spontaneously as a new and very interesting daughter of the family. From the first day, with many smiles and embraces, my mother-in-law, whom I had begun to look upon as my Indian mother, began teaching me with infinite patience to speak Punjabi. She presented me with a brilliant scarlet and blue sari embroidered in sequins, and the other aunts gave me the Punjabi dress, *salwar kameez* and gold-bordered *dupattas* to frame my face.

The Bedi family was unusually broad-minded and accepted his foreign wife together with their dangerous political ideals. The two Bedi brothers were like opposite sides of the same coin. As a high-ranking Indian Civil Service officer, Bedi's elder brother Trilochan Das had the professional duty to maintain the existing law and order of the British Raj. The brothers "were like a Bollywood film," said Kabir.

My uncle became a Sessions Judge and here was my father, the freedom fighter. My uncle was a Nationalist at heart and got

CHAPTER THREE ❖ A Passage to India

into great trouble for helping my father. He would lend him his car and my father would use it in a demonstration. My uncle came through three enquiries and emerged unscathed. They loved each other dearly and supported each other. My uncle was interested in people getting justice. He would wear his Indian clothes to court and in court he would wear his wigs and go back to his chambers, then change into his clothes and go back home.

Today Kabir lives in an apartment in Mumbhai's prime Bollywood area, Juhu Beach. We were settled comfortably into two sofas opposite each other in his apartment with views of the skyline. With its antique furniture, painted scrolls, an array of bronze busts, family photos, books, bottles of wine, a desk, it was not the sumptuous decor of a Bollywood celebrity, but the hideaway of a creative, engaged artist and intellectual. Freda recognized a marked philosophic streak in her second son. Now at the age of 70, he seemed deeply spiritual: he was at home in himself, composed, quiet inside and natural on the outside. "I believe I have always been spiritual," he reflected.

Kabir's paternal grandmother (Freda's mother-in-law) was born into an aristocratic Hindu family and given in marriage to a prominent Sikh family at the age of ten, although it was not until many years later that she bore two strong sons. Her husband died when she was still young and she fell on hard times. Yet she was defiant for her time, a rebel in her own way. She refused all proposals of marriage for her sons from wealthy parents, telling them, "My sons will choose their own brides when they are old enough to do so."

As it happened, Freda was the chosen one. It was as if she possessed the magic potion that the whole family was waiting for. Like Cinderella, her foot fit the slipper.

Kabir commented,

It's probably because she was English that our family accepted her. If Freda had come from Africa it would have been different. Mummy was also an exceptional person. I have encountered countless people who believed they had a special relationship with her. She had that capacity of focusing on you and taking in everything you stood for. She was very empathetic, in tune with the person's entire psychic being. You felt she cared for you and that you knew her.

The past suddenly came to life when Kabir narrated the family's mother-in-law story in a mesmerizingly deep, resonant voice.

Mummy was warmly welcomed into the house and given great respect. My grandmother was the matriarch of the family. There were stories of how when she entered her matrimonial home her father-in-law's sister made her life and that of her mother-in-law hell. In one apocalyptic scene my grandmother picked up a glowing log from the fire and hit the sister with it, seized the keys from the sister and said "I am in charge." So she was never an interfering mother- in- law.

For the first year, they lived as an extended family with Trilochan Das, his wife, Freda's mother-in-law Bhabooji, and her adopted son named Binder, the child of her deceased brother. Freda regarded the boy as her own child, the perfect playmate for Ranga. There were difficulties, Freda confessed, for someone used to independent living, but they all became accustomed to each other and grew close, and she quickly picked up Punjabi. Bhabooji became a fixture of her life. "The beautiful relationship between my husband's mother and myself has

CHAPTER THREE ✣ A PASSAGE TO INDIA

deepened and strengthened with time: we can talk together now and make jokes with each other, and we have weathered storms together too."

Like a perfect Indian bride, she truly became the daughter of her husband's family. Every morning she greeted Bhabooji by respectfully touching her feet. At her request, Freda promised never to eat beef and became vegetarian for the rest of her life.

One incident that she kept in her heart inspired her to serve her Indian mother.

> Two years after my arrival in India my mother came to see us. It was the day when she was leaving again for England. While saying goodbye to my mother-in-law, she cried and said," Tell her to look after you." The reply was: "Tell her she is my own daughter, as dear to me as my son," and they both cried together.

Wherever they moved, Bhabooji came with them – to a fine house with servants in Lahore, into thatched huts in Model Town, from villa to houseboat in Srinagar, and all over Delhi from a grungy flat in Karol Bagh to a well-appointed government apartment in Moti Bagh. There was even a period inbetween houses when they lived in elaborate tents in the Ashoka Vihara at Kutub Minar. Freda attended her until she passed away in 1958 at the age of seventy at the family home. "It was a beautiful peaceful end to a life that contained much suffering but brought us in the family circle much blessings," Freda wrote to Olive Chandler. "We were great friends. Her loving presence in the home like a great tree constantly there was a source of great joy to the children and to me."

◆ ◆ ◆

Freda in Lahore in the 1930s   *Courtesy of the Bedi Family Archives*

CHAPTER THREE ⚜ A Passage to India

When Freda's imagination took flight, she could conjure images of Lahore in the '30s in evocative scenes like those in the fabled romance of A Thousand and One Nights.

In the Shalimar Gardens the fountains played and women crowded the Colleges, but the Purdah Club still met in garden settings. In Dubbi Bazaar, history lived. Wizened craftsmen with embroidered caps fashioned marvels of beauty out of gold thread.

They lived in Model Town, the brainchild of Dewan Khem Chand who designed a co-operative modern housing estate. "It was a perfect place to live," said Freda, separated from the Lahore of the sahibs by a long dusty road that had all of Punjab in it: "donkeys, with potters on them, bearded walkers wearing checked lungi cloths, fantastically uncomfortable buses with their cargoes of good companions."

She lived partly in the world of her imagination and partly in the everyday world, feet firmly on the ground. They had to survive as a family and maintain their political principles as well in order to create the brave new world of independent India. Freda befriended some of the English foreign wives; her sisters-in-law provided her support group. "We had a fine villa, servants, and all commodities that life could offer," said Bedi. Soon after, in 1935, they joined the Punjab Socialist Party.

Freda was offered a position as Head of the English Department at Fateh Chand College for Women, where nationalism was approved and accepted. She lectured three hours a day, contributed articles to Contemporary India and The Tribune and became a book reviewer for All India Radio in Delhi. No propaganda was allowed, "but I manage to insert something." She disliked teaching, because the routine work was boring, but "I manage to make the girls a bit more radical."

Bedi, however, could not find work as an economics professor unless he renounced his nationalist ideals since these appointments were government supported. He turned instead to leftwing journalism and brought out a successful, outspoken journal called Monday Morning. They were both busy writing and lecturing on every subject imaginable from "Libraries as a Factor in Western Life," to "De Valera and What We Can Learn From Russia." In their free moments they organized publicity for a boot company. "So whatever else you can call life, you wouldn't call it empty or boring," Freda told Olive. Sometimes she didn't know if she was standing on her heels or her head.

> Life is one long work with rather less than more reward in the way of money but that is inevitable if you are living in an imperialist country and have the temerity to fight the government (the vast majority of paying jobs are government or toadying to the government) but our lives have a great joy in them... Being a Socialist in India is no joke... We all of us live on the edge of jail...

She was also living fully and sincerely the ideals of her generation. The leftist intellectual world of Oxford had formed her at a time when the intelligentsia believed Marxism to be a bulwark against Fascism. The Nationalist movement of India then impacted on this sacrosanct belief system.

Kabir explained,

> My parents were two Oxford graduates. They could have had the best jobs in town, but they lived for their ideals. Whether the cause was the freedom struggle or their religions or their family, it was an ideal. They might have been unworldly, but that's what they were. In this day and age it's hard to see people living entirely for their ideals.

CHAPTER THREE ❖ A Passage to India

After they built up a minimum income on which to live, they settled into the more serious goal of radicalizing the Sikh peasantry of the Punjab, instilling in them a spirit of rebellion. Freda became known both as a writer and a radical political speaker in student and worker unions. With her husband at her side pushing her onto the platform and with memories of the rousing student debates at Oxford, she overcame her fear of speaking to masses. When she recalled her activities, she added sotto voce, "I almost don't like to go back and think of it all again."

> The first meeting I was asked to speak at was an assemblage of students, young people, and nationalists in Lahore. When I got there I was almost petrified to find 24,000 people waiting who had a definite opinion about what you should and shouldn't listen to. If they didn't like the speaker they would beat the ground with sticks and soles of the feet and make a noise so that the speaker would have to get down. I decided the reason they didn't like a number of speakers was they couldn't hear them and the best thing would be to speak very loudly into the loudspeaker. So I stood on the platform like a martyr awaiting execution and I suddenly started speaking about the proctorial system in Oxford or something like that. ... I could still hear the shock that went through the 24,000 heads when this rather slight Western-looking person suddenly bellowed into the microphone out of sheer fright. I found I could go on speaking as I was not drummed out of existence by the sticks and feet. That established me as a speaker.

Gradually she travelled into the villages to help peasants fight for civil liberties. When she became the secretary of the Civil Liberties Union in the Punjab, she was called on to protect them against beatings by police officers who were in fact Indians working under the guidance of the British. The Punjab peasants became friends. She addressed hundreds of thousands in village meetings. "It's the truth," she said. "It became a way of life. I didn't particularly enjoy doing all this," she admitted. "I would have preferred sitting at home and having a more peaceful family life, but it was the way life was and I had no choice."

At the same time she loved it. Writing, speaking, and being heard by the Indian people gave her a sense of satisfaction. "I am happier here," she wrote to Olive, "for all the hardness of life from the point of view of Western amenities, than I ever was before. The more I see of India, the more I realize I was not built to live in the West. The kind of happiness I feel in an Indian bazaar I never felt in an English street."

She explored Indian village life where poverty was a way of life; people were living on one paise per day, "ground down by starvation and the money lender." With her finely- tuned poetic sensibility, she filtered unbearable suffering through reflections of the grandeur of nature, seeing at the same time "the wide Punjab plains, surrounded by grain fields with the Himalayas stretching covered in snow in an unbroken line... in the melting heat of a summer day, suspended, as it were, in the haze of hot air..."

In 1936 a second son was born, Tilak Zaheer, named after famous Indian nationalists. In spite of the astrologer's predictions of an outstandingly lucky destiny, he died unnecessarily four months later. A common summer diarrhea turned into a fatality in Freda's absence. She was shocked, then philosophical, "I see too much of life in all its forms not to believe that such troubles are all in a day's work." Bhabooji helped her survive the guilt she would carry for many years. "It really was a turning point in our lives and we decided in the life we had dedicated ourselves to, it wasn't fair to have children unless we could give them our whole-hearted attention and I didn't have to go out to

CHAPTER THREE ❖ A Passage to India

work to feed the family." They delayed having their second child until 1946, a year before Indian independence. Kabir was thus twelve years younger than Ranga.

"There wasn't much money around," said Kabir, "but there was an abundance of good will."

> It was an extraordinary time. I remember my father telling me that when Tilak was ill he went to the chemist and said, "I don't have money. I'll pay you later" and the chemist said, "Sahib, you are doing so much for us." Years later, in Delhi, my mother would take taxis and often taxi drivers said to her, "I won't charge you."[2]

In the late afternoon of a hot summer day in Lahore, Freda and BPL were awakened by their servants who, not wishing to disturb them, had kept their Socialist comrades outside waiting for some time in the blazing sun while sahib and memsahib were sleeping.

Simultaneously the Bedis awakened to a moment of truth – that their lifestyle did not suit their ideals. BPL had already given up his share in the family property, believing it was unprincipled to own land. In his memoirs he recalled

> ...in that moment, we took a dramatic decision to renounce that lugubrious way of living. Freda was the first with all her heart and the nobility of it, to make the suggestion. So the servants were said a goodbye, the villa was returned, the large number

---

2 By the early '60s Freda had earned the respect of the Choegyal of Sikkim. When she could not pay Kabir's entrance fee to attend St Stephen's College in Delhi, she advised her son to ask the Maharajah. Kabir said, "Your Highness, I need a little money, 10,000 rupees to pay for my college entrance fees. He said, 'Are you sure that's all you need?' I said, "Yes." He said, 'Are you sure you don't want more?' I said, "No thank you."

of books we had brought from England were donated to the library. With a few packages, we rented an acre of land in Model Town and built a hut made of bamboo and straw, keeping one servant with us.

"In India there are always too many servants because they are so cheap and inefficient," Freda remarked in a memsahib moment. Their cook lived with them for fifteen years beside the kitchen hut. A smaller hut next to it sheltered a buffalo with its adorable baby Clarabelle tethered to it.

Their political ideals had placed them so far from respectable middle-class society that it forced them to adopt a self-sufficient, alternative lifestyle. Bedi's Monday Morning "rag" went the way of all left-wing journalism, financial defeat; while Contemporary India went under due to the prohibitive price of paper. It meant Freda was the main breadwinner. Ranga's first childhood memories of home are thatched huts in agricultural fields. One room was a combined dining room, bedroom, sitting room; another hut was for Bhabooji and Binder.

> They started in that and they had to leave because they didn't have the money to pay the rent. Then we moved sixteen miles outside Lahore to a totally new block of straw huts. We never lived in a house. No electricity, no running water. That's how we lived. I used to study from kerosene lamps. Pump it and it gives more light. No fridges or anything else. That was childhood.

Moving to the border of Model Town under the trees and mustard fields meant they would live the simple life of the poor. On the other side of the border was an upper middle-class area of palatial bungalows. Freda confessed to Olive she dared not invite her mother to visit since she would have been too distressed to see her daughter living in rural poverty when she had so recently extricated herself from it.

For Freda it was not rural poverty but a source of inspiration. Like that of the romantic poets, her lyricism was quickened by her living in a natural setting. At Oxford she had likened the leafless boughs of poplar trees to the hair of Botticelli angels; now she sang in praise of the idyllic country life in rent-free reed huts with plastered mud floors.

She grew vegetables and tended the roses, on guard for the wild deer who enjoyed munching them; Bedi cared for the poultry and they ate the eggs; Ranga kept the two shepherd dogs, Punt and Snug. In the evenings they sat under the trees on string cots. "Those cool dawns and the evenings under the trees when I'm near the earth and countryside more than made up for living in a small house in the center of town."

Their home soon became known as a center for "seekers of the truth," artists, poets, writers, and revolutionary politicians. Bhavesh Sanyal, an illustrious artist, and Dr Raghvera, linguist, scholar, and Hindu nationalist were close companions on the path. Raghvera's home in Lahore was a safe house in which to hide from the British. Hafeez Jallundhri, later to become the poet laureate of Pakistan and the composer of the country's national anthem, was one of their circle. Their happiest hours were spent in art galleries and listening to the poets, she said.

> Babaji and I seemed to find our way into the circle of scholars and artists and spent hours and days discussing history and books and writing and looking at paintings. Those were the days of political overtones but we lived in the books and the colours and the folk life of the villages.

Irish playwright Norah Richards, early 1940s *Courtesy of the Bedi Family Archives*

A close friend and mentor during this period was the Irish playwright and activist Norah Richards who followed Gandhi's model of simple living and high thought.

"Both women were utopians," said Frank Miller, a Peace Corps volunteer who met Freda and Norah decades later when Norah was 90." Freda admired Norah's focus on living in harmony with nature which would now be called environmental sustainability.

> Norah had wanted to prove that one could live in the countryside Tolstoy fashion and needn't go to the town for intellectual life. She proved one could live in mud cottages with thatched roofs and plastered floors without mod cons and that one could make clean bathrooms with bamboo and buckets. She taught me a great deal. She was interested as I was in the simplicities and beauties of rural living and cooking and not using anything

CHAPTER THREE ❖ A Passage to India

except local products, earthen plates, and home spun cloth. Ours was a long friendship. When she passed away at 94 our friendship had ripened for over thirty years.

Most of the friends they attracted, however, were old revolutionaries. After serving time in jail, they came to the huts to recover, descending from the hills in the winter months "like migratory birds." There was the soft-spoken, bearded Balochi Gandhi wearing homespun cloth and many of the important Kashmiri leaders: in particular, Sheikh Abdullah who would become the first Prime Minister of Kashmir and Giani Zail Singh, another visitor, who would later become President of India. The General Secretary of the Communist Party turned up frequently, as did Balraj Sahni, a famous Bollywood actor. Presiding over it all was Baba Pyare Lal Bedi who took to wearing the traditional salwar and kurta with a shawl thrown over his shoulders, giving him the look of "a biblical figure."[3]

"The huts became a gathering spot for a lot of leftists," Kabir confirmed. Unsurprisingly they caught the attention of the police who pulled them off their bicycles and beat them. It was a test of their endurance and they bore it as part of the struggle.

Bedi was a Marxist from his Oxford days and when he returned to India, he established connections with the Communist Party of India based in Lahore. "I am not sure if my mother was active as a Marxist," said Ranga, "but she was with him as a Communist sympathizer." In the late '30s and early '40s the Communist Party and the Gandhians parted ways. Ranga explained:

> The Communist Party did not agree with Gandhi's passive resistance and felt the only way to get the British to leave India

---

3   Som Anand, "Portrait of a City," extract The Times, 1998

was revolution and this involved violence – blow the trains up – that attitude. At that point she severed all connections, even as a sympathizer with the Communist Party and became a Gandhian. She was a congresswoman. Whatever activity she took was as a Gandhian. As to Gandhi's launching of Satyagraha, the Communists would have countered that with saying, "It will not work, get on with the action."

Bedi was more radical, a nonviolent saboteur. In September 1938 he was addressing an anti-recruitment rally in the Punjab, an extremely politically sensitive issue due to the onset of World War II and the urgent need for Indian troops in the Allied Army. He was in the midst of a particularly provocative speech at a peasant conference when hirelings of the Punjab government broke up the meeting and in the commotion, a lathi stick landed on his head leaving him with a deep cut. He was arrested with twenty-seven other protesters on charges of rioting.

Kabir commented,

> My father didn't believe in violence. He was a rabble-rouser, arousing people to fight for independence, railway people to fight for their rights, but never violent. He was never a saboteur in the legal sense. The British would call him a saboteur because he was sabotaging the rule of the British Government, but he never resorted to violence.

He was set free on bail and the case was dismissed within months due to lack of evidence. A stalwart figure, he maintained a cheerful stoicism throughout.

◆ ◆ ◆

CHAPTER THREE ✣ A PASSAGE TO INDIA

The Kangra Valley holds like a hidden land the tiny village of Andretta where Norah Richards maintained her Woodlands estate. There she had established a community of craftsmen and artists in the mid-30s. Even the tourist guide waxes lyrical about the setting: "a perfect bowl surrounded by thick forests and bamboo groves of the Shivalik Hills on one side and the looming Dhauladhar on the other. Standing in its fields, you feel you are in the womb of creation — where nature itself conspires to create a gamut of colors and perspective."

Richards built a Kangra-style mud hut for herself, set up a proscenium stage for her theater, and invited artists and potters to create a settlement of simple dwellings. The village was known to the locals as the Memsahib Village although inspired by Gandhi. The foremost resident was the Sikh portrait painter Sardar Sobha Singh who lived in Andretta for thirty-one years.

Freda had discovered Andretta while out walking in the valley with a friend. She loved the landscape of the Kangra Valley, so unlike the hill stations with the wealthy notables at the mountain's top and the ordinary townspeople below.

I got to my spot by chance. It was in February that I paid it a visit and took with me a friend who had come from abroad. We got out of the small train at an even smaller station and threaded our way by paths across a new and attractive countryside. It was very green and a stream tumbled along below us. Blue flax flowers and yellow mustard mingled among the grass, and the wild pear was white with blossom – as white as the snows that were blossoming on the hillside above us. We didn't speak much as we walked along, following the sturdy man from the upper mountains who was carrying our bedding. By the time we arrived at our journey's end though, we all had shining eyes, and

Freda Bedi's restored Andretta cottage 2016   *(photo by the author)*

I think we were all saying to ourselves, "Here is a lovely homely place."

In 1938 Norah gave the Bedis a plot of land on the hillside and invited them to build a mud cottage with the warning not to bring their politics with them. Freda reassured her that they came to Andretta simply to rest. She boasted that the cottage they built had cost a total of £25, including furniture and labor.

With her many connections in politics and art, Freda fitted perfectly into the community of artists and intellectuals. She was not only a friend of Norah but also of Sardar Sobha Singha who would design the extraordinarily haunting cover of her book of political essays, Bengal Lamenting.

CHAPTER THREE ❖ A Passage to India

It became an idyllic hideaway from the politics of Lahore for the Bedis. They celebrated all the religious festivals of India but the Kangra Valley was where they loved to usher in Christmas, even planting a pine tree transported by a coolie from the forests in Kulu directly into the mud floor of their beloved Kangra cottage. Local children came and sang Hari Om, ate almond halva, and felt the Christmas spirit.

We were standing on the fringe of that circle of light - the poet who saw Christmas for the first time, the young wife who saw it for the first time in India, we two, hand in hand, illumined for a moment by those clouds of glory and that ageless spirit of childhood.

After a few years of makeshift Christmas trees of baby cypresses, Freda was longing to recapture her lost life as an English girl. For all her love of India, Christmas made her homesick for England. She felt like hanging holly and hearing Bach in New College Chapel. Both were as far away, she said, as the mountains of the moon. "War makes familiar things remote. It's only peace that can give them back to us." The war stretched between her and the country of her birth.

The outbreak of World War II brought Freda to a significant moment in her ambiguous life as a British Indian nationalist. On August 19, 1939, the day that war was announced in India, she was on holiday with Ranga in Andretta where Bedi visited on weekends from Lahore. She bought a newspaper and was sitting on a bench at possibly the most scenic, peaceful railway platform in India – that of the two-gauge toy train that runs through the Kangra Valley – when she read that war had broken out again. Memories of the first war flooded her mind. With her mother in London and a brother in the Navy, she agonized over the bombings. To her great relief, she could communicate psychically in dreams.

Jack in the Navy during World War Two   *Courtesy of the Bedi Family Archives*

I had a vivid dream of going to my mother's house. She wrote to me after that and said she had a dream of me and I came to her as a young girl as I was before I left England. Various experiences came to me and I realized the years of meditation had not been unfruitful and I was able to communicate with friends through dreams.

CHAPTER THREE ❖ A Passage to India

The war could have triggered a conflict of interest in her between Indian nationalism and the enormous suffering of her friends, family, and country, but it was as if a past life had been activated from the time she set foot on Indian soil. England was her childhood and girlhood, she said, but India was her womanhood and her wifehood, her home and her future.

> I am still the same as I have ever been; fundamentally I don't think India has changed me at all. But I am Indian now, to all seeing. Anti-Fascist though we all are and have been for years, it is hard for the average British citizen who isn't very interested in politics to understand what resistance to Imperialism means, what India is really feeling, how severely her national self-respect has been wounded, how she is ready and willing to fight all oppression and aggression and vindicate her denied nationhood.

India was where Freda reached political maturity as a nationalist. The most important test of commitment to her ideals now beckoned. Gandhi used the war to stir up the Quit India movement. The driving force was not pro-Hitler, but anti-British colonialism. Freda explained:

> The deep-seated impetus toward Nationalism in India took the form of antiwar propaganda and in Gandhi's hands the movement turned into a Satyagrahi movement, the movement of seekers of the truth who were willing to protest peacefully against being forced to do things they didn't want to do. Gandhi said India had the right to choose whether it should fight or not. In terms of Nazism and Hitler, no humanist or democrat could do anything but shudder at the idea of it spreading in Europe.

At the same time as Gandhi seized the moment, the Government acted to curtail Satyagraha. On December 4, 1940, the lights of the oil lamps in the thatched huts went out. Bedi was arrested. As one of the leaders of the first all-India railway strike, he was deemed a dangerous political dissident. Leftists, terrorists, Communists, congressmen, and Punjabi peasant workers were all placed in a preventive detention center, the infamous concentration camp at Deoli in Rajasthan designed by the British for Japanese prisoners of war.

Ranga commented:

It was in the middle of the Rajasthan Desert. There was no means of escaping. There was one dusty road where a bus used to operate once a day and that was a mile away from the camp. But if you had only prison clothes, how were you going to get there?

Freda was so shaken by Bedi's disappearance and its political motivation that she decided to join in with her own action. Satyagraha, a force born of truth and love or non-violence, seized her imagination. With Bedi in long-term imprisonment since no one could tell when the war would end, it was the right time. She was suddenly alone in the house with only Ranga, the adopted boy Binder, and Bhabooji. She was a doting, even "dippy" mother as Bedi called her, but she could trust Bhabooji to look after the children and Trilochan Das to support them. She yearned for Bedi's embrace. They were comrades, lovers, soul mates, leading almost mystically intertwined lives, like "the peepul and the banyan twining upwards in close embrace." Her last night in the huts she started to feel the pangs of a loneliness that would remain throughout his absence. "I could have wept for my sheer aloneness. I wanted to talk to Bedi, to have his cheery voice near me." Rather than wait outside prison walls, as he had cautioned she might do in his marriage proposal, she decided to go inside herself.

CHAPTER THREE ❖ A Passage to India

Gandhi handpicked the individuals he trusted to offer Satyagraha and Freda's dedicated work as a nationalist had touched his heart. She had seen him publicly two or three times. The last time would be in the garden at Birla House where five weeks later three bullets would blast through his body. She gave in her name and was the fifty-seventh to be chosen.

She decided to make her statement as the first British woman to offer Satyagraha in her husband's ancestral home at the small village of Dera Baba Nanak rather than in Lahore. An English woman's solitary defiance of the Raj would spread rapidly throughout India. Her prison diary Behind The Mud Walls tells the story. Real-life characters like a documentary interrupted by entertainment like a Bollywood musical make her tale of arrest, trial, sentencing, and imprisonment more Monsoon Wedding than The Gulag Archipelago, but her diary pulses with the heartbeat of a young woman on the streets, lamenting the sudden loss of her loved ones.

With her keen powers of observation she painted portraits of the women in prison as well as a revealing self-portrait. The three months she spent inside showed that her black and white politics was oversimplified. Many of the jail officials were nationalist at heart, but to maintain their families, they had to serve the British.

The journey began when she got onto the train from Lahore garlanded in flowers like a celebrity, then continued with having to explain to the passengers that she was going to offer herself for imprisonment.

I said, "It is degrading that India should be treated like this. Somebody had to do something: we can't just all sit down and keep quiet about it." 'But what does your husband say about it?' one matron asked. "He is in jail himself," I replied. 'Ah,' her eyes turned in pity toward me, 'now I understand.' It was the wife following

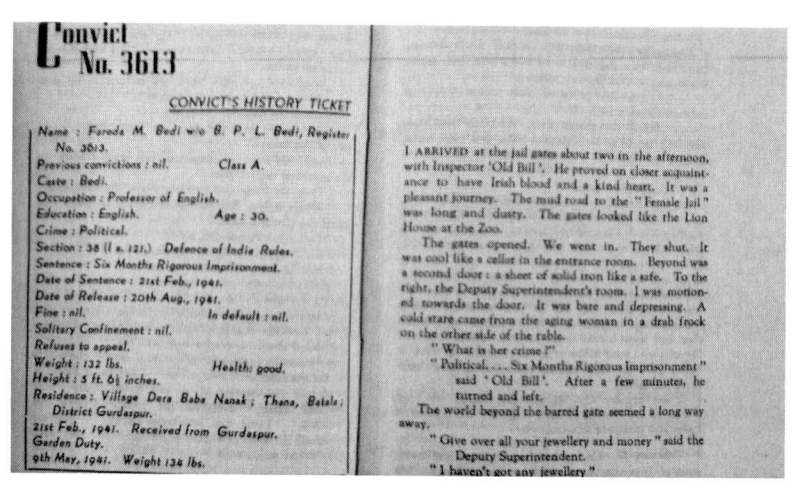

Freda's penal document, copy of original in Beyond the Mud Walls Courtesy of the British Library, London *(photo by the author)*

her husband. That was as it should be. It was a strange thing that a woman should choose to go to jail, but if her husband was there, then it was only natural after all. I smiled with her.

On the day she was to offer Satyagraha, the local officers had to send for a special policeman from Amritsar who knew how to arrest a British woman because they had no experience. How would a British woman react?

At eight thirty they arrived. In the center was the local Inspector with a beard. He came forward politely, "regretting it is my duty but I must arrest you." The turbaned police officer on his left had a half-smile. To the right was the European inspector from Amritsar in an unwieldy toupee. He was surprisingly small and had a walrus moustache. He looked like Old Bill: I wanted to laugh, and the corners of my mouth twitched. "Yes, I am quite ready. Take me along with you."

CHAPTER THREE ❧ A Passage to India

The trial was conducted by a red-faced Englishman who, Freda recalled, "looked like he had been to Oxford." It took all of fifteen minutes to deliver a guilty verdict and a sentence of six months rigorous imprisonment. Unforeseen circumstances conspired nicely to shorten the term to three months since letters had been sent announcing a speech but the orators were arrested before they made their speeches and therefore legally they had never broken the law.

The gates of the prison, Freda thought, looked like the lion house at the zoo. Maintaining her principles, she turned down the offer of preferential treatment as an English woman. "Give over all your jewelry," said the Deputy Superintendent with a cold stare. Freda looked at the aging woman in a drab frock on the other side of the table and turned the tables. She was twenty-nine years old, seven years into her marriage. Never had her wedding ring left her finger and she refused to remove it to comply with prison rules. Switching roles from common Indian woman to memsahib, she reminded the Deputy Superintendent that she was a class A prisoner. Her wedding ring remained on her finger.

She shared a cell with two "lovely Indian women, examples of beautiful Indian womanhood – self-sacrificing, cheerful, and simple." Both were Brahmin and vegetarian and they insisted on making maize cakes and vegetables also for her. In the early dawn before anyone awoke, she practiced meditation and yoga and once became entranced by the sound of two parrots mating. Her rigorous work assignment was to be gardener on a plot of ground that separated political prisoners from convicts. She imagined it as The Secret Garden, recalling her childhood rapture when Margaret O'Brien's book was read aloud to her. In the cool hours of morning and evening, she planted vegetables and flowers and before retiring, they all spun cloth which was Gandhi's way of keeping his little army together, sang nationalist songs, or read from the Gita. The food was plentiful and they could cook it themselves. Political literature was not allowed so she read Steinbeck's Grapes of Wrath and Huxley's Many a Summer. Sometimes a friend would bring her flowers, pink and red roses that she floated in two bowls.

On the other side of the wall they could hear the enchanting songs of the women convicts, many of whom had killed their old husbands, the consensus being, Freda concluded wryly, that jail was preferable to living with an aged husband. When they heard of the birth of an inmate's granddaughter, they made a special feast with extra rations of ghee, then sang and danced.

Sometimes a day seemed like an eternity. The torture of jail life was never being alone, "always on top of people. However nice they are, they 'permeate' me too much and I begin to lose myself in an odd way; I feel like a plant uprooted. I was brought up in a quiet home, with my own room where I could keep my books and personal things, a pot of flowers, a picture, photographs. After leaving home I still managed to get it. But in jail, there is no room to myself."

The worst thing about jail life was going to the toilet with the choice of either hiding her face in a dirty curtain to shut off the mud cubicle or throwing up the curtain and being caught unexpectedly.

She thought continually of Bedi locked up in the detention camp in the barren countryside.

> My thoughts burn like a flame sometimes and we are no longer apart. All together, Ranga and he and I, the family, even if at three corners of a triangle. It gave me some satisfaction that if my husband was in the concentration camp at least I was not shirking although I had intense longing to see my son.

Her wish to see Ranga came true. He was allowed to enter the jail and for one weekend slept with her under the mosquito net. Bedi for

CHAPTER THREE ❦ A Passage to India

his part was in good company at Deoli. As a high-ranking political prisoner he was sharing a cell with the barrister Rajni Patel, the youngest member of the nationalist movement. Patel was Cambridge and Bedi was Oxford, so they had light blue and dark blue curtains, respectively, separating their cell.

When Bedi's letter finally came she felt her insides turn over. On his birthday she lamented it was the first time they had spent it apart. At the same time she carried the sorrowful state of the world on her head like a dark cloud, "It is almost unbearable to think of the brutalities and stupidities of man to man." And the dark thought of her mother under the bombs in London was horrifying.

There were plenty of jail holidays, even one to celebrate the fresh ripe mulberries. On the first day of the Hindu New Year they sat out in the garden together and ate especially prepared food, with delicious sweets offered by a Bengali family. On May Day as temperatures inside the prison soared, they gathered to hear readings from Lenin and the meaning of the Russian Revolution. There were more telegrams from Bedi.

> Everybody was happy with me and the Delhi women started singing and dancing and plump Raj Dulari with her typical Delhi charm was in the middle of the circle moving her arms with infinite grace and beating her feet on the ground. It rained in the evening – it seems almost monsoon weather. Some of our family sent apricots and a pineapple.

When the weather cooled they danced in a spirit of festivity, banging buckets and pitchers like drums, moving and swaying to the beat.

Freda also managed to accomplish some important work, getting the name of the jail changed from female jails to women's jails. As she pointed out humorously, jails do not have genders. When their prison term ended after only three months, a round of farewell parties began, "an atmosphere of regret: we were parting, after so long together, in an intimacy that only jail life gives. Who knows whom of us will meet again, have the same talks."

All the villagers of Dera Baba Nanak came out to greet her with cascades of flowers, a brass band played, and a crush of well-wishers enveloped her. After the quiet of the jail, it was overwhelming.

> Early in the morning we all went to the garden to Bhabooji. She received me in traditional style, putting the red tikka on my forehead, garlanding me, presenting me with sweetmeats. It was bliss to be in the quiet of a home again. Ranga and I slept unashamedly all the morning and afternoon, relieved of all care.

After her release Freda stayed with Ranga briefly in the Bedi ancestral village. The old huts on the border of Model Town which they had abandoned were no longer home. She sought solace in the hostel of the college in Lahore where Mrs Pandit, the superintendent, "acted like a real mother to me. I deeply love her. Even now I can't remember those days without emotion. In my loneliness she gave me a feeling of security and allowed me to bring eight-year old-Ranga to sleep in my room in the hostel."

Bedi went on a hunger strike in the detention camp in 1941 and was released in April 1942 on the grounds of compassion. Ranga had been stricken with typhoid and had developed abscesses. When they returned to Model Town to pick up the threads of family life, they had to construct a completely new set of huts in the Green Belt where they lived until 1947.

Bedi continued active political struggle right up until independence, spending six years of his life from 1936-1945 intermittently

CHAPTER THREE ✤ A Passage to India

confined in prison, including detention in Deoli. In acknowledgment of his dedication and intimate knowledge of Lahore, he received a publisher's commission to write a biography of Sir Ganga Ram, the brilliant architect-cum- engineer who was the founder of modern Lahore and Model Town. The publisher's advance for *Harvest from the Desert* finally released Freda from the burden of family breadwinner. She published Voltaire's *Fragments of India* translated from the French and *Bengal Lamenting*, a collection of essays on the Bengal famine.

On the lighter side, she continued to compose *Rhymes for Ranga*, a book of nursery rhymes in which their two dogs Punt and Snug, the pony Badami, and the adorable baby buffalo, Clarebelle Cutty "with eyes of blue who lived in her personal private hutty," all played star parts. *Rhymes for Ranga* is not just a book of nursery rhymes. Freda was never one to disguise her emotions or to hide her ideals. One of the poems is a sweet vision of Indian Independence.

"The Dawn of Freedom, 1942"
Mother, see how the bird flies
Joyful, full of song.
I want to be like that, Mother,
How long will it be, how long?
"Son, as the river is flowing,
From the mountain to the sea,
As to his hive, unthinking,
Travels the honeybee,
So India is marching
Straight to her Freedom Day,
And nobody shall stop her
And nothing shall bar the way.

Freda in Derby with Kabir, 1947 *Courtesy of the Bedi Family Archives*

CHAPTER THREE ❊ A Passage to India

And you shall be free as the bird is
Free as the air, my son!
The bars of your cage will be broken,
And your journey just begun.

♦ ♦ ♦

In spite of the Satyagraha antiwar movement, by the height of the war 2,500,000 Indian soldiers had volunteered to fight the Axis forces, earning seventeen Victoria crosses. The British commander-in-chief stated that the Allies could not have won the war without the Indian Army.

In 1945 peace was declared in Europe. A year later, January 16, 1946, Kabir was born in the thatched hut of Lahore. In May 1947, when he was just over a year old, Freda bundled him in her arms and

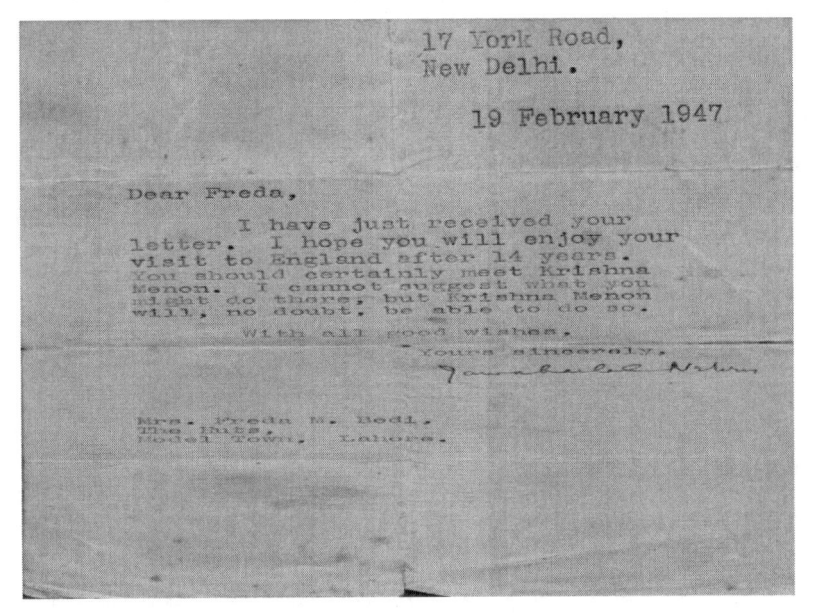

Original letter from incumbent Prime Minister to Freda Bedi *Courtesy of the Bedi Family Archives (photo by the author)*

103

finally made good her promised passage to England, the first in fourteen years. The incumbent Prime Minister Nehru sent her a brief note upon her departure.

Two years after India's victory, the British returned India to its nationalist leaders. On August 15, 1947, Independence Day, the British Raj divided the continent into Pakistan and India, and the new nation was born in the blood of partition. On January 30, 1948 Gandhi toppled to the ground, breathing out RAM after a round of gunfire. He knew it would happen. His work was done.

CHAPTER FOUR
Breakthrough in Burma

I was walking through the streets of Akyab in North Burma when suddenly I experienced the first real flash of understanding - the interconnectedness of everything that changed my whole life. When I got back to Delhi I told my husband, "I have been searching all my life but the Buddhist monks have shown me and I am a Buddhist from now on."

It was a circuitous road that led Freda to Burma. Lahore was where she saw political engagement give rise to an independent India, but it was in Burma where she had a vision of interdependence which would change the direction of her life. The route to it lay through the desecrated remains of religion and war torn lives in the refugee camps of Kashmir. India's independence was the end of a great political mission for the Bedis, but it was not the end of their work. She was in England at the stroke of midnight August 15, 1947 when the awaited moment of liberation unleashed the greatest upheaval the country had ever known.

When she returned to India in November, she discovered that all their possessions in Lahore were either looted or stored and could not be retrieved. "We had to rebuild from the ground up." Dangerous as it was, they began life anew in Sheikh Abdullah's vision of a new Kashmir.

> It had never been our fate since our marriage in 1934 to live a particularly safe life in the political conditions then obtaining in India, and we had hoped that with the dawn of Independence we should have the chance to settle down to solid constructive work to build up free India, with so many millions of our fellow countrymen and women. But there was a stretch of danger and

difficulty still to be crossed, and we landed in Kashmir at the end of November 1947 to contribute what we could to the Resistance.

Greater Kashmir which included Hindus in Jammu and Buddhists in Ladakh with a Moslem population the majority in the valley was the new war zone. The rules of partition allowed the Maharajah of each princely state to choose accession either to India or Pakistan. In Kashmir, Maharajah Hari Singh, a Hindu, chose to align with India and Sheikh Abdullah, Bedi's close friend, was appointed first Prime Minister of the state. After partition the Sheikh summoned Bedi to act as an adviser. His experience in drafting the New Kashmir manifesto outlining a state with democratic and socialist values made him an invaluable aide and his ability to converse fluently in Urdu, Hindi, Punjabi, and English enabled him to pass from the Hindu to the Muslim sides incognito. As the horror stories started trickling in from both sides, he made two trips from India to Pakistan, helping people in each place. He was also in charge of counterpropaganda against Pakistan. By this time he had severed all connection with the Communist Party of India and was not a radical, but leaned strongly toward socialist democracy.

Following the Kashmiri decision to align with India, invasions of tribal raiders from Pakistan plundered, looted, raped, murdered, and desecrated holy images, much like the Taliban today, in protest against a Kashmir aligned with India. The priest and nuns of Baramulla, the oldest Catholic Church in Jammu and Kashmir, were murdered and thrown into an open well. Freda led a party of volunteers to clean the church where the holy icons had been either beheaded or mutilated. "It was grim. A very brutal tribal invasion."

In the Kashmir Valley itself where a Muslim majority existed, Freda was working day and night in the refugee camps attending to

CHAPTER FOUR ❖ BREAKTHROUGH IN BURMA

Freda holding Kabir with Ranga sitting on the dog, Women's Civil Defense Corps, 1948   *Courtesy of the Bedi Family Archives*

Kashmiris who were uprooted as a result of the raids. She was in charge of relief supplies arriving from all over the world. "We had 17,000 refugees in the city and ran twenty-three milk and relief centers. There wasn't time to breathe and I lost over a stone." It was a long bleak winter with the worst snowfall for forty years cutting off Kashmir completely. Snow fell for three months uninterruptedly and planes could not land on the muddy airfield.

She liaised with the Sheikh and government officials and was part of a Kashmiri women's civil defense force trained by the Indian Army to use "3 north 3" rifles, the same weapons the army was using to defend local areas.

She wrote to Olive,

> It has been a new world, harrowing and yet inspiring.... and a lot of propaganda from the Pakistan side has been trying to make the state communal-minded. Hindus, Moslems, and Sikhs fought together to keep the raiders out. Last week I divided my time between the Kashmiri Women's Army, military training, and refugee relief.

She had a month off in the summer and then returned to the relief centers for the unemployed. "Living in Kashmir is like sitting on the edge of a precipice. I sometimes wonder what it must be like living in a world with some sense of security. Then I tell myself I should feel lost and bored... security is a relative situation. How many in this war-torn hungry world have got it?"

Her faith in the new Kashmir of Sheikh Abdullah with its Socialist government and young leaders was now her sustaining vision. Her proclamation rang with the high-flown rhetoric and ideals of the revolutionary.

CHAPTER FOUR ❖ BREAKTHROUGH IN BURMA

Freda and B.P.L. Bedi with Kashmiri leaders c. 1949   *Courtesy of the Bedi Family Archives*

We are both of us convinced that the present government of Kashmir, headed by the Moses- like figure of Sheikh Abdulah who has with his party led the Kashmiris out of the virtual slavery of kingly rule to Responsible Government, has given a new self-respect to this gifted people... To this country whose beauty is tragically silhouetted against the great unchanging poverty of its peasants and working classes, he and his Government have brought fresh faith and a new approach.... a great deal has been done to change the feudal face of this traditionally backward area. Land legislation has given land to the tiller of the soil... trade has been canalized into the emporiums... and we are

Gulie and Kabir with Freda, Srinagar 1950   *Courtesy of the Bedi Family Archives*

now giving priority and a bigger percentage of our budget to education than almost any other part of India.

We feel happy living here and working here... and are sure that we shall welcome and win a plebiscite that will join Kashmir permanently to India.

On January 1, 1949 the first Indo-Pakistan war concluded with an agreement that Kashmir was part of India. Freda occupied herself with preparation for the birth of a new child, Gulhima, Rose of the Snows, born in September.

She wrote to Olive,

It's rather a lot to take on a new baby in the midst of present day Kashmir, but Kabir needs someone his own age - and they have a lovely garden to relax in. Her name was fitting for a child born in the valley of the Himalayas, famed for its snows, flowers and lakes.

CHAPTER FOUR ❖ Breakthrough in Burma

Freda in Delhi in the 1950s *Courtesy of the Bedi Family Archives*

The next year 1950, Freda was back at work teaching English at the newly founded Kashmir University in Srinagar. As head examiner for English, she was up until two or three at night, conscientiously marking every exam paper. It was a strenuous period.

Talking with Kabir as he delved into his earliest memories was like watching the actor in him tuning into a part he had played in an absorbing drama long ago. It took a few minutes to unwind the circuitous road of his childhood. He was born at Model Town, Lahore at two huts set up on a barren piece of land with two tethered buffaloes.

> I was a little over a year old when we returned to India. My earliest memories were of Kashmir where the family moved after independence. In Kashmir, we were in a two-storey house,

Jack, Freda, Kabir, and Nellie Houlston in 1947 in England   *Courtesy of the Bedi Family Archives*

Freda and B.P.L. at a Srinagar garden party, 1949   *Courtesy of the Bedi Family Archives*

CHAPTER FOUR ❧ BREAKTHROUGH IN BURMA

a reasonably nice house which had a sitting room, dining room, kitchen, big garden with apple trees, a driveway ringed with daffodils. I would be taken to school every day by our cook on a bicycle and dropped off.

It was an idyllic time for me. I remember being taken to Shankar Acharya Temple, Gulmarg, and all the wonderful resorts around Srinagar. Mine wasn't a family that took holidays; we were very hard-working people. We had a large car, a Packard, which Papa had bought secondhand in which we would run around. Memories of a lovely time there... houseboats, shikara rides on Dal Lake, always tourists but never to the extent that grew later. It was a place that people came because Kashmir was regarded as the Switzerland of India. We were there till I was about seven years old.

For all her relentless schedule working in the camps and military training, Freda still possessed a striking elegance. Their house was down the road from Rumer Godden, the famous novelist (*Greengage Summer, Black Narcissus*). Godden often invited Freda and the children for traditional English high tea with scones. By this time Freda was famous throughout India as a radical firebrand but when she came to tea, Godden was taken aback to see a gracious English lady. Her manners, propriety, and feminine grace complemented by children who were perfectly English created a completely different impression.

By 1949 the refugee crisis had ended and normal life made Freda feel a little lost. She needed to live for an ideal and throw herself into strenuous activity. She then turned to religion and began to study the different faiths, first Islam, but she could not find a copy of the Koran in English. She then decided to practice the Hindu faith for one year, reading the Bhagavad Gita, the Mahabharata, and behaving as

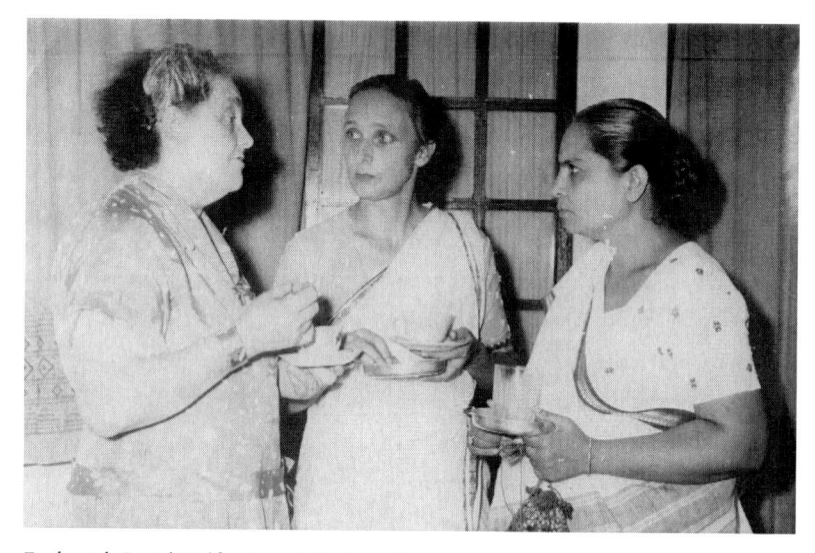

Freda with Social Welfare Board, Delhi 1950s *Courtesy of the Bedi Family Archives*

a perfect Hindu. By then Bedi had succeeded in obtaining a copy of an old Koran that he inscribed. The heavy black book with his loving inscription on the inside front page is sacrosanct, kept as a treasure on the family shrine. She then practiced the Muslim faith, praying five times a day, observing the rules and rituals. At the end of the year she came to a standstill.

At the same time, Sheikh Abdullah began to manuever his position with India, proposing greater independence. Bedi advised the Sheikh against it; the consequences would be severe. The Sheikh was not a radical but a Socialist who believed in land reform, breaking monopolies, the need for a social conscience. A breach opened in their relationship and before the disagreement became definitive in 1953, Bedi made plans to leave for Delhi. The two comrades who shared the same ideals and had survived imprisonment during the freedom movement suddenly separated. As Kabir put it, "There was no point in staying in Kashmir."

CHAPTER FOUR ❖ Breakthrough in Burma

President Radhakrishnan, B.P.L. Bedi and Freda   *Courtesy of the Bedi Family Archives*

Burmese Mission, 1953   *Courtesy of the Bedi Family Archives*

In Delhi they moved eventually from a squalid flat in Karol Bagh into a modern government flat complete with fans and showers in Moti Bagh when Freda became editor of Social Welfare, the magazine of the Central Social Welfare Board.

She was more than an editor. She traveled all over the country into villages from Kerala to Himachal, teaching handicrafts, literacy, childbirth preparation, and running nursery schools. "I would tag along with her," said Kabir, "and see a lot of rural India which very few boys of my age had the opportunity to do." Through her work on the magazine, Freda became the voice of India's volunteer social workers for which she received an award from Indira Gandhi.

She was now a government officer with trusted friendships based on shared ideals with the most powerful political leaders in India, Nehru and his daughter Indira Gandhi. These far-reaching links into the corridors of power in Delhi would serve her well.

It was then that a simple twist of fate brought her to the next and most meaningful stage of her life. In 1953 she arrived in Rangoon as part of a three-member United Nation's mission to reorganize social services in Burma and entered Swadgam Pagoda where the head priest was the great master Sayadaw U Titthila. She had explored religions but never the locked door of the mind. Suddenly that door opened.

Kabir was closely intertwined with the Buddhist part of his mother's life.

> There was a very close mother-son relationship, because we shared a journey. When Mummy began her Buddhist odyssey, I was with her most of the time. She was always a seeker, genuinely looking for the right belief system. She had studied the Koran, Vivekananda, a lot of Vedic teachers, Tagore, all the writers. It was a continuous search. We had a very secular home where

CHAPTER FOUR ❈ Breakthrough in Burma

respect was given to all religions, but in terms of a belief system for herself, it became Buddhism in Burma in 1953.

Buddhism in India, the land of its birth, was virtually extinct by the end of the nineteenth century. Realized masters experienced in meditation were essential to transmit the Dharma and at that time Burma, Thailand, and Sri Lanka where the monastic tradition of Buddhism received state support kept the flame alive. Although she had started meditating as a young girl in the church near her house in Derby and continued throughout her life even when imprisoned behind mud walls in Lahore, it was not until she entered Burma, a Buddhist country, that she experienced a living tradition. She became a regular visitor to the pagoda and became deeply influenced by the meditation master U Titthila who taught her Vipassana or insight meditation.

After practicing for eight weeks, she experienced what she called "a flash of understanding that changed my whole life." She was walking down a street in northern Burma, Kabir recalled, together with other members of the mission, when she suddenly fainted and dropped to the ground unconscious. Kabir was only seven years old and it influenced his life.

Mummy herself said it was an ethereal feeling, like everything was pulsating, shimmering, all sounds and sights becoming extremely acute. She was not able to function. Not much was told to the children but it was a nervous breakdown. She was brought back to India and hospitalized briefly, not for long, just a few weeks to allow her to recover. We were not allowed to see her for a few days, maybe a week or so, then taken in and she recognized us. Then she started studying Buddhism with great earnestness, diligently, methodically, understanding all the principles.

Ranga who was nineteen years old recalled how Freda was brought back to Delhi.

> My father and I were in Delhi as well as Kabir and my younger sister. My father had been in radical left-wing politics all his life and did not have a passport. My mother and father were closely associated with Prime Minister Pandit Nehru. My father went to Panditji and said: "I don't have the money or even a passport to travel to Burma." Panditjji arranged for his ticket, money for his expenses, and an emergency travel document within forty-eight hours. He left for Burma and five days later returned with my mother who had had a severe nervous breakdown. She would sit all day on her cot in Delhi staring into virtually nothing, would eat when shown food but wouldn't speak a word or make any signs. It took about three months for her to return to normal, no medication, psychiatrists, nothing, a natural return. She was totally passive, no danger to the children. She would eat when she felt like eating, sleep when she wished. Gradually there was more and more consciousness in her reactions to environments. She came out of it.

Freda always referred to this experience as her first glimpse of enlightened mind. Many years later she told a group of students in California how she had "perceived the scene around her in amazing clarity and expanse, seeing the interconnectedness of everything." She became intricately and visually aware of interdependence. It was, she said to another student, "an experience of mystical intensity" that lasted several hours. Tears poured down her face. She never disclosed that it was diagnosed as a nervous breakdown.

Whatever the terms, the doors of perception had opened. Had Freda been of the '60s generation, she would have called it cosmic

CHAPTER FOUR ❖ BREAKTHROUGH IN BURMA

Freda and Burmese ambassador at Delhi reception, late 1950s   *Courtesy of the Bedi Family Archives*

consciousness, possibly enhanced by hallucinogens. In her case there was no question of mind-expanding drugs. She had found her way to the ineffable, the doorway she wanted to enter for so long, through meditation; it was a taste of emptiness or transcendent wisdom, impermanent like a flash of lightening in the summer sky.

From around 1954-55 she read Buddhist texts, met prominent Buddhists in Delhi, and made offerings for monks. The first Buddhist monk that entered their house, said Kabir, was the head lama of Ladakh, Kushak Bakula.

In 1955, U Nu the first Prime Minister of a Burma that had been freed from British rule in 1948, visited India and met Freda at the Ashoka Vihara near Kutub Minar, eight miles from the center of Delhi.

A rural-cum-Mogul setting, it was a Buddhist teaching center with five ordained monks from South East Asia and an Indian Youth Hostel. When they were inbetween houses the Bedi family would camp in the gardens in elaborate tents. "When I think about it," Kabir reflected, "we were living in tents; however glorious, it was still a tent... but I never felt deprived."

U Nu invited Freda to the foremost meditation center in Burma headed by Mahasi Sayadaw. Regarded as a living saint in Burma, he had trained many of the great Vipassana teachers, including Goenka who brought Vipassana to the West. U Nu, whom Freda admiringly called the Lion King of Dharma, sponsored her trips several times and gave extra tickets for five monks to come and study. One ticket remained, and when Kabir pleaded, "I want to be a monk," he was added to the trip in 1956.

> We went to Rangoon where Mummy studied Vipassana with Mahasi Sayadaw. I was told that in Burma a lot of children would take the robes for a summer vacation so I thought, why don't I take the robes? I was about ten. I asked my mother and she said yes. I was ordained, given a begging bowl, and went on the alms round with a crocodile of monks. I was the youngest so I would be at the end of the line. At five in the morning people would come out of their homes and give them a scoop. I was right at the end so if it filled up they got upset and had nowhere to put it. So mine was always the fullest. There were various ways of disposing of the food - animals, birds, the ground. But you ate only once a day. You were allowed a little jaggery with your tea in the afternoon but no solid foods. I did it for a couple of months. I had my own room which I shared with another monk and Mummy and I would meet every day over tea. I was taught Vipassana meditation.

Mummy was delighted that Kabir behaved so beautifully. When Freda formally disclosed her decision to become a Buddhist to Bedi, he was not surprised. He knew, even before she did, that she had been

CHAPTER FOUR ❖ Breakthrough in Burma

Freda and B.P.L. Bedi, Delhi, mid-1950s   *Courtesy of the Bedi Family Archives*

a Buddhist in past lives. "This was bound to have repercussions on the more conservative members of the family, but my father said he was with her all the way," said Kabir.

It was a defining moment in their journeys. They were two extraordinary, unconventional, intelligent, and active people who had their differences and led separate lives, although they lived together until the early '60s. Theirs was always a deeply symbiotic relationship bound by ties more lasting than sexuality. Bedi had discreet relationships with other women, but the couple was always respectful toward one another.

"Mummy was observing the celibacy of a nun even before she became a nun," said Kabir. "There was always a sense of great mutual respect."

Gulhima agreed.

My father adored my mother. He was charming, charismatic, an amazing speaker, very handsome, very attractive to women, but he never disrespected my mother in her presence. I imagine she was aware of his relationships. She said she was celibate after my birth. When she came to Delhi she would stay wherever my father was staying. They never got a divorce. It was just like a separation, but not a legal one. My mother told my father what she needed to do.

And he honored her wish. He was a man who marched to the beat of his own drum.

Kabir paused for a few minutes to collect his thoughts for the next episode.

My father has a parallel story. The reason I'm talking to you is that I want the memory of my mother and the memory of my

CHAPTER FOUR ❖ Breakthrough in Burma

B.P.L. Bedi, Delhi, 1954   *Courtesy of the Bedi Family Archives*

father to be passed on for the idealists they were, the parents they were, the difference they made to the world they lived in. Mummy did it in the world of Buddhism, Tibetans. My father did it at a more esoteric level, a sense of what matters in the universe and how it functions and (he) brought laughter, joy, and healing.

I had strongly suspected that the hidden figure behind Freda Bedi's remarkable life story was the extraordinary Baba Pyare Lal. He had given her a respected name, a cause, a country, and a supportive, loving extended family. Kabir confirmed that his mother's spiritual journey was not a solitary one but the result of a highly evolved union.

After his break with Sheikh Abdullah, Bedi turned away from political activism. He was physically debilitated from the time he had spent in prison camps and walked with a staff to support his injured spine. When the family came down from Kashmir, his elder brother Trilochan Das died. It was a traumatic event for him. Suddenly he went through a number of radical spiritual experiences.

His spiritual guide was Nizamuddin, an ancient Sufi saint whose mosque was across the road from the Oberoi Hotel. Every Friday evening he would go to listen to devotional music, although he was not religious. He developed an interest in séances. One day the table went out of control and smashed various objects in the room. On another occasion, Ranga came home to find his father sitting on a settee and lifting a heavy table off the ground with his fingers. "His behavior puzzled everybody," said Kabir. "He would stare into space endlessly, not eating for long periods of time and remaining silent for long periods."

Finally, said Ranga, he found his father standing on the terrace of the house with his hands uplifted. He did not talk or respond to any stimulus and remained standing like a stone statue for thirty-six hours

CHAPTER FOUR ❖ BREAKTHROUGH IN BURMA

in spite of having been injected with three shots of morphine to relax his body and bring him out of the trance.

Abruptly he turned around of his own accord, went into a room and lay down on his back on the bed. Other than having no movement in his joints, he was warm and firm. A doctor carried out all the tests and said he was normal. Later he got up, went down into his room, washed, opened the fridge, and ate.

Said Ranga,

That was the end of it. Throughout this period, his eyes were like two stones, expressionless; he had no recognition of the family. He would sit at the head of the table, but there was no conversation. Nor did he show any signs of hearing anything. It took a few months before he started to return to normal. Mummy just accepted it for what it was.

Kabir continued the story of his father's recovery.

At the end of this whole process which took a couple of months the doctors couldn't figure out what was happening; then he stated automatic writing. People would come to him and he would look at them and start to write something. People would get to know about him. He was channeling something. After a year or two of that he stopped writing and started speaking directly. That became his path for the rest of his life. He had an interest in the esoteric and founded Enquiry Into the Unknown and then spent the last thirty years of his life in Italy.

In Delhi he held an open house from five to seven every evening. People including businessmen and politicians were coming to him asking for advice on all sorts of matters. He would sit there and

Baba Bedi in Italy *Courtesy of the Bedi Family Archives*

communicate his understanding of universal energies and he began to be treated like a fortune-teller or an astrologer: "Will my daughter get a good husband?" "Will I get a good job?"

In the '60s when interest in Eastern mysticism was at its height, an Italian professor came to hear Bedi talk. Sometimes twenty or thirty Westerners would be sitting on the floor quietly listening. The professor returned for three consecutive evenings on his way back from Nepal. A few months later he invited Bedi to Italy. They arranged meetings and seminars that became very successful. After six months, Bedi took up residence in Italy.

There he was a healer, not a fortune-teller. He had appointments every hour, five days a week. Eventually, after Freda passed away, he married an Italian woman, Antonia.

> He was interested in the meaning behind things, light, sound, color. He found the work in Italy very satisfying. He was helping

CHAPTER FOUR ❖ Breakthrough in Burma

Baba Bedi in Italy, late 1970s *Courtesy of the Bedi Family Archives*

Baba Bedi in Italy, late 1970s   *Courtesy of the Bedi Family Archives*

CHAPTER FOUR ✤ Breakthrough in Burma

anybody and everybody who came to him. He thought that blocking your creative side causes disease and letting out those energies causes a positive flow. He had great gifts of healing in his hands, a vibrational energy which was tangible. I met so many cases in Italy where people who were in wheelchairs began walking. Another woman was diagnosed with cancer and came back to die. That was four years ago. He was able to help terminal cancer just with touch. The main thing to him was larger energies, channeling energies in the universe to be the best you can be.

He became a guru and adapted his clothes from the Punjabi salwar kameez to a long robe. With his staff he looked like Moses.

He was a man who had insights. When I asked my father how do you reconcile being a flaming Marxist at one moment and a spiritual guru the next moment, he said, "There is no contradiction. It is just helping people." He didn't see it as Marxism versus religion. Whether he did it as a fight for independence or enlarging psychic sensibility, it was to make people more complete.

At the same time he was very down to earth with an impish sense of humor. He smoked, drank wine, and was always laughing.

There was a woman called Raj who had a relationship with my uncle Trilochan Das who had asked my father to look after her when he passed away. I would imagine there must have been physical intimacy between them.[4] He lived with Raj when Mummy was in Dalhousie. Mummy had moved beyond a sexu-

---

4   Raj's daughter Seerat does not agree that her mother was physically intimate with Bedi. He was a brother figure she claimed, as Trilochan Das's wife was the sister of Raj's husband.

Sister Palmo and her husband, B.P.L. Bedi, Delhi 1965   *Courtesy of the Bedi Family Archives.*

CHAPTER FOUR ❖ BREAKTHROUGH IN BURMA

al relationship much before. She knew about Raj and that she was looking after Papa when Mummy was doing other things. His path after his brother's death was already underway, so when Mummy said she wanted to be a Buddhist, he said, "You must."

Freda continued to include updates on Bedi's activities in her family letters at Christmas. In 1960 she said, "He continues to take a deep interest in the occult." They corresponded until 1975. Her tone was the same as when they were a couple, as if he were standing right there beside her. Only the signature on her letters changed from Freda to KKP – Karma Khechog Palmo or Lady of Realization – after the closing phrase "with the blessings of the Triple Gem," the Buddhist refuge formula, the belief system she now adopted as her lifelong guide.

In 1966 when she told Pyare Lal she wanted to be a nun, he gave his blessing and wept. Throughout all his years of marriage to Antonia, he kept a picture of Freda in the center of the sitting room. Only years later did Antonia remove it.

❖ ❖ ❖

Bedi returned on a last visit to Delhi before he died in 1993, to the house in Jangpura Extension where he had lived with Raj Narendra and her daughter Seerat. It was a home packed with memories. The entire Bedi family, including Freda, who had a childlike love of Christmas, had gathered there every year after they had given up their flat in Moti Bagh, to celebrate the festival. At Bedi's request, Seerat invited Giani Zail Singh, former President of India and Bedi's comrade-in-arms, whom he had not met for twenty years.

She recalled,

Giani-ji was thrilled when I called him to come to see Baba-ji. He said, 'It didn't please me as much or make me as happy on becoming the President of India as to meet Baba-ji after all these years.' That is how much he was respected. He told me that Bedi had saved the lives of two presidents of India, Dr Zakir Hussein's and his own.

In 1953, after twenty years of political activity, Pyare Lal Bedi renounced politics and took to a mystic life. In 1961 he founded the Institute for Enquiry into the Unknown. When he moved to Italy in 1972 he founded the Aquarian Center in Milan. He presided over the International Congress for Reincarnation held in Milan in 1981. Bedi spent his last days in a wheelchair and died of a heart attack in Italy at the age of 84.

His publications include: The Pilgrims Way, *with an introduction by the President of India, Dr Krishna;* India Analysed *edited jointly with Freda Bedi, published by Victor Gollancz, London;* Mahatma Gandhi, Saint and Statesman, *jointly with Freda Houlston Bedi, published in German by Rheinhardt Verlag, Munich;* Harvest from the Desert, *published by Sir Ganga Ran Trust, Lahore;* The Prophet of the Full Moon *by Guru Gobind Nanak published in Punjabi, English, and Italian;* I am the Soul Consciousness; The Total Man; Man in the Age of Aquarius *published in Italian;* Mystic India, *Unity Publishers, Delhi. He gave more than 250 public lectures while in Italy.*

CHAPTER FIVE
The Tibetans

The fact is I'm called Mummy. All Dalhousie calls me Mummy. Everywhere you go I'm called Mummy - even when I became a nun. I became a mother figure.

The Tibetans who escaped to India from the Chinese invasion of their country in 1959 were fortunate in the timing of their exodus. India was now independent, the horrors of partition had passed ten years before, and Pandit Nehru was the first Prime Minister of a new nation. Although they came over the borders by the tens of thousands, they had a unique refugee in their midst, the Dalai Lama. He was welcomed by Nehru bearing a long white ceremonial greeting scarf at Mussoorie, a hill station north of Delhi. It was unprecedented for a refugee leader to be so warmly received by such a prestigious head of state.

The bamboo village of Misamari in Assam became the transit camp for the weary mountain people descending through the leech-infested jungles. In the summer of '59 while the rest of the world was marvelling at the first photo taken of the earth from a satellite in space, twelve thousand refugees came seeking a dry bed, food, and medicine in the camp of one hundred lofty huts each sheltering eighty or ninety people. Nehru welcomed the refugees like a father advising his children: "I want to see doctors, technicians, and educated men and women among you," he said on a visit to Misamari.

Indian independence meant that those previously called saboteurs were now the leaders and with that shift, the Bedis were welcomed into the establishment. Freda became a personal friend of Nehru and his family with frequent invitations to visit Teen Murti Bhavan, the renamed former residence of the commander-in-chief of the British Forces in India. Her children called him Uncle and she called his young daughter, whom she knew before her marriage, Indu. Indira's nickname for her was Fridapa.

Freda often took Kabir with her to play with Indira's children Sanjay and Rajiv Gandhi when she went to visit, and he was invited to their birthday parties. "They would get lots of gifts from visiting foreign heads of state. They had a whole floor covered in toy trains and we would play with them," said Kabir.

The discrepancy in their living standards was at times frustrating.

> Mummy used to take the bus to work. We didn't have a car. The Packard disappeared long ago. One word to them would have got us a telephone, but they were too principled to ask or to bribe. It would infuriate me. There was a four-year waiting list, sometimes seven, but we would use a neighbor's phone and then one day a phone just happened to turn up.

Freda, who had become a respected confidante of Indira, toured the northeastern border of India with her where the Tibetans were crossing into Assam by the thousands. Now that she was a Buddhist and had proven her abilities in the refugee camps of Kashmir, she fitted perfectly the post of Welfare Adviser to the Ministry. She offered her expertize and got the job. It was a grueling, heart-breaking assignment but the outcome of her experience in the camp was the creation of two far-reaching organizations, The Tibet Friendship Group and The Young Lamas' Home School.

From Assam, Freda wrote a letter describing her work at the refugee camp to her friend Muriel Lewis, a theosophist:

> The last year, since October 1959, has been a busy and memorable year. Looking after six thousand refugees from daybreak to

CHAPTER FIVE ✤ THE TIBETANS

dark for months in Misamari camp is something I cannot forget. Technically I was Welfare Adviser to the Ministry. Actually I was Mother to a camp full of soldiers, lamas, peasants, and families. Women and children were barely 1300 but how precious, for on them the continuance of the old Tibetan Buddhist culture depends. We struggled with barley to save babies whose mothers' milk had dried up during the journey or out of their suffering. Others had worms and diseases contracted on the long journey down. There were no office hours. Sunrise was the signal for the first visitors.

We had no electricity so work slowed down when the dark came. But even after that we used to go into the barracks and around the hospitals with volunteers and interpreters to pick up the sick and solve the day's problems. Every morning and night the chanting of the incredibly soothing and rhythmical prayers of the lamas filled the air. Each home group had its private shrine. Butter lamps were burned even if rations had to be sacrificed – their piety and devotion meant more than bread.

I can't begin to tell you of the tragic stories all carried in their hearts. We even avoided inquiring so that old wounds would not be torn open and gave instead positive hopes of work and resettlement. Much of my time was spent in keeping friends and family groups together when the dispersal to work sites and centers was taking place. For those who have lost home, country, almost every possession, family and village ties are all that is left and they assume tremendous importance and significance.

Characteristically, she looked on the bright side. Misamari was a haven, she wrote in the 1960 Journal of Social Welfare.

It was a place to rest and think about the relatives left behind and the agonies past. But it was also a place where people smiled and showed a courageous face. In the evening the youths would come out of the huts and walk down the central road wearing washed clothes, strapping Khampa boys with wide brimmed hats at an angle, and sometimes a Tibetan coat slung with careless elegance, over a camp bush shirt. The children would grin happily and cry little. They were an engaging group.

She adopted a fourteen-year-old Tibetan girl who had appeared unexpectedly at Losar, Tibetan New Year's Day, wearing a fur and brocade hat perched attractively on her smooth black hair. "I used to be a rich girl in Lhasa," she said. "I had a lot of clothes and a good house. Now I have only this," she said fingering her striped woolen apron and her long robe, "but it is better to have a bed in Misamari than to be in Lhasa now."

The richness of the religious tradition with the earthy simplicity of decoration attracted Freda: the small shrines improvised from wood and paper and adorned with brass or clay images and "silver caskets of the kind they used as protection against the terrors of the way." She admired pictures of buddhas cut out of magazines and newspapers, oil lamps that burned in spite of the rationing, and jungle flowers and seeds used as offerings in the pujas.

Every evening and morning the prayers of the monks would resound with a deep rhythmic hum through the dusk and bring a sense of peace and fitness and comfort into alien surroundings. The discipline and orderliness of the monks reminded her of the crew of a big ship or a sports team with group loyalty and cheerful spirits: "If they took decisions they took them together and not individually."

It was in the Tibetan refugee camp that Freda metamorphosed from British freedom fighter to an iconic Mother India. When Kabir

CHAPTER FIVE ❧ THE TIBETANS

visited the camp he saw his mother's hut surrounded by Tibetans seeking help and intervention; "She was going through the camps and getting to know them on a human level. I called her Mummy and the Tibetans called her Mummy-la. It was the easiest thing for them to say." The name stamped her identity indelibly, fusing the disparate aspects of her personality.

Back in Delhi, Freda's mind was still with the Tibetans and she made a heartfelt plea to Muriel Lewis to keep it all going through her Mothers' Group. Politely, simply, eloquently she came up with a plan: spread the word among friends to adopt a lama pen friend, write letters even if there was a language barrier, send parcels.

> Last year my son adopted a small lama of twelve, sent him a parcel of woolen yellow cloth, sweets, and picture books, soap, and cotton cloth. This time when I went to Buxa, Jayong gave me such an excited and dazzling smile. He was brimming over with seeing me again. It was of course most touching to see the "Mother-love" in the faces of the tutor lamas and servant lamas who look after the young ones. They are very tender with them.

Her plea was successful. Her letter to Muriel was reprinted in The Middle Way, journal of the Buddhist Society founded by Christmas Humphreys and mailed around the world. From the huge response it received, the Tibetan Friendship Group was born with the mission to spread Tibetan culture. It continues to this day in India, Australia, South Africa, America, and Europe.

Said Ngodup Burkhar, translator for the Karmapa,

> The Tibetan Friendship Group was doing two things. It was connecting well-off Westerners who were curious about spirituality

His Holiness the Sixteenth Karmapa seated outdoors with Ani Karma Kechog Palmo *Courtesy of the Shambhala Archives*

with Tibetan monks and lamas and she was introducing Buddhist culture and spirit to them. For Westerners, it was a way to support the Lamas and for Lamas it was very exciting to communicate with Westerners. In those days it was simple, basic, and beautiful. Maybe they gave ten dollars, but it meant a lot. It was very precious. I wrote a number of letters for Thrangu Rinpoche to his pen friend in South Africa. It was very simple, at a very grass roots level. She had all these little handouts.

Freda sent hundreds of individually handwritten letters. She never had a secretary and all the donations would come in as one, two, five, or ten dollars. "It was literally pulling dollar notes out of envelopes and writing thank you letters." Said Kabir, "All the people who

CHAPTER FIVE ❖ THE TIBETANS

Chögyam Trungpa *Courtesy of the Bedi Family Archive*

Akong Rinpoche *Courtesy of the Bedi Family Archives*

knew her knew how hard she was working for this, so they would have parties to make money. It was hand to mouth."

Even more touching than the simplicity of its origins was the gratitude of the Sixteenth Karmapa. The establishment of The Tibetan Friendship Group that helped integrate the refugees at such a critical moment endeared her to him. "This work you are doing to link the lamas with friends all over the world excels any of the other work you are doing for the refugees," he said. "It is of the greatest significance."

CHAPTER FIVE ❖ THE TIBETANS

Her attention turned to the incarnate lamas whom she observed were "the bearers of a tradition that dates back to the seventh century, a spiritual richness we can as yet only partially realize. I am sure the whole world will ultimately be enriched." Ngodup Burkhar said, "More than the state of the people, she understood the preciousness of Tibetan spirituality."

Freda set about categorizing the characteristics of the monks and lamas in the camp and made notes: there were 2500 dedicated monks of a high standard of learning, among them two hundred incarnate lamas with a smaller group of forty adolescents and children of "extraordinary intelligence and physical beauty."

One of them, an incarnate tulku whom they called Tongpa, approached her one day and passed her a sheaf of papers. They turned out to be copies of prescriptions from doctors the originals of which he had found while rummaging in waste paper and had skillfully copied in English. He made it clear that he wished to read and write in that language. She soon realized not only was he very bright but also highly motivated. His plan was to come and live in her house to learn English and he insisted that his "pal" live with him. Tongpa's mispronounced name was Trungpa and his pal was Akong.

Trungpa was to become the most brilliant, albeit iconoclastic, lama to emerge from the Tibetan diaspora. His mastery of English far surpassed anything he could have learned from his teachers in India. When he linked a traditional phrase like "licking honey from the razor" to describe the Vajrayana path with his own phrase "licking the clitoris of the heart" to indicate the arousal of bodhichitta, he zeroed into the zeitgeist of the peace and love generation and made his name as an incisive Tantric teacher.

Apart from these special incarnates, she noted simpler "country monks," nearly a thousand strong, who had volunteered for road work in Himachal and Arunachal, as well as soldiers from Kham who had worked in Sikkim. In the mountainous areas of Simla, Kulu, and Ladakh entire Tibetan families were earning a minimum wage building roads in order to be independent of government help. "My parents were working on the road in Manali," said Burkhar, "and they would come home at the end of the day covered in dust looking like ghosts; trucks were thumping up and down outside their tattered tent. They earned three rupees a day and lived on oil and bulgur wheat."

At the time of the Tibetan exodus no one in the Indian bureaucracy understood the difference between ordinary Tibetan monks and reincarnate lamas. In the Hindu caste system, mountain people were on the fringe. They were lumped into the category of primitive uneducated peasants and metaphorically dumped into a mass grave.

"She was the only one who understood the Tibetan culture and the importance of its continuity," said Professor Lokesh Chandra, President of the Indian Council for Cultural Relations and a prominent Vedic scholar. He was the son of Acharya Raghuvera whose safe house had sheltered the Bedis when they were on the run from the police in Lahore. His ninety-year-old memory retained the impression of Freda's work with the Tibetans:

> The people who came to help the refugees did not understand the Tibetans. The Tibetan language came after Sanskrit in sophistication of expression and thereafter Greek and Latin, and after it came Chinese and then Arabic. Most of the terminology of Tibetan was based on Sanskrit. Without this understanding, the Tibetans were just refugees without any culture or education. They were just tribals.

With discriminating intelligence, Freda then implemented a vision conceived by the Dalai Lama of a school where incarnate lamas from all four sects of Tibetan Buddhism could be educated in the

CHAPTER FIVE 🏵 THE TIBETANS

profound tradition they had inherited. Great effort, unswerving perseverance, and more than a touch of the British memsahib converted the plan into a reality, and at a stroke freed the lamas from hard labor on the roads. They did not have to endure the dust, disease, and poverty of the ordinary refugees bound to "food for work."

Ranga described the frustrations of the bureaucratic process that his mother had to endure. India was a secular country and could not support religious institutions. When the system struck her in the face, she resigned her position immediately.

> The principle was food for work. Because they were a strong rugged people, they were all assigned to building mountain roads. When she realized you cannot do that in respect to lamas and Rinpoches, she requested the Government of India to set up separate camps for them where they would continue with their religious activity and that the food for work formula should not apply to them. They could be set up alongside the labor camps but the young ones and their teachers should continue with their religious activity. This was what she recommended.
>
> In typical government fashion Delhi ignored it. She then enlisted the support of some political friends in Delhi who tried to implement her plan but did not succeed. She got frustrated and took a flight to Delhi on an Indian air force courier plane to which she was entitled as a government servant and met the powers that be in Delhi. She returned to the border with an assurance that the plan would be sympathetically considered. Nothing happened for three to four months. When she again returned to Delhi she pursued the same subject.
>
> Then she realized she was getting nowhere. As a result she resigned her government job with the Social Welfare Board and started raising money from well-to-do friends and sympathizers.

She rented two bungalows in the hill station of Dalhousie, went back to the border at her own expense, and drew up a list of Rinpoches and their lama teachers, giving them priority and made arrangements for them to go to Dalhousie.

Joanna Macy, author, environmental activist, and Buddhist scholar met Freda at precisely the moment she was trying to get the school underway and witnessed the particular combination of qualities that Freda possessed – a thoroughly British upper class application of serenity and sheer nerve.
Joanna Macy said,

The school at Kailash (in Dalhousie) was the topic she wished to pursue with Fran.[5] What was precisely needed now was a Peace Corps volunteer to teach English to the young tulkus (but not Indian-English, with its idiosyncratic vocabulary and intonation), to prepare them to take the Dharma into the modern world. She was aware that the government of India was being a bit difficult about all this, but surely in such a good cause....
Fran and I looked at each other and laughed. 'You're getting it from all sides,' I told him, for I had already been after him to try to transfer Logan to work with Khamtrul Rinpoche's group.

Freda smiled, 'I shall speak to my friend Mr. B. in the cabinet. I already know the volunteer I want; his name is Ray. When, do you think, we can expect him?' In that moment I viewed her with a satisfaction almost equal to her own. Yes, I could learn a lot from this woman, confidence, for one thing, the marriage of serenity with sheer nerve.

---

5   Fran refers to Francis, Joanna Macy's husband and Deputy Director of Peace Corps India at the time. Logan was a Peace Corps volunteer from Clearwater, Florida, a member of the group that Frank Miller was assigned to.

CHAPTER FIVE ✤ The Tibetans

By the end of our lunch, Fran had assured her he would do what he could, and she had invited the whole family up to Dalhousie when school let out: "You must all come to Kailash then, to get out of the heat. May and June are unbearable in Delhi. I know just the place for you — a lovely old cottage a short walk from our school, four or five rooms, I think, with lovely views. Just bring your cook along to buy food; it's a mile uphill from the topmost bazaar." As she left, she turned to me and said, 'By the way, I have an idea for Khamtrul Rinpoche's group. There are some abandoned houses in lower Dalhousie that should do fine with a little repair. I will see what I can do about a loan; I think His Holiness will be glad to help.'[6]

Frank Miller was the young Peace Corps volunteer who accompanied Joanna Macy on her pilgrimage to Dharamsala and Dalhousie. What had struck him about Freda at their first meeting the previous year in Andretta was her strong will and aura of purpose, "the penetrating look that combined depth, determination, and great kindness, a countenance that we might describe today as combining feminine and masculine aspects."

Toward the end of my Peace Corps assignment in 1966, I travelled to Dalhousie to visit Mummy. This time it felt like a journey to visit a guru. I was twenty-five and had never considered myself on a spiritual journey or had a spiritual guide, but this visit was to mark the end of spiritual loneliness.
Seeing Mummy in the context of the YLS added a new dimension to the image I held of her in my mind. She was definitely in charge of the school; you couldn't doubt her earthly

---

6   Joanna Macy, Widening Circles, A Memoir

authority there for a minute. She cowed some of the younger monks who worked at the school with her. Everyone behaved – or felt like behaving – around Memsahib, the principal.

Authority and fortitude was not all she possessed. No one could visit the Dalhousie School and miss the reasons why she was known and loved as Mummy. The radiance of her warm, wry smile of Buddhist tolerance and love fitted the role of mundane and spiritual mother to all who approached her. She was firm, kind, brooked no foolishness, yet was not afraid to express her sensitivities, emotions, vulnerability. Mummy was the kind of person who could feel inklings of spirituality in people who didn't know they possessed any or who would deny any suggestion of it.

A life-changing moment came when Mummy suggested I visit a monastery in Bangkok, as I was travelling to Thailand on my way from India to the US East Coast. I remember the moment she handed me a handwritten letter of introduction addressed to the abbot of Wat Bowoniwet Monastery where the late Thai King Rama IX spent time as an ordained monk.

In this letter, Mummy suggested to the abbot that I might want to remain as a lay resident for a period of several weeks, maybe longer, "who knows." This was more her idea than mine, but she felt certain it was meant for me to really experience life in a Thai wat for myself.

After ten days at Wat Bowoniwet of adhering strictly to temple regime, I greeted the outside world with renewed wonder and enthusiasm. When I returned to my family's home in New Jersey and began to create an adult life on foundations rebuilt in India, I informed my military draft board that I was unwilling to participate in the American war in Vietnam. I had left the US a striving, searching young man and returned with

CHAPTER FIVE ❖ THE TIBETANS

Chögyam Trungpa, Freda, and Akong Rinpoche *Courtesy of the Bedi Family Archives*

utopian dreams, spiritual yearnings, and a love of India which has never left.

At Freda's own home in Delhi an experiment was in progress. Ranga returned from work as manager of a tea plantation in Assam to find two young monks, chosen from among the incarnate lamas, living in his family. The plan was for them to be tutored in English and exposed to the outside world. The two monks were Chögyam Trungpa and Akong.

> My father was very mischievous, and took advantage of my mother's definition of exposing them to the outside world. He bought them each a pair of shorts, shirts, shoes and socks. He would give them some money and say "Go to the shops, buy what you want, eat what you want, and have a ball." This happened twice a week. My mother had no idea.

Tulku Major and Tulku Minor, as Freda named Trungpa and Akong, lived with the Bedi family in their two-bedroom flat for over a year with one room occupied by the aging and ailing Bhabooji. Kabir remembered the somewhat undefined living arrangements.

My father had a shack where he could sit and write and they lived in the verandah or the sitting room. They lived here and there. Whenever we could, we all slept outside on these charpoys and we rolled out our things. Winters in Delhi you could not sleep outdoors. At first I resented their presence. I wanted undivided attention, normal stuff. I particularly liked Akong. Trungpa was clever and brilliant, a rebel of sorts. Akong was very humble. He did everything. Trungpa was more in his head, Akong was more grounded.

Freda was positive they would learn conversational English with the children. Instead they learned what it was like to live in a family with sibling rivalries and a mischievous father who was more like another child. Kabir played pranks on them. Sugar was a novelty to Tibetans and they would go into the kitchen and steal it, particularly Trungpa. It would infuriate the cook. One day Kabir put salt in the bottom of the teaspoon and covered it with sugar. Then he put it into Trungpa's mouth.

It was Mummy who taught them English when she came back from work. She would put her hands on the table and say slowly with perfectly clear enunciation, 'I put my hands on the table' and they would parrot, 'I put my hands on the table.' She loved having them in the family: 'To work for the lamas is blessing unlimited.'

Freda set to work enlisting her influential connections to place the tulkus in higher education. With the endorsement of her Oxford friend, Barbara Castle, then a prominent Labour MP, and Christmas

CHAPTER FIVE ❖ THE TIBETANS

Young Lamas at YLHS with Kailash School in the background   *Courtesy of the Bedi Family Archives*

Humphreys who belonged to the Tibetan Friendship Group, she eventually succeeded in obtaining a scholarship for Trungpa Rinpoche to attend Oxford University. Akong Rinpoche accompanied him and supported them both by working as a hospital orderly.

After this interim period, she rented a beautiful new house and called it Kailash, located at L-7 Green Park in Hauz Khas. Lama Zopa described his meeting with "a tall English lady with blue eyes, dressed in a yellow sari" at the transit camp in Buxa and attending her Home School in Delhi for four months. He didn't learn much as the teachers spoke no Tibetan, but enjoyed sightseeing. At weekends the staffs of various embassies invited the students to the zoo or to watch movies, "taking us around in nice cars and giving us delicious food, so that we had a very good time." They played with Western children and kicked around a football until a representative of the Dalai Lama pronounced it incorrect for tulkus.

The Dalai Lama at Kailash School *Courtesy of the Bedi Family Archives*

The school for lamas in Dalhousie found a home in a stately but dilapidated colonial house with nine or ten bedrooms and a picture postcard view of the Himalayas. Justice Dickchen, the owner, agreed to a nominal rent. At the official opening on October 25, 1961 the Dalai Lama offered his blessing and support while the Indian Government volunteered an initial grant plus provisions. Freda was named Honorary Director and promised the Dalai Lama and Prime Minister Nehru to run the school for five years.

The Dalai Lama wrote to the heads of all the lineages, asking them to select students for the new school. All five Tibetan religious schools, both Buddhist and Bon, were represented: ten Nyingmas, ten Kagyus, ten Sakyas, ten Gelugs, and two Bonpo lamas. As well as their scriptural studies, thangka painting and rituals, the lamas were taught hygiene, mathematics, and geography. They met Westerners and

CHAPTER FIVE ❖ THE TIBETANS

Young Lamas Home School *Courtesy of the Bedi Family Archives*

Ringu Tulku on the left and Akong Rinpoche on the right *Courtesy of the Bedi Family Archives*

learned other languages to help their adjustment to the world outside Tibet and monastic life. Among the first year tulkus were Chögyam Trungpa, Akong Rinpoche, Tulku Pema Tendzin, Geleg Rinpoche, and Lama Zopa. Chime Rinpoche, Ato Rinpoche, Tarthang Tulku, and Ringu Tulku also attended. It was the start of the spread of the Dharma from East to West.

The school transformed into the first inclusive five-sect Tibetan monastery, renamed Mahayana Monastic House on May 7, 1966 with Ato Rinpoche as assistant principal and Geshe Tenpa Tenzin as head master. "There is a real monastery-family feeling in the new group which transcends sects," said Freda with maternal pride.

Ringu Tulku was the youngest of the lamas, sent to Dalhousie in 1961 with his cousin and teacher Khenpo Rinchen, a highly qualified lama and close friend of Chögyam Trungpa. In his two years of study, he saw the school grow from twenty-eight to forty students.

Ringu Tulku's gaze was far away as he recaptured memories of his school days as a tulku refugee fifty years before.

> I was nine or ten but I was never a child. From two years of age I remember everything very clearly. I remember Freda Bedi wearing a maroon sari and a shawl, like a zen. She had long hair that she used to tie up, very blue eyes, very fair skin and she was nice, soft, and kind. I didn't feel anything striking or shocking that impressed me about her, although it was probably the first time I met a Western person. She was nice, that was my impression. We used to call her Mummy and we really felt she was Mummy, nice and kind. I didn't feel anything different or special but there was a sense of familiarity. Sometimes in the evenings we used to stop beside her window and make a funny clacking noise to get her attention and she would call us in for hot chocolate. Nobody had his own family nearby.

CHAPTER FIVE ❖ The Tibetans

Freda *Courtesy of the Shambhala Archives (photographer unknown)*

Freda with President Radhakrishnan, Delhi 1962   *Courtesy of the Bedi Family Archives*

Mummy was not teaching but she was busy with the administration while we had classes with the teachers. She had already studied Tibetan and could read and write. She had a mortarboard from Oxford, a graduation hat which she wore on one occasion and we took photos of her wearing it.

She was very close to Indira Gandhi, who was much younger. She was in her thirties and because Nehru had no other children and his wife was dead, Indira played the role of hostess. She also knew Nehru's sisters. I used to visit Indira with her sometimes. She was only afraid of one person – Nehru and a bit afraid of Radha Krishna, the President of India. Otherwise she wasn't afraid of anybody. She knew how to deal with people; she was strong. When she talked she would argue. She was strong-willed and independent and possessed a certain kind of power.

CHAPTER FIVE ❖ THE TIBETANS

When she spoke everybody listened to her. She had a presence. She knew what to say and what not to say, what to do and what not to do.

We stayed in Dalhousie during the spring and summer. Just before the winter we would go to Delhi. There we stayed in the newly built Ladakh Buddh Vihar. At that time the '62 border war with China was raging and many Tibetans who were near the borders came to Delhi to the Ladakh Buddh Vihar. That was the start of Majnukati-la.

In Delhi we met the great dignitaries. It was then that I met Radha Krishna, the President of India, and learned the national anthem from him. The President gave her a free ticket to go everywhere in second class trains whenever she wanted and she could take someone with her. I also met the Vice President of India, Zakir Hussein and of course Nehru. We also met many other ambassadors - American, English. They gave us tea, showed

Freda with Sri Lankan ambassador, Delhi 1958   *Courtesy of the Bedi Family Archives*

us films. Because she had such important connections, we were treated like VIP's.

On holidays she rented a big bus and a few cars and off we went to Dharamsala to meet the Dalai Lama, then through the Kangra Valley to the Punjab (at that time Himachal Pradesh was also Punjab) to Amritsar. When we got to the Golden Temple the war was so near we had to leave. The tour lasted one month and the itinerary covered all the interesting places. We stayed in gurudwaras at night and took our meals there because they were free.

Some people said she was Marxist but she was actually Gandhian. Maybe she had had some interest in Marx at Oxford before she followed Gandhi, but when she came to India she was more influenced by Gandhi. Gandhi had a very complete philosophy, including economy and lifestyle. Economy is small scale home-based, self-sufficiency. It is based on contentment, rich and poor working together, simple living, high thinking. Simple accommodations.

She took us to many Gandhi places where the houses were made out of mud and bamboo. We observed how they made bathrooms, toilets without water and all kinds of simple things like that. You had to make your own clothes so everyone has to spin. It was Gandhi who started the khadi industry. All of us wore maroon khadi robes.

In 1962 during India's border war with China, Freda took a group of twenty-three tulkus and three nuns from Dalhousie to her hermitage cottage at Andretta in the Kangra Valley, a safe place, halfway between the tea estates of Palampur and the Tibetan community of Tashi Jong. It was a great responsibility, she said, to have so many future leaders and guides of Tibet grouped together in one building in

CHAPTER FIVE ✤ THE TIBETANS

Dalhousie when the sound of gunfire was only sixty miles away. She planned to set up an evacuee school to keep classes going and advised the volunteers at the Young Lamas' Home School to go to the plains.

Chime Rinpoche, now in his mid-70s, was another of the young lama refugees who was selected for the Young Lamas' Home School. Freda Bedi insisted he call her Mummy, he said. In a small chamber of his Buddhist Center in London, he recalled his school days at Dalhousie:

> I came out of Tibet in 1959. In 1962 I went straight from Sikkim to Dalhousie to meet Freda Bedi who was starting the Young Lamas' Home School for reincarnate lamas. I was a monk, yes, absolutely.
>
> My first impression was surprise. I said, "Shall we call you Freda Bedi?" She said, 'No, call me Mummy.' She insisted all of us call her Mummy. We didn't understand why but she really insisted. If we said Freda Bedi, she got upset. Now I understand why. Mother is so important, especially for Tibetans.
>
> She was dressed in a sari but she was a Westerner. I didn't think of her as a Westerner, and although she was wearing saris all the time, I didn't think of her as Indian either. She was dedicated to India and went to prison for Indian independence. All of India loved her and called her Sister. I too felt very comfortable with her and did not feel like she was a foreigner.
>
> We were all refugees and she was very genuine in helping us. It was wonderful that someone was looking after us, feeding us. I definitely feel gratitude to her. She was disciplined and ran the school very well. We had classes in English, German, all the Western languages, as well as Punjabi, as she was married to a Punjabi. The most important point is that all the lamas who came to the West were from that school. Not only Akong,

Group photo c. 1960-61, Young Lamas Home School, Dalhousie, Chögyam Trungpa Rinpoche in back row with Sister Palmo, Akong, et al. *Shambhala archives*

Trungpa, and me but three Gelugpa lamas who went to Germany all came from that school. Now looking back, I can see that all Tibetan Buddhism in the West was the result of her school.

Certainly Karmapa recognized her as an important lady in bringing Buddhism to the West. Some people said she was an emanation of Tara but I don't think I saw her as an emanation. Of course I knew she was a wonderful lady and a very important person. How she connected with all the reincarnated Tibetan lamas, the heads of all the sects, is almost unconceivable. Even His Holiness the Karmapa came to visit our school.

Chime fixed me with a direct gaze and said emphatically, "We are all here through Sister Palmo. All the Dharma coming to the West is rooted in Sister Palmo. Me, you, all of us. She is amazing. The Dharma you have right now is due to her."

CHAPTER FIVE ❖ The Tibetans

Freda did not stop her activity with the Young Lamas' Home School. There was much more work to be done to save Tibetan spiritual culture.

Said Professor Lokesh Chandra,

> She put each and every Tibetan into place. She put in a lot of hard work, a lot of effort. We had all worked very hard in politics and it continued with her work in Tibetan culture. She was one of the very few Europeans who helped. There were only four or five Europeans who were in the freedom struggle and she was very close to Nehru and Gandhi. She was very much a part of our lives because very few people were actively involved with helping the Tibetans and promoting their culture and helping the monks so they could make their lives as in Tibet. She was a graduate of Oxford and had all the fine qualities of a British lady. She was charming, very gracious. She wore saris most of the time. Later on when she became a nun she dressed in robes. She was impressive, meaning as in the presence of compassion.
>
> She was always organizing things for everybody. My father was interested in Tibetan artists. We wanted to make a library of Tibetan deities. She was always trying to find a place for Tibetans artists or scholars. Whenever she found an artist she would phone my father and tell him. We were making a complete compilation of the iconography of Tibetan deities. We had about five artists here and we published their work, copying all the illustrations. The archival work went on for about fifteen years. We published a lot of Tibetan works now continued by the Library of Congress. About eight thousand works were published under this scheme. I myself published about six hundred texts. The LOC would buy eighteen copies of each publication and send them to different libraries in the US. It was always in

Tibetan so the literature was not lost. It was not easy. The originals were woodblocks. About thirty Tibetan lamas were doing the touching up for publication.

Something she felt deeply was the destruction of Tibet. That hope became despair as time went on. It turned into a cultural transformation. Now nobody speaks Tibetan. They have become Chinese. This worried all of us. The Chinese took away everything. She felt so sad when she saw this. It touched her so deeply. There is an inner feeling. Why does that inner feeling arise? That is expressed by saying she is an incarnation of a bodhisattva.

♦ ♦ ♦

Mummy, bodhisattva, memsahib – Freda's multifaceted personality was like that of Alice as she gazed through the looking glass: "I know who I was when I got up this morning but I think I must have changed several times since then."

In 2016 I returned to the Kangra Valley where I remembered the eco-architect Didi Contractor who had lived in Andretta telling me, when I had first visited there in 1980, of her friendship with Freda.

I remembered Freda's cottage set back from the group of huts, higher up on the furthest hill. It looked cool, dark, and utterly simple, like a cave with high ceilings. In the late '60s and '70s she would come frequently with Ani Pema Zangmo for short retreats. Her mud brick hut inspired the design of my retreat house at Sherabling with its mud floors and bamboo ceilings.

I wondered how the mud bricks had weathered the years. I climbed up the hill to view the three directions of the Kangra Valley she had dramatized, looking through each window, animating it with scenes and characters like a stage play. The hut was completely bare, recently restored to its original simplicity. I peered in the window to see

CHAPTER FIVE ❧ THE TIBETANS

Freda's original hut in Andretta with views of the Dhauladhar Mountain range *Courtesy of the Bedi Family Archives*

Freda's restored retreat hut, 2016 *(photo by the author)*

Sister Palmo   *Courtesy of the Bedi Family Archives*

CHAPTER FIVE ✤ THE TIBETANS

the only ornament, a framed photo of Karma Khechog Palmo beatifically smiling a warm welcome, but the door was locked.

"She said she had a good meditation space in Andretta," said Didi, "and she liked it." Khamtrul Rinpoche with whom she had a close connection came and blessed it.

Didi's portrait of Freda reflected a multitude of perspectives. Here was a Western woman in front of the looking glass and in the prism of reflected light seeing a kindred spirit. They had much in common. Each had a guru: the Sixteenth Karmapa and Muktananda. The historical meeting of the two gurus at Muktananda's ashram in the late '60s was their joint venture. Both were highly educated Westerners married to Indian husbands, in the same political, social, intellectual, artistic, and spiritual circles although separated by a generation.

Didi said,

> I was part of the assortment of people in the intellectual movement of that time as strongly as she was a member of the Buddhist community. She presented a context in which I could talk with her about the things that interested me. Our conversations about Indian culture were animated.
>
> We hit it off like a house on fire. I was delighted by her, amused by her Englishness, loved that she was also a foreign wife. We became good friends. When we look at a many-faceted figure like Freda Bedi, we see only one or two facets, but what is remarkable and memorable about her is she was full of ambiguities and paradoxes. When there are paradoxes you are closer to the truth. The ambiguity sits at the center. There was an ambiguity of ideology in the generation when her ideology was formed. The movement of the intellectuals in Oxford underwent massive orientations and changes. I'm fascinated by seeing her in the context of her background.

The more ways in which you can see how a lovable and laughable human being can have both frailties and ambiguities with consistency and sincerity, the closer you are to the truth. She was not all of a piece, but she tried to be. There was nothing fake about her. She was naively sincere. At every stage of her development she was fully there. She was an early feminist, experimenting with Marxism, Gandhi, poverty, and that restlessness brought her to Buddhism.

I remember her saying "my first enlightenment" about when she was in Burma and discovered Buddhism. She came back and was changed by that experience. She referred to her epiphany as if it was an enlightenment experience. Embracing the experience of living with a joint family in a Punjab village was also a wholehearted experience. In the Lahore years, she lived in a hut and slept on the floor and had oil lamps; and then Norah Richards in Andretta was one of her older people whom she admired and emulated. Everything she undertook she did completely and wholeheartedly. The whole bouquet is what Freda was. She kept moving as people do when they are on a journey.

Freda changed the horses she had hitched her chariot to a number of times and we have to see her in the context of those times. From the beginning she was a romantic looking for a noble cause. At the same time, she was very determined; if she wanted something it happened. There was always about her the English schoolgirl – the epitome of the English schoolgirl. In the short war with Pakistan she remembered what you do when there is an air raid, and she taped all the windows. She was a Head Girl. She carried the Head Prefect with her into the nunnery, into the school that she founded. The teachers were quietly smoking dope in the corners and Freda was totally unaware.

CHAPTER FIVE ✤ The Tibetans

There were many parts that went together. She didn't turn off any of them. She didn't turn off the English working class woman who knew how to make jam properly. She was particular about the way things were done, a practical earthy woman with her mind in the sky. Her knowledge of the spiritual was way over the top. She was a little excessive in everything. She was a participant, not an observer, ready to get up and start playing the game, but always interested in the rules.

There is always the hope that the spiritual traditions of the world will get us out of where we are and take us into the next dimension that will be somewhat miraculous. What people would like to hear about the spiritual life is that it is magically transformative. Freda liked to see herself as magically transformed and many people saw her in that way.

We would like to read about Freda, the English woman who comes to India experimenting with leftism, ideological movements, finds her place in the spiritual world and dies within it in such a way as she is affirmed by the supernatural. We don't learn much from success because we may not be able to emulate it. We may not be able to emulate the absolute ridiculous single-mindedness of her belief, a certain naiveté.

She adored the Sixteenth Karmapa just as one might have a crush on somebody. All of us have crushes on our gurus. When we were going to receive darshan from the Karmapa and were taking roses to him, she busied herself taking off their thorns, because she wanted us to present the flowers as representative of our actions. So we were pulling off these thorns and I was amused by her literal interpretation in picking off the real thorns.

She was a great romantic all the way through, ready to believe in any miracle that one brought up, with herself as having a glorious role in it. She saw us as part of the great unfolding

Freda Bedi   *Courtesy of the Bedi Family Archives*

CHAPTER FIVE ✤ THE TIBETANS

of the religious history of the world. She liked to see things on a grand scale. She was not deeply intellectual. She was a big-hearted person.

The last time I saw her was when Karmapa was in America and Muktananda was in hospital with a heart attack. She met me when I came to Bombay and we had darshan with Muktananda. Then we went home. At that meeting she said, 'I don't like you dressing in all these colorful saris, you should take robes. You're dedicated to the spiritual life and we should be able to see this.' She was larger than life, an aggregate, very amusing, with a genuine loving warmth, but she also took the time to put you in your place and tell you how to do it. 'Look here Didi, you are leading a spiritual life. You should be wearing robes.'

The last time I saw her, a month before her death, she knew she was on the way out. She was very aware of it. She didn't feel that she had to do a lot more. It was more important to be in the moment. She was ready to risk the future. She knew she was taking chances. Anyway, she didn't mind if she died; she was ready to go whenever it happened.

As Didi spoke, I began to see a figure in continuous transformation – an English head prefect, a memsahib, a fearless activist, a selfless bodhisattva, a solitary contemplative, and a universal mother. One face was a profile sharply angled in an oval Victorian ivory pendant; another was a black and white '60s poster of an iconic revolutionary, the next was rectangular, a thangka of a renunciate enclosed in maroon khadi, sitting silent in a darkened hut, and a fourth was circular, a madonna, softly smiling, handing out trinkets. Through them all was drifting the graceful long-haired figure of a romantic almost pre-Raphaelite figure in a sari, holding a lantern to light the darkness.

Whatever Freda was before India, she took it with her on the path. Then Mother India, "earthen pitchers on her head, bangles on her feet, and babes in arms" got under her skin and lightened it with the stroke of compassion.

> *Mother India,*
> *Mother, Mother India[7]*
> *She walks along the village path*
>
> *She walks along the street*
> *With earthen pitchers on her head*
> *And bangles on her feet.*
> *And always little footsteps*
> *Are following her own*
> *And little ones are crying*
> *Or welcoming her home.*
>
> *She is Mother India*
> *The real one that we know -*
> *Giving all her blood and sweat*
> *For love and not for show*
> *Her face is lit by household fires*
> *Worn by the earth her palms.*
> *Mother, Mother India*
> *With babes in her arms!*

---

7   "Mother India," *Rhymes for Ranga*, Random House 2010.

CHAPTER SIX
Meeting the Guru

The bodhisattvas rely on the Perfection of Wisdom and so with no delusions, they feel no fear and have nirvana here and now. The Perfection of Wisdom is the greatest mantra. It is the clearest mantra, the highest mantra, the mantra that removes all suffering.

Tayata Om Gate Gate Paragate Parasamgate Bodhi Svaha
Gone, Gone, Gone Beyond, Completely Gone Beyond, Awaken. So Be It.

The opening lines of the Heart Sutra on transcendent wisdom, the most famous of all Buddhist teachings, refer to the five perfections that merged to create the circumstances for Sutra to come into this world: the perfect time, the perfect teacher, the perfect retinue, the perfect teaching, and the perfect place.

Freda Bedi met her guru during a parallel juncture of the five perfections. In 1959 the Sixteenth Karmapa came out of Tibet through Bhutan to India with his sacred lineage treasures just two weeks before the Chinese invasion, thus avoiding a long dangerous trek over the mountains. The great Tibetan master was suddenly available to Western laypeople in a way he had never been to Tibetans. It was the perfect time. It was the Karmapa who could show miraculous powers just by his presence. He was a buddha and thus the perfect teacher had appeared.

The perfect retinue or assembly of monks is defined as a harmonious group that is not easily split into schisms by external forces. The devotion of the monks and laypeople who followed the Karmapa into exile was further strengthened by his power to predict the right time to escape. They formed the perfect retinue. The Karmapa embodied the teaching beyond words: the transmission of enlightened mind through presence and when he spoke the miraculous power of being heard in the language of the listener.

The perfect place was Sikkim, an independent Buddhist country, one of the hidden lands concealed by the eighth century Tantric Buddha Guru Padmasambhava who designated it as a place of meditation for practitioners. A Buddhist king or chögyal had ruled there for centuries and in 1959, fifteen years before India invaded, he was still in power. In a historical precedent the Ninth Karmapa had established a monastery on a remote hillside above Gangtok in the sixteenth century.

In 1961 Freda Bedi journeyed to Sikkim, the same year that the king of Sikkim and Hope Cooke, a New York debutante, made international headlines by announcing their engagement, having met at the colonial style Windermere Hotel in Darjeeling. Freda was still a layperson with a husband and family. She had heard of the Sixteenth Karmapa through the Indian diplomat Apa Pant who, like her, had been a freedom fighter. Pant had a serious interest in Tibetan Buddhism and visited the great monasteries of Sera, Drepung, and Ganden in Tibet. His own guru Jamyang Khyentse Chökyi Lodrö known as the master of masters was at the heart of the ecumenical or Rime movement in Tibet. Lodrö had exchanged empowerments and teachings with another great master, the Sixteenth Karmapa.

In the latter part of his life Jamyang Khentse lived in Sikkim at the Palace Temple together with his consort. In 1959, two weeks before the Chinese invasion, the Karmapa had come to India via Bhutan and around the same time, Jamyang Khentse passed into parinirvana. Pant met the Karmapa in Sikkim and was deeply impressed. Freda was in Sikkim on refugee work when Pant told her, "You cannot leave Sikkim without meeting the Karmapa."

> There was no road to the monastery. Apa Pant sent me on horseback. I remember the journey through the forest. Most beautiful.

CHAPTER SIX ✤ MEETING THE GURU

His Holiness the Sixteenth Karmapa in his Rumtek chamber *Courtesy of Lama Surya Das*

His Holiness the Sixteenth Karmapa with white cockatoo *Courtesy of Dale Brozosky*

CHAPTER SIX ❖ Meeting the Guru

As we neared the monastery His Holiness sent somebody with a picnic basket full of Tibetan tea and cakes. It was about twenty miles on the path leading up to the monastery.

In a letter dated July 17, 1961 she described the timeless wonder of the hidden land and the discovery of Rumtek Monastery as the opening of a spiritual odyssey, reminiscent of Alexandra David-Neel's entry into Lhasa in 1924.

Sikkim is in India, and yet out of it. As Indian citizens we enter without passports. A beneficent old world maharajah in Tibetanized dress ruled this beautiful little hill country. There are prayer flags outside houses and in the markets the inevitable stream of refugees, lamas, monks, nuns, all with shaven heads. We didn't stay there long. The next morning we made our way by jeep to the foot of Rumtek Hill. There we were met by the ponies of the Head Lama, the famous Gyalwa Karmapa, head of the Kagyupa Order in the line of spiritual descent from Milarepa, the Tibetan yogi. I always enjoy riding on Tibetan mountain ponies. In about two hours we reached the monastic settlement. On the outskirts of the colony I was taken to a small room with a shrine, which was to be my home and my meditation cell for the next fortnight. It was in the evening that I was taken to see the Head Lama. He was seated on his ceremonial square cushion on the top floor of the simple country monastery, surrounded by birds. He greeted me with a smile full of happiness. In the days that followed I was to meet the Great Teacher daily.

Just at that time the Burmese changeover took place and the gates of Burma were shut. I was feeling a great sense of loss that I could not go and ask my Burmese guru, so I asked my question that I was saving to ask my guru to His Holiness, 'How

His Holiness the Sixteenth Karmapa   *Courtesy of Lama Surya Das*

can one combine saying the rosary with mindfulness, given that in mindfulness you have to give away all concepts and ideas and just sit?' He said, 'Just be mindful that you are turning the rosary.' It was a deep answer and so simple. I thought it was one my guru in Burma would have given me.

The amazing part of the whole visit was the complete lack of dependence on language, yet we managed to understand one another, the secret being of course that the transference of teaching and ideas was on the transcendental level, anuttara or

CHAPTER SIX ❖ MEETING THE GURU

beyond the reach of words. It was an experience too deep to be written but as natural as the sunlight. Often the "little lamas" came in; there was always an old monk attendant to serve tea, Indian (sweet) or Tibetan (salt), and to hand us sweets and biscuits. Often it was only when I got to my room and again took up the thread of meditation that I realized the teaching that had been given.

Just before leaving we called on little K.T Situ Rinpoche, very sacred, in his last incarnation the Teacher of the present Karmapa. When I asked the delicate little child what he wanted, he said, unprompted, 'Holy books, pictures of the pilgrimage shrines, and a pair of binoculars.' "What for?" 'To see as far as Rumtek where my teacher lives.'

On the same visit she witnessed the reunion of nineteen members of the Karmapa's family – cousins, nieces, nephews, and a brother and his family –

after an epic escape, fighting all the way, that had gone on for two years. What a joyous moment it was to see them all reunited after the intermediary separation and suffering!

The Karmapa's way of empathizing with the enormous suffering that enveloped his people was unusual. Years later Freda's friend and devoted student Barbara Pettee recorded an incident in her memoirs:

She was speaking of His Holiness who had left Tibet two weeks before (everyone else), due to his insight and took out many things that other refugees could not. Quite a while afterwards a party of 350 struggled to get through the mountains.

Cosmic laughter of the Karmapa *(photographer unknown)*

Out of that group 150 survived. They came to the Karmapa and gathered in a great group to tell him their story, proceeding one by one to say this one died, another was shot, that their food had run out, and a child had frozen to death, the whole tale of woes.

As they told it, His Holiness smiled and began to laugh, an extraordinary warm embracing laughter that has the effect of sun shining. As they told these tales of woe and horror, his warm laugh continued and finally they began to catch it and they laughed. Finally everyone was laughing. A huge cosmic paradox in this moment of extreme tragedy. Later on he told Mummy or rather she commented, that if he had taken them seriously or wept with them, it would have been a mass case of sorrowing and that this way they were all lifted up into the laughter and huge compassion that he surrounds everyone with.

CHAPTER SIX ❖ MEETING THE GURU

Some of the nuns from the original nunnery *Courtesy of the Bedi Family Archives*

When she met the Sixteenth Karmapa, Freda was already advanced in meditation. "She had not only very high knowledge but also a kind of inner realization," said His Holiness Sakya Trizin who knew her both before and after she became a nun. With intuitive insight into the teaching beyond words, she recognized her guru. "When His Holiness moves and walks and is with his people, I can see the Buddha quality. If the Buddha was here he would have walked and talked and done things just like that. Even physically, there is a certain radiance."

He requested her to found a Tibetan Mahayana Nunnery, the first in India, and she did it with her whole heart. It was also an important part of her own vision. His Holiness mentioned to her that in the past when he was on pilgrimage in the region around Punjab, he had visited a site sacred to Master Tilopa. He had seen suitable land near there. If a nunnery could be established, it would be excellent, he said. The place the Karmapa had seen was high above a village called

His Holiness the Sixteenth Karmapa ascending the steps to Tilokpur nunnery with Sister Palmo   *Courtesy of KTD Archives*

Tilokpur, more like a bus stop than a village with an untidy row of tea shops opposite a deep boulder-strewn ravine. The reason for the bus stop was a pilgrimage site, a sacred limestone cave next to the river where the eleventh century mahasiddha Tilopa practiced in the crazy wisdom tradition of the most advanced yogins. It is said that when his disciple Naropa met him, he was spitting out the entrails of fish and bringing the fish back to life. Tilopa was the guru of Naropa from whom the lineage passed to Marpa who, after going to India, transmitted it to the great yogin Milarepa.

In 1963 together with Karma Thinley Rinpoche Freda established a nunnery to save the nuns from extinction, at first in Dalhousie. Of the 20,000 nuns in Tibet, not more than 150 had escaped to

CHAPTER SIX ❖ MEETING THE GURU

India. A year later, she gave back the rented house in Dalhousie and moved to the new land. The buildings were made of flammable straw bales and a few months later, as Freda was leaving the nunnery, a sudden fire consumed everything: precious dharma texts, personal belongings, shrine objects. At her request, the Dalai Lama gave food and Dharma robes and instructed the Office of Religion and Culture to offer the most sacred objects of the Kagyu lineage, statues of Marpa, Milarepa, and Gampopa.

Before the next nunnery was built the Sixteenth Karmapa and his young regents stopped on their way to Tashi Jong to bless the Buddha statue that was lodged temporarily in a shelter. Freda waited humbly until His Holiness called for Mummy-la and took her by the hand. She then presented the plan for the new buildings. He consecrated the land and wrote out the name of the nunnery, Karma Drubgyu Thargay Ling. In the afternoon, he continued on his way to Tashi Jong.

Freda put all her energy into raising money for the construction of a new shrine hall, nuns' quarters, and community kitchen. At one point, the Dalai Lama stopped by unexpectedly en route to Dharamsala, climbed the 164 steps, each about two feet high, to the hilltop site. He stood in silent prayer, threw rice, and blessed the ruins to protect the future of the nunnery. An invaluable source of pure drinking water for locals in the surrounding area had run dry. When he blessed it, the water flowed again. Since then, the nuns say, it has never stopped.

A few days later a party of notable lamas came from Tashi Jong – Khamtrul, Dorzong, and Choegyal Rinpoches and the Tokdens. They drew a mandala showing the lines of power in the land and made prayers to remove obstacles.

All the nuns worked together with the coolies and skilled laborers, carrying building materials up the stone stairs to the topmost elevation with its breathtaking view of the boulder-strewn river. Pack

Boulder-strewn river viewed from Tilokpur Nunnery, 2016   *(photo by the author)*

New shrine room at Tilokpur Nunnery, 2016   *(photo by the author)*

CHAPTER SIX ✤ MEETING THE GURU

animals carried gravel and sand strapped to their backs on another path. Freda came to oversee the construction, stayed a few days, and then left.

In 1968 the Karmapa inaugurated the nunnery, giving audiences and teachings to the nuns. He emphasized that both practice and study were essential to establish a true foundation of the Dharma. To facilitate this, he appointed teachers from his seat in Rumtek: Khenpo Khatar, Karma Thinley Rinpoche, and other masters who came in turns to provide spiritual guidance.

◆ ◆ ◆

What was once a little hilltop nunnery accessed by an arduous climb is now a living, breathing, pulsating Gompa standing grandly at the end of an undulating paved road. An entirely new complex with a shrine room flanked by nuns' quarters, guest rooms, kitchen, and reception room centers around an open sunlit courtyard. Inside the great shrine hall, images of the Sixteenth Karmapa and the mahasiddha Tilopa sit on either side of a magnificent towering golden Buddha.

A special shrine to Machik Labdron, female Buddha and holder of the Chod lineage is aglow with white tormas in one corner. Two khenpos and one geshe supervise a shedra or college where the nuns can study to acquire academic degrees.

In the early morning I awakened to the sweet chanting of the long life prayer for the Seventeenth Karmapa while the nuns hoisted the Sixteenth Karmapa's flag which had first appeared to him in the dream state. He had declared, "Wherever this banner is flown, the Dharma will flourish."

At the original site a few kilometers away, the shrine room was lit by sunrays that sprang from a crystal chandelier, turning it into a sparkling Buddhist fairyland. The simple retreat house in which Freda lived and practiced had been faithfully restored.

Shrine of Machik Labdron, Tilokpur Nunnery, 2016 *(photo by the author)*

CHAPTER SIX ✤ Meeting the Guru

Karmapa's Dream Flag, original made by Deborah Luscomb   *Courtesy of Deborah Luscomb*

I walked through each tiny room looking for something personal and found a container of miscellaneous items saved from the fire. A well-thumbed book, The Six Yogas of Naropa, with penciled annotations around the diagrams used to illustrate the practice of Phowa revealed her advanced study of meditation.

Ani Wangshuk Palmo, the senior nun, said:

> Her greatest characteristic or quality was her wish to benefit others. That is clear and the most inspiring memorable thing about her. She had more concern for the well-being of others than herself. She was a visionary. She had a sense of what was coming in the future. She foresaw the importance of a well-rounded education; it became the single most important emphasis of the nunnery. If she had lived longer, she could have benefited people on a large scale; she had the ability to elevate them toward spiritual well-being. It would have been good for the world. When she was alive many important people came to visit. When she passed away they stopped. That made us feel her loss even more.

Sister Palmo's retreat house, 2016, front view   *(photo by the author)*

Restored retreat house   *(photo by Dennis Harrap)*

◆ ◆ ◆

In 1966 when Freda left worldly life and took ordination, she remarked, "All my life was a preparation for renunciation." She had raised her children while living in thatched huts without running

CHAPTER SIX ✤ MEETING THE GURU

Nuns at Tilokpur Nunnery, 2016   *(photo by the author)*

water or electricity. She had experienced economic hardship. While Bedi did time in prison, she was the breadwinner for the family, the responsible adult. When India won independence and she became a government employee, she had to commute to work by bus in the sweltering heat and monsoon rains of summer and the dust storms of winter. "She got a scooter but the business of kick-starting it was too much for her heart," said Kabir. "She had a heart problem even then."

She had also enjoyed a fulfilling family life, a soul mate relationship with her husband, and had entertained VIPs at her dinner table, sitting together on occasion with her servants contrary to the Indian rules of caste. She was surrounded by children and dogs. "It was a very full life," she said. By 1966 these comfortable ties to worldly life were coming to a close and Freda craved the happiness that came only with the peace she had experienced in deep meditation.

After receiving her husband's blessing, she told Kabir and Ranga of her decision. They were old enough, she thought, to manage their own lives. Kabir was twenty and Ranga, a married man of thirty-two.

His Holiness the Sixteenth Karmapa flanked by Chögyam Trungpa and Akong Rinpoche, and Freda and B.P.L. Bedi, Delhi, c. 1961   *Courtesy of KTD Archives*

CHAPTER SIX ✤ Meeting the Guru

Kabir initially felt a mixture of pain, anger, and a sense of abandonment, mainly for his sister. To his question, "Why didn't you wait longer for Guli to grow up?" she replied, "Who decides when an apple drops from the tree?" A letter she wrote to "My darling son Kabir" expressed the vulnerability she felt on taking such an irreversible step. She opened wide her motherly heart:

> I have been in a maze of pain, feeling yours and Guli's. There is a special link between us, a trust. You all knew one day this step would be taken. We even joked about my losing my hair. Somehow now had to be the time. The inner renunciation was complete long ago.
>
> Basically it's Guli you are thinking of. Guli is deep inside me in an inner way. In her childhood, I gave her all the protection I could; now I am giving it to her in a higher way. But she is always with me... Mother love doesn't just dry up. I can still see your little face as it was when you drank my milk and Guli at her first birthday with that full moon face of hers. You needed me then, you need me now. I am still there. If Papa at any time in advancing life needs me I am also still there.
>
> To take an ordination in a direct line from the Buddha is an inexpressibly sacred thing... There is an inner time, a ripeness, a realization of the impermanence of life, of the suffering of others, not only oneself. A reflection of the great compassion of the Buddha. At that time the knowledge of the approaching birth comes. I thought that the birth could be painless. I had not realized that the cutting of the birth cord must cause pain. It heals. The link between the baby and the mother does not cease. It continues. Nothing ceases. In a way, this time I am the baby. And I need you all, your love and protection, even physical help, if in another way.

But Guli was unprepared and the shock of seeing her mother gone turned into anger:

> She never told me she was becoming a nun. I was sixteen. I felt irritated. It hadn't been discussed with me. She knew I could be a volatile little woman. She let Kabir and Ranga know and she asked Kabir to tell me. I was very annoyed to start with. In retrospect, I realized it was a good thing because I was headstrong and would have had a tantrum. I accepted it at some point. She would have known that. It didn't take a long time to get used to it. When my mother came shortly thereafter, we were fine, we never had words about it. My mother was a prolific letter writer. I got a letter from her every week.

In later years, Guli understood that her mother had not renounced her family ties or given up her children.

> She didn't give up everything, she gained everything. It was what she was looking for. She was looking for this, to have a guru of that kind. She had lived that part of her life and she was moving on to another part of her life, continuing her journey. She never gave me up or gave up the family. This was just a different stage. She deserved it so much and she had wanted it and searched for it. She found it. She was concerned that I was her little one, but I had two loving brothers. She felt I was old enough now.

Freda's decision resulted in Guli meeting the Karmapa at Patiala House where he was staying as a guest of the Maharani of Patiala, Freda's friend; his all-encompassing love released her from the pain of abandonment.

CHAPTER SIX ✤ MEETING THE GURU

When I arrived there were Tibetans all over the place. He laughed and was so happy to meet me. He said, "Why don't you become a nun also?" Being a young college girl, I had no intention of doing that. In retrospect I should have, although I'm not religious in the least. He was wonderful, laughing, big hugs, a great guy. When he was in Delhi, I would meet him and he was always most loving to me.

The Karmapa was said to be always in meditation. It was a state called non-meditation in which there is no doer, doing, or thing to be done, no reference point. In his presence everyone could feel the powerful psychic energy arising from the state of samadhi.

Ranga said,

We went to Rumtek to meet His Holiness Karmapa for the first time,. "I'm not psychic but the energy I felt, even as a young man of thirty-eight, was just amazing. I've never felt it before or after.

With the family united again in spirit, Freda could take the next step on her spiritual odyssey. After receiving novice ordination from the Karmapa, Freda Bedi was given the name of Karma Khechok Palmo and lived at Rumtek with her guru. From now on Freda Bedi disappeared and she was known either as Sister Palmo or Mummy-la.

In 1972 when she was sixty-one years old, she journeyed to Hong Kong to take the highest ordination, that of gelongma or bhiksuni, from the unbroken lineage maintained in China throughout the millennia. Both the Dalai Lama and the Karmapa had requested her to bring back the ordination to the Tibetan tradition. The King of Bhutan sponsored her journey.

After the eighth century in Tibet the bhiksuni or gelongma lineage of transmission had been broken, leaving a gap in the sangha. It was like a pillar missing from the foundations of a Buddhist temple. In the chaos of the Tibetan diaspora of '59, the position of nuns in relation to that of monks was even more diminished than it had been in Tibet. Entrenched opposition from the monastic hierarchy to the full ordination of nuns existed particularly in the Gelugpa sect. As in the Church of England's resistance to women's entering the priesthood, the established order felt threatened. Sister Palmo was a successful Western woman accepted in Indian society, but as an outsider escaped the critical eye of the conservative Tibetan elders. A dignified upholder of the Dharma as a novice nun, Oxford-educated, and trained in Vipassana meditation, she was a worthy vessel to return the highest ordination to Vajrayana Buddhism. The requests themselves were an honor, a sign of the esteem in which she was held. They marked the pinnacle of her Buddhist life.

◆ ◆ ◆

When she disembarked at the airport, she suddenly realized she was alone. No one had come to greet her and she didn't know anyone in Hong Kong. "I hadn't a clue where I was going." It cost fifty Hong Kong dollars to reach the temple where the ordination was to be held. On the day, the temple filled with young students and the media, creating a great buzz of activity. At first she found it disconcerting that the entire ceremony was to be televised for everyone in Hong Kong to watch and then concluded, "It increases the faith of those who watch and creates great respect for the monks and nuns."

> We had to sit for long periods of time. In the prayers to Amitabha which go on all the time, there is a constant kneeling which is difficult for knees like mine. Extremely painful. Very strenuous, from early morning till midnight, doing constant prayers and bowing. One was quite dizzy, must have lost pounds. Then a half

CHAPTER SIX ❖ MEETING THE GURU

hour rest, taking a cup of tea. Ritualized taking of meals. One had to learn it all. Teaching how to behave as a monk or nun.

The Venerable Ming Chi of the Chan Line, one of ten Buddhist schools in China, gave the ordination together with Venerable Sek Sai Chung. Twenty lamas were present, some living in the outlying islands around Hong Kong.

> We were absorbed in our ceremony. Six incense sticks were inserted and lit and kept on the head. I was told if I meditated rightly I should not feel the burning. I did feel it at the beginning as it came down on my skin but then I meditated with great concentration, thinking of the Buddha as inseparable from HH Karmapa and Amitabha, and after that I did not feel the burning sensation at all. I don't know how long it went on. When they said it was over, I was conscious of a little soreness. The scar was not healed until ten days after in Rumtek and still there was no pain.
>
> It was so wonderful. We had a terrifically strenuous day on matters of the Vinaya. At midnight when it finally stopped, they gave us delicious chunks of Hong Kong watermelon. It was so refreshing. At the end of this I was physically tired but light and happy in a way I can't explain. The effect of the whole ceremony is something no words can express. Lightness and light, when one realizes that the unbroken line goes right from the Buddha like a stream of history. I feel purified and enriched in every way since taking the ordination and able to communicate the meaning.

Before leaving Hong Kong she was given a guided tour of Mahayana temples. She found that climbing up stairs was more difficult and prostrating to every monk and nun made her exhausted, but it did

Sister Palmo, Delhi *Courtesy of the Bedi Family Archives*

not dampen her elation. Gelongma Palmo was flying, and when she boarded the aircraft, she praised Air India, feeling proud that the national carrier of her country compared favorably to any airline in the world. In five hours she was back in Calcutta.

When her family saw her, said Ranga, they were amused. She had bright red stains all over her head. "True to her British upbringing the first thing she did when she emerged from the shrine hall was to go to a pharmacy for Mercurochrome which she dabbed on the slits and the seven or eight burn marks. These stains lasted for several weeks."

When she reached Gangtok, she spent the night at the palace guesthouse and met the crown prince "who was beautiful, just as a crown prince should be." She was eternally grateful to the Choegyal and Queen Hope, she said, for allowing her "the luxury of sinking into a dazzlingly clean bed with a marvelous mattress and waking up

CHAPTER SIX ❖ Meeting the Guru

to a hot bath in a tub," after travelling for days on the train and enduring a day-long bus ride up the hill to Rumtek.

Next morning Anila came to fetch her and she heard the news that her benefactor, the King of Bhutan, had just died.

> I would have loved to share the experience with him. I share the merits with him and pray it will help him on his journey now. When we reached the temple of Rumtek on the hill, the monks ran out with scarves to welcome me. After, I went to His Holiness and prostrated. He was happy and delighted I had been able to do the work. The second step is to raise the nuns so the tradition can be re-established.

◆ ◆ ◆

"This Karmapa is an incredible one," said Ngodup Burkhar, a Tibetan translator who met Sister Palmo in 1973 when he first arrived in Rumtek. He felt like a second foreigner, an outsider like Sister Palmo, magnetized into an extraordinary but alien environment. Karmapa was "a nonhuman human."

> As a child you heard so many stories. He was there, he was not there. My heart was thumping. I just wanted to serve the Karmapa. The Sixteenth Karmapa had such an incredible presence. No one came close to it. Jamgon Rinpoche, his heart disciple, would say he was like the Buddha. Sister Palmo had been exposed to other Buddhist masters, Hindu and Burmese, but his presence spoke to her heart more than the convenience of language. She could talk to His Holiness the Dalai Lama and Sakya Trizin in English. And the Dalai Lama had good PR. He was the main lama to be connected with. His Holiness Karmapa didn't know English and even what he knew, his pronunciation was really poor.

When I went to Rumtek in 1973 there was hardly any one there. Who wants to come and give up everything and settle there? Rumtek was not an easy place. A Westerner, a woman, a family person, all the barriers of language, customs, culture. She gave up everything to be with the Karmapa, to practice and be an extension of his activity. It was a combination of good karma and the magnetizing quality of the Karmapa.

What was most striking to me is how much she seemed to feel at home, especially with the Karmapa. Mummy-la did the Mahakala puja every night with the tulkus and Karmapa. It was an odd gathering. The little Rinpoches, the heart sons – Tai Situ, Jamgon Kongtrul, Gyaltsab, Shamar – and Mummy, older than the Karmapa. She was made a part of it and felt a part of it.

The environment around His Holiness was not so friendly, everybody was so big and special, I didn't fit anywhere. I didn't know anybody. Slowly I was able to make connections. Then I went to see Sister Palmo. As things began to settle, it was amazing to see her with Karmapa. Under some circumstances there are contradictions in harmony. His Holiness was as traditional as you could get. He didn't want the young Rinpoches to learn English or make connections with the outer world. It could do away with the third person barrier.

He would call 'Mummy-la.' And there she is, this English woman, an activist, in a situation where the hierarchy is very strong and male with all the protocol that goes with it, and she is coming from England - maybe the Queen helps a bit? "Yeshi Norbu (Wish-Fulfilling Jewel)," she replies, and melts in front of him. 'Sister Palmo, do you know anything about these people?' he asks. 'The first thing they say is "Where can I get the red string?"'

She told me this story. She was there when some army captain came to see His Holiness and then Karmapa gave him a red

CHAPTER SIX ✤ Meeting the Guru

Ani Pema Zangmo, Prime Minister Indira Gandhi, and Sister Palmo   *Courtesy of the Bedi Family Archives*

string. He said, "Bulletproof" and then he laughed. So the captain was a bit puzzled. He put the string around the neck of the goat and shot it. He wanted to experiment. Luckily the bullet didn't go through. Then the word spread. 'They always come for the red string, Yeshi Norbu,' she said, and started laughing.

From what I remember of her, she was simple, humble, motherly, very incredible when she mentioned Karmapa. Her face lit up with devotion. She had this very caring voice. I did not need more formalities, more aristocratic keeping your distance kind of thing. Did she keep all that protocol with the Karmapa? Yes, more than that. It was very natural, very real. It was delightfully, truly genuine. No question about it. She was incredible and he was more than incredible. He blew her mind. He transmitted awakened intelligence to her and she was forever grateful. That is why she was in Rumtek. Otherwise, it would have been a very lonely place. Her only companion was Ani Zangmo, her very sincere servant. She cared for Mummy.

Because of her good karma, supporting the Tibetan cause out of the goodness of her heart, she felt his spiritual presence. If you have experience, integration, that's what matters. If you have humility, gratitude, appreciation, that's what matters. All the differences do not matter because there were more important things in harmony, in common. The communication that she had with Karmapa and the transmission she received, nothing else mattered. When you are at home with your mind and are able to look at the face of your own Yeshe Norbu as a reflection of that, then there is common understanding. This is more than being treated like a tulku. She was treated for whom she was, respected for whom she was.

Those days are like centuries ago. The change has been so big. At that time this woman finds herself there, and it's like she finds her home on Mount Kailash. It's quite something. It's not like she didn't have other places to go. She wasn't rejected, ostracized. She was full on, standing there on her own. Coming from where she came from, she knew quite a bit about the world. She had seen corruption, rebellions, intermarriage, and all of that, so she was entitled to her strong opinions. But when she was in the presence of the Karmapa, could anyone appreciate him more than she did? She wasn't of that culture. It was uncontrived devotion.

I heard that she knew she was going to pass away and that before she died she talked to the Karmapa and she died while the Four Session Guru Yoga of the Karmapa was being played. She had received transmission and was a heart disciple, but favorable circumstances can enhance the passing.

That she passed away in Delhi while she was in meditation had many profound dimensions to it. One thing is the ability

CHAPTER SIX ✤ MEETING THE GURU

Sister Palmo at Rumtek   *Courtesy of Goodie Oberoi (photo by the author)*

and power of the mind, irrespective of language, culture, societal differences. Everyone is endowed with buddha nature. The potentiality of the mind is the same for everyone and by the truth and power of interdependence, communication can result. The guru's transmission of awakened intelligence and the disciple's ability to contain it out of pure devotion and confidence are how awakening can occur.

He would say, 'Mummy-la sit down.' It was like the greatest thing had happened to her. She knew she was in the presence of the Buddha. It was not a belief or a faith. Her sense of gratitude was boundless. Every time she was with His Holiness she had the experience of being in the presence of the Fully Awakened One. Through her good karma, her intuition, merit accumulation, and through the transmission she experienced more than glimpses. She knew that she was on her way. The proof of it is that when she died she was sitting in meditation.

Gelongma Palmo held the transmission for the rest of her life and conveyed it to others. In an amateur recording made in Milan in 1971, her barely audible voice was soft with motherly love. She sent the recording to Jane Taylor, a retired administrator for the federal government who was born and lived all her life at 501 Edgwood Road, San Mateo, California, the place of the first fledgling Dharma center of the Karmapa.

> Jane Dear, I was so happy to receive your letter about the dream in which you received the refuge ordination with all the appropriate feelings of the transfer of power, the deep current you felt. I do feel frankly that although you haven't taken the refuge in the outer way you have received it in the higher way. It is definitely a case of spontaneous higher refuge and ordination.
>
> I know of this because at some earlier part of learning from His Holiness and when my language was not very good, I was relying on the feelings I received through His Holiness and I also had some such powerful experience. I don't know whether this indicates you have had this ordination in a former life or will have it and become a Buddhist in this life, but it is of profound significance. As the years go on you will understand it.
>
> I think that the combination of the study of the Guru Lama Yoga which is now in a beautiful translated talk called the "Supreme Illumination" and the "Contemplation on the Divine Mother," these two in combination will be very beneficial for you for your own personal happiness and those who surround you. All blessings to you and to the circle around 501 Edgwood Road.

I play the tape again and again. Her voice is beguiling.

CHAPTER SEVEN
Freda Bedi In Her Own Words

My vision of Freda's life was emerging through images. I scrutinized her photographs to understand the different stages she had passed through. The pictures each told a different story, enough for several lifetimes: the downcast eyes and Mona Lisa smile of the Oxford girl, the demure look of the fair-skinned, blue-eyed Indian wife and mother in graceful sari standing next to her strong Indian husband, the strident woman in khaki trousers holding a rifle in Kashmir, and the maroon robes and shaven head of the Buddhist nun, blissfully radiant behind the Sixteenth Karmapa. I had read her letters to Olive Chandler from 1931 - 1962 all delightedly English schoolgirlish, to her "Darling Son" Kabir, and to her husband, "Respected Baba-ji."

In September 2016 another part of her story came to life when I learned of some tape recordings in a remote hillside cottage in mid-Wales. I drove on the narrow lanes to an original Welsh dwelling with bulging walls and lopsided floors. There, in an office behind the workshop outside the main house, were two reel-to-reel magnum tape recordings of an interview with Freda.

In 1968 Olive Shapley, Freda's close friend from Oxford and BBC radio pioneer broadcaster of the first on-the-street interviews, visited Rumtek Monastery carrying an Uber tape recorder, accompanied by her son Nick Salt. After Olive's death, scores of tapes came into his possession. They lay in an anonymous stack in his hillside home in Wales until he got around to cataloging them.

It was like discovering gold. At last I would hear a professional sound recording of Freda describing her spiritual journey in her own words. After she became a Buddhist, she spoke only in passing about

Sister Palmo at Rumtek, 1972   *(copyright Tamara Hill)*

her early life as a freedom fighter and social worker. All of it was gone, as if she had awakened from the dream of ignorance.

"I'd just like to ask you by what road did you come to this? Here you are in Sikkim, in a very remote part of the world. What has brought you here?"

Olive Shapley's voice is sharp and crisply modulated in a middle England BBC accent. Freda had become a nun two years earlier but she had not yet received full ordination as a Gelongma. She was now braving the barriers of gender, culture, and language to live in a primitive Tibetan monastery at Rumtek in Sikkim. In spite of Freda's shaved head and maroon robes, Olive greeted her friend with the standard courteous opening line, "You haven't changed a bit."

It was 1968 but Olive noted that "it was rather like being transported back to the Middle Ages." The monks chanted prayers in the prayer hall while the smaller ones chanted their lessons, and all about her, cows and goats rooted around as wood smoke from the kitchen fire wafted in the air. The Tibetan exodus was only nine years old; the

CHAPTER SEVEN ❖ FREDA BEDI IN HER OWN WORDS

Sister Palmo, Rumtek   *Courtesy of the Bedi Family Archives*

first lamas had just arrived in the West and here was Freda from Derby sitting in a cool, dark room with red walls and windows opening onto the mountainside.

She slept in a box bed and meditated on a mat. A table functioned as a shrine with her texts wrapped in cloth, a picture of the Dalai Lama, a vase with peacock feathers, and a butter lamp. Her personal possessions were few – photos of her children, paper, and a fountain pen. Her smiling attendant Ani Pema Zangmo made the tea and served the guests. Once in sheer joy she walked in holding a monastery peacock and set it down in front of the guests.[8]

Freda laughed briefly before replying,

"You mean what is my life story?"

The sound was startling. Her voice cut through time. It was soft and clear, tuned to a perfect pitch like the exquisite handcrafted bells used in Tibetan rituals. It had the clarity and depth of water in a still pond and the confidence of a stream bubbling onward to the ocean, sure of its direction. It was gentle and caring, soothing as a mother's lullaby.

"Of course. What brings you to the life of meditation of a Buddhist nun?"

It's a deepening and goes on for years and years and it doesn't come quickly. It was like a subterranean stream that flowed underground all the time while I was leading a very active life and it finally emerged. At that point I realized it as the mainstream.

I listened, riveted by the sound. Freda's voice was an attribute that could magnetize people. I found myself drawn ever deeper into the conversation.

"How strong was your Christian background?"

It was always interesting, especially the Old Testament when I was a child. At fourteen I was confirmed in the Church of England and I took great interest in the mystical side of the

---

8   Olive Shapley, Broadcasting A Life, p. 195, Scarlet Press, 1996

CHAPTER SEVEN ✣ Freda Bedi In Her Own Words

Christian religion. I don't like the word mystical by which I mean the deeper side. My first interest in meditation stems from there. I felt I needed peace. When I got to Oxford, one thing I was sure about: the Christian religion wasn't the final answer as far as I was concerned. I led an ordinary life at university. As you know I met an Indian student at Oxford and I felt a natural interest in everything connected with India. As a Buddhist it may have something to do with samskaras, the thought formations coming from former lives. That's how we explain inclinations. Then I got married shortly after taking my degree and came to India about a year later in 1934.

When I reached India, although I should have felt strange, I felt very much at home. I loved it from the moment I put my foot on Indian soil. It was a real home for me - not that I didn't love England. I still feel something very deep for the land of my birth. But there was something very deep for India, though I couldn't speak the language. At the beginning I lived in the Punjab, my husband's home. It was a time of great stress, the time of the freedom movement. Both of us were full of idealism about the independence of India and took part in the movement. It was a very busy life. I was bringing up a family. My first child was born in 1934. I was a lecturer in one of the first colleges for women, in Lahore. I used to write and move about a lot in the villages, mostly work connected with the independence movement. It was a very full life. But still that feeling persisted. I must find out the meaning of life, the meaning of suffering. Why? What? How?

About 1957 I met a very interesting English woman, I don't know if she's still living. She used to be a pianist at one time. She later became a Hindu swami. She said, "If you're interested in deeper things, why don't you meditate?" She told me a few things and from that – it was just an ordinary conversation not a lesson – I started meditating on my own and found it so absorbing, so revealing, so satisfying, that I tried to keep on doing it. I used to meditate also before writing. It helped me a lot. It helped the creative side of life. When I went to the Himalayas in the summer I used to have periods of meditation. Nobody knew about it except my family. I used to take interest in all the Eastern religions. I didn't get converted to any of them. I used to read Shri Ramakrishna's life, and the life of Guru Nanak – my husband comes from the family of Guru Nanak – and the Koran Sharif which is the most holy book of Muslims and the Bhagavad Gita, the main book of the Hindus, and some mystic poems from different religions, and the Bible still. I used to keep the books on my table and pick them up and think about them and meditate. But the meditation was not on anything. It was an attempt to reach beyond the mind.

I had a very busy life and after independence we remained in India. We were living in Kashmir and in Delhi. I was working as a social worker, writing most of the time, bringing up my children. I had three children by then. The interest was still very deep in my mind. In 1953 I had an opportunity to go to Burma for six months with the UN Social Services Planning Commission. I had to leave my family behind. I had more time to meditate. I met the most remarkable Buddhist teacher, a remarkable monk who had lived in England for fourteen years, though the last war had been in ARP. He taught me meditation at my request and it was then after about eight weeks that I got my first flash of understanding. More than that, it changed my whole life. I felt that really this meditation showed me what I was trying to find. I got great happiness, a feeling I'd found the path. I didn't know much about Buddhism. I felt that the Buddha had been the supreme guide and therefore I should take the

CHAPTER SEVEN ❖ FREDA BEDI IN HER OWN WORDS

Buddhist faith. I told my family about it and they were very understanding. I became Buddhist in 1953.

Then in 1956 His Holiness the Dalai Lama came to Delhi with a lot of Buddhists from all over the world for the 2500 year anniversary celebrations of the Buddha. I got his blessings then. In the meantime I was studying meditation with another very wonderful Burmese guru, Ven. Mahasayadaw and I went to Burma two or three times and was carrying on a full life as a mother, social worker, and editing The Social Worker magazine.

This went on till 1959 when the Tibetan refugees came over. I had a great wish to help them and I felt it with my particular background as a mother, social worker, and Buddhist. So I was sent at my own request to one of the transit camps near the frontier and I worked with the refugees for about six months, helping the mothers and babies doing all the things that women can do and also getting to know the lamas and their problems. About a quarter of the total refugees were lamas. Nobody knew what to do with them or could understand why they shouldn't do the ordinary sort of work. They thought they shied away from work but it wasn't true because they worked hard in their monasteries, but they had to have the right sort of work because they had given up everything – home, family, comfort, freedom of moving around – to be a lama. And why? There had to be some reason for it. They're not going to give it up without a wrench. There are a few who coming into contact with modern life relinquish their robes and take to a lay life. But for those who are really dedicated, we have to find out how to help them keep the tradition alive because it's very deep and very beautiful.

We say the teaching of the Buddha is beautiful in the beginning, beautiful in the middle, and beautiful at the end. It's the way across the ocean of suffering of the world. When you once realize the suffering of the world and you realize there is a way across it, that is the time when you accept renunciation and feel the only thing that's worth doing is not the work in the world but helping the minds of people to overcome the suffering every human being has.

In the West there's a great deal of mental suffering. I feel that the Buddhist way has a great message for those suffering from mental conflict. In the East we have less material things, are poorer, not so clean but there is a great content in the East which is not in the West. At first I didn't see it but I see it very clearly now and I have been seeing it through the years in spite of all the troubles India has had.

To come back to myself, I finally started a school for lamas whom I felt were the key point in the education process for Tibetans as they wouldn't be touched by the programs started by the government and the Dalai Lama for the younger children and children of lay families. So I consulted His Holiness the Dalai Lama. I couldn't do anything without consulting him and the Government, and they both agreed that a school for the incarnates would be a good idea.

"What do you mean by incarnates?"

An incarnate lama is a special lama, a child whom the Tibetans believe has been a big lama in a former life. The Tibetans are highly evolved spiritually. Extraordinary people. They do find the special child. They know the signs. In the West we talk about especially gifted children. They were doing that in Tibet for hundreds of years. There has to be a special way of bringing up these children with special gifts. It's a long story. Anybody who reads the life story of the Dalai Lama will discover how such children are found. I also feel, having worked among them for some time, they are very special.

(As if on cue, on the tape could be heard the haunting music of Tibetan horns in the background proclaiming the arrival of the Karmapa, the Dharma King, to his monastery.)

I began the school in Delhi. His Holiness the Dalai Lama felt it would be better in Dalhousie so we went up there and got quite a nice house, and we are still there. Over 100 incarnate lamas and monks have taken training in English in the school and a nucleus has remained. Many of them are now in different parts of the world. Once they got a little language everything was clear.

"Do you feel the Tibetans are naturally very intelligent?"

The lamas are the intelligentsia. Everyone who was intelligent gravitated to the monastery. I think there's a lot to be said for a good monastic system, The people who don't want to remain monks naturally go out and they become good lay people because they had a good religious training in the monastery. In fact many times I thought of Oxford and Cambridge in the Tibetan monasteries in terms of discipline, and their system of tutors. All kinds of things keep on reminding me... this old system of guru and disciple. The oral tradition: the book is there but the teaching is given by a teacher who has taken the teaching from another teacher, who has taken it from another teacher and so forth who has an oral tradition. You can't get anything from a book compared to what you can get from a good teacher. They won't teach the book if they don't have the tradition of teaching the book. It's not like they read the book and teach the book. They say no I can't teach it because I haven't been taught it. That book I can't teach because that was not taught to me.

After founding the lamas' school I found out there was a problem with the nuns. There might have been 20,000 or more in Tibet and I don't think more than 150 came out and I realized unless we took a few and tried to keep them as nuns many of them would go into lay life or live quiet lives here and there and the tradition would be lost. Again there is an oral tradition, not only a book tradition. So I started a nunnery with five nuns and ended up with forty-five with some young ones now. That was in Dalhousie and now we're going down to a permanent nuns settlement.

So altogether it's been a very interesting experience. I've put a lot of work and thought and energy into it. It's been the most wonderfully rewarding experience for me. I feel very humbled by the great learning I've seen and the great religious realization and the great gurus.

In the course of the year when I was living in Dalhousie, it just happened that when a moment of maturity came, worldly life appeared quite meaningless and I felt that I'd done everything for my children whom I dearly love, but that now I had to make a choice between helping all and helping just a few. I was blessed with a wonderful family who understood this. So renunciation had been there, I became a nun, but we're not cloistered as Buddhist nuns and I do meet my family. The love of the family has extended into a bigger family.

"Tell me what you're doing now in Sikkim."

I took my ordination two years ago and I decided the time had come to have a retreat, a deepening of spiritual experience. In the

CHAPTER SEVEN ✤ Freda Bedi In Her Own Words

West we have sabbatical years. I had been learning the Tibetan language and translating too. Between meditations I was writing it down to help the students. I had the wonderful opportunity of going to the Dharmachakra Center of my guru who lives in Sikkim and is the head of the Kagyupa tradition There are four traditions in the Tibetan Buddhist tradition, like four churches. This one specializes in meditation and the famous yogi Milarepa is a member of our line of gurus. His Holiness the Karmapa is such a radiant personality, so warm and human, a marvelous teacher in the oral tradition. He carries on the great tradition I explained. It is a great opportunity to study under him.

"What are your days like here?"

I get up at four in the morning. The early morning is very good for meditation and I go on meditating and have some tea in the middle. We don't believe in too much asceticism.

"I notice there is a lot of tea around."

Yes, There is a lot of tea. At 7 I have breakfast, then I go back to meditation and meditate until 11:30 and then have another break for lunch. At about 1:30 I meditate again for an hour-and-a-half and then I have a three-hour break for writing and all those things. It's quite an easy program as far as meditation is concerned. Sometimes we have a much tougher one but His Holiness thought this is good for me. Then at 6 in the evening, I start prayers again. Meditation includes prayer. In deeper meditation we combine prayers and visualizations with the silent meditation. Protector prayers remove hindrances. Meditation isn't sitting being peaceful. It is quite hard to meditate. It's quite an effort. Sometimes hindrances do come. These prayers protect and are very helpful. Then I go to bed at about 10 and have an hour free before sleeping.

"And you have a little nun to look after you?"

Yes. I couldn't meditate like this unless I had her. She's both Tibetan and Indian. Racially Tibetan but she's always lived on the Indian frontier. She knows Hindi and cooks the food I like, Punjabi. She is very cheerful and uncomplicated.

"But you hardly go out of this room for a year?"

I go out when I take a lesson from Guruji, His Holiness the Karmapa. I may go three or four days without taking a lesson. It depends on the stage of the meditation. If I feel the need to ask a question or I need his help I send a message. He's very busy but he's very good and helps in a wonderful way. To struggle alone for realization, the lonely meditator, is very hard. It may be very beautiful in its own way but somebody of whom you can ask questions, a real living teacher, or even without asking questions, just sitting in front of him and somehow from that which is beyond the mind, something comes. The Buddha is the greatly compassionate one. There are systems of meditation that are not as compassionate as this method. It's a combination of compassion and wisdom which leads to the enlightenment of the Buddha.

"Do you have regrets at all for what you've given up?"

I have no regrets because what had to be given up was given up. It fell off naturally like an apple falling off the tree. We don't have to give up loving. We have to give up attachment. To be attached is a great burden not only for you but for the people you are attached to as well. Love is the great thing and that doesn't change. It expands. If I have caused any suffering to my children I am very sorry about it and I think they understand it. But by the blessing of the Triple Gem everything has gone on so well since I left and the older brothers are taking more interest in their sister. Really there's no loss, in fact I think there's a gain. It's impossible to explain this. If you see my family I think you'll understand.

The main point is to help others not just for myself. It's not to get enlightened for myself. This path is: I take refuge in the Buddha, the Dharma and the Sangha and until enlightenment is reached, by the merit of generosity and other good deeds, may I attain enlightenment for all that lives. It isn't for oneself alone. How well I do it I can't say. I only pray that whatever I've done may be of use to others. I don't think for one minute of myself.

"Do you go back to a more active life or don't you know?"

Life outside is very active. A lot of people come with their problems. Sometimes I have to travel about. I can't say in advance what I'm going to do. I've given up planning. The only thing is we shall have to build our own nunnery and that is quite a job. We will start on faith as we started the school on faith.

His Holiness the Dalai Lama has taken a great interest in this monastery we founded and he's now the patron. It's the first monastery to have the five sects all together. Next year it will move to Dharamsala so it can be nearer to him and he can take more day-to-day interest in the work of the monastery. There we

Sister Palmo   *Courtesy of the Bedi Family Archives*

will teach languages, English, Sanskrit, and maybe some European languages too.

"So you see a very busy life ahead of you."

Again I can't say what is ahead, who knows? We may be dead tomorrow. We may live twenty or thirty years. Nobody knows. It

CHAPTER SEVEN ✤ FREDA BEDI IN HER OWN WORDS

Sister Palmo   *Courtesy of Tamara Hill (photographer unknown)*

is the realization of the impermanence of life that makes a Buddhist nun.

On Olive's next visit to India Freda arranged a meeting with the Dalai Lama who asked her, "Tell me, what do you call Khechog Palmo?" Olive replied that she still called her Freda, to which the Dalai Lama replied, "I call her Mummy."

In 1977 the two friends met again and lunched at the YMCA in Delhi. It was a happy reunion but it was to be the last. Freda died unexpectedly two weeks later. She died as she had lived: consciously, sitting upright in deep meditation.

CHAPTER EIGHT
When The Iron Bird Flies

When the iron bird flies and horses run on wheels the Tibetan people will be scattered like ants across the face of the earth and the Dharma will come to the land of the red men.

Padmasambhava, eighth century

In the early '70s when Sister Palmo was living in Rumtek Monastery, practicing extensive retreats in the remote mountain kingdom of Sikkim, cosmic consciousness was permeating the West. Light from the dawn of a new age was spreading. In 1968 the Beatles, kings of rock and roll, had abdicated to Ravi Shankar and the Maharishi and were practicing Transcendental Meditation, proclaiming it as a drug-free high. David Bowie had been to Chime Rinpoche and asked to become a monk. Leonard Cohen dropped in at Samye Ling. Allan Ginsberg had beaten his drum and chanted OM on the banks of the Ganges in search of drugs and enlightenment. He turned up at Rumtek and asked the Karmapa whether taking LSD was a valid spiritual path. In 1974 in San Francisco when Chögyam Trungpa introduced the Beat poets – Ginsberg, Ferlinghetti, and McClure – to the Karmapa, he received the reply, "The use of drugs creates an artificial sense of higher consciousness. Only mind in its natural state, a complete openness, the practice of Mahamudra, achieves this."

It was in this new spirit that Padmasambhava's eighth century prophecy was popularized and quoted to mean the coming of Buddhism to the West. "It was predicted in Tibetan scriptures that the teachings would go to the land of the red-faced ones when the iron bird appeared," said Sister Palmo. "What was a calamity for Tibet appears to have been an inspiration for us." Suddenly meditation, the

215

guru, and enlightenment appeared in the public consciousness, available for exploration. "Buddhism is based on meditation." explained Palmo, having found her spiritual path based on mind.

> The root and base of the practice is that.. This scientific way of finding out the truth of being in the universe has had a profound influence in the West in this generation. It is not accepting it from somebody else, but experimenting with it yourself. It has emotional and artistic aspects but the younger generations are not for the older ways of practicing religion. Basically most people if they are not the kind who work on themselves leave quickly.

There was a great explosion of Dharma activity as East met West. The tulku protégés Chögyam Trungpa and Akong Rinpoche who had lived like brothers at the Bedi home in Delhi founded the first Tibetan Buddhist center in the lowlands of Scotland at Johnstone House donated by a Burmese-trained meditation master Anandabodhi, later known as Namgyal Rinpoche. They called it Samye Ling, the place of the inconceivable, after the first monastery in Tibet. In 1970, after an acrimonious disagreement, Trungpa moved to the United States and established new and thriving centers in Vermont and Boulder, Colorado. Many of the graduates of the Young Lamas' Home School were taking the Dharma into uncharted waters.[9] Tarthang Tulku was actively working in California to connect the Dharma with science. Chime Rinpoche had become a popular lama with a center in Saffron Walden in England, and Ato Rinpoche, the head of the nonsectarian Mahayana

---

9 Ringu Tulku, the youngest lama, would later found Bodhicharya International, a nonecumenical Dharma organization with branches throughout Europe; and Lama Zopa would found in 1976 the FPMT, Foundation for the Preservation of the Mahayana Tradition.

CHAPTER EIGHT ✤ WHEN THE IRON BIRD FLIES

Monastery that originated in the Lamas' Home School, was teaching privately while working as an orderly in a hospital in nearby Cambridge.

Palmo was filled with a sense of urgency to bring the Karmapa to the West where he could sow the seeds of Dharma and sprinkle the water of blessing to make the seeds sprout, but the Karmapa wouldn't budge. "His Holiness seems to be able to move only when the cosmic time for moving comes," she remarked.

When we met in Delhi in 2016, Anila Pema Zangmo revealed how Sister Palmo had tried to persuade the Karmapa to travel to the West. Sister Palmo asked, 'Yeshe Norbu, please make a tour and give teaching in Europe and the USA.' Yeshe Norbu said, 'There is no Dharma in foreign lands.' He didn't want to go. Then she said, 'Yeshe Norbu look and see with your own eyes, then you will know.' She touched her fingers to her eyes. Again she said, 'Yeshe Norbu, go and see with your own eyes.' Sister Palmo asked for two years, continuing to wait for him to reply. Invitations were no problem.

Palmo had another reason for wanting to take the Dharma westward. Her spiritual search was now an acceptable way of life. She had left her family and homeland in the '30s under the stigma of a socially unacceptable interracial marriage. Her nostalgia for Europe had been dimmed by the Great Depression and the rise of Hitler, and she had made her life in India, becoming the "daughter" of her Indian mother-in-law. When her own mother Nellie died in 1966, Palmo was in Rumtek. She had translated a history of the Karmapa's sacred Black Crown and dedicated it to her, hoping it would have been a comfort in the absence of a daughter by her side. Her only brother Jack, a submarine commander in World War Two, was torpedoed off the coast of India, surviving many hours in the ocean. After his rescue he had been reunited with Freda in India. He passed away in 1968 after a heart attack. Palmo was in Delhi. Although she had visited her niece Mary in Scotland in 1973 when she made a Dharma tour of Europe, in a sense she still had unfinished business. She had to come home again, and it was the new spiritually attuned generation whose journey mirrored her own that inspired her.

When Freda Bedi became Gelongma or Sister Palmo it seemed that she was living out another identity. The first was as an Indian nationalist, "a jailbird and political activist chased by the police and watched wherever she went," said Ranga. Then came the social service period, followed by Buddhism. "There were three totally different lives," Ranga concluded.

An Italian journalist Cristina de Stefano used a similar demarcation in a profile of Kabir for ELLE magazine in 2000. Freda's three names showed three different lifetimes: born the English girl Freda Houlston, she became Freda Bedi, the wife of an Indian Communist revolutionary, and died Gelongma Palmo, a pioneer of the international revival of Buddhism.

The thread that connected Freda's triple lives was meditation. She was on a spiritual journey her whole life to reconnect with her previous Buddhist lifetimes and everything on the way to her destination was preparation, like rites of passage. She believed fervently in Gandhi's ideal of ahimsa or nonviolence to bring about political change: "I feel proud to claim my own little part in Gandhi's great movement with its motivation based on love, not on a struggle with hatred. I learned a lot."

> Outwardly I was a social activist and a follower of Gandhi, but inwardly meditation was beneath it and I don't think I could have borne those years with all their difficulties and strains unless I had done so.
>
> The basis of a Dharma life is nonviolence; it is the message of Gandhi also. If you harm others, the law of karma will strike and you yourself will be harmed. The ripples of harming go far. If

CHAPTER EIGHT ❖ WHEN THE IRON BIRD FLIES

through meditation people come to understand the importance of nonviolence it will be a great thing for peace in the world and for peace in the country. This knowledge will be constructive whatever you do. I feel that not to harm is the seed of Dharma.

When I saw the stupas and the monks in their golden robes with their begging bowls in Rangoon going out in the morning to take enough food only for the day and met my first gurus U Tittila, a great Bhikku and Mahasi Sayadaw, a saintly monk, then that was home. It rang a bell. It was a movement of the heart toward the path of meditation and the way of the monks. I knew that I had been a Buddhist in many former lives.

Freda did not live three lives but had three parts to her life and each part corresponds to the three vehicles of the Buddhist path: the Hinayana, the narrow path of focus on ethics and renunciation, in the Gandhi years; the Mahayana or Great Vehicle, the path of boundless compassion, in the refugee years in Kashmir and Assam, and the interim social welfare period in the villages. Within the Mahayana is the third path, the esoteric Vajrayana.

Mahayana brought in another aspect that fit me like a glove because it brings in compassion for all sentient beings and the great cosmic point of view. The enlarging of frontiers pleased me very much as a social worker. The Mahayana was my way.

My responsibilities have changed from the physical plane to the spiritual plane. The world now is my family. There is a great broadening of the mind and a great feeling that whatever the situation there is a sharing with all. If we examine the mind, where is "I," how can you isolate it? The I is changing constantly as the child changes from babyhood to teenager, adult, then elder. Just as the body changes, so the mind, the thoughts, change. The pure mind remains. My search was always inward. I had a strong feeling that I had lived before and had always been looking for solitary meditation.

The bodhisattva ideal of self-sacrifice to benefit all beings was the message of Freda's poem "The Ballad of the Golden Deer"[10] written in 1942, eleven years before she became a Buddhist.

The Golden Deer sped through the fragrant wood to the palace of the King to offer himself to the butcher's knife in place of a doe suckling her fawn, but the King dismissed him. The deer replied with the altruistic statement of the bodhisattva,

I will not move,
Said the King of the Deer,
Until every fish
Each fowl of the air,
Each deer that hides
In the woods its sorrows
Is safe from the knife
And the hunter's arrows.

Then to the eyes
Of the King there came
Tears of pity
And tears of shame.

'None shall kill
And none shall harm
The forest creatures

---

10 "The Ballad of the Golden Deer," *Rhymes for Ranga*, p. 76

CHAPTER EIGHT ❖ When The Iron Bird Flies

O gentle One.'
(Lotus heart,
So late to bloom,
Open your petals
Toward the sun.)

Freda's life was her path. Through her activities and bodhisattva motivation, she connected with the Vajrayana or Diamond Vehicle that contains profound secret methods to attain liberation in one lifetime. The merit accumulated in the first stages of her life brought her to the Tibetan lamas and into direct contact with her guru. Preparation for the esoteric Tantric path was by this time complete. Life had wrought and shaped her into a practitioner of the highest level, one with little dust in her eyes.

The most perfect is the Tibetan Buddhist way, the Mahayana way. The lamas were extraordinarily developed behind those mountains. For centuries they were undisturbed and were living the lives that the disciples of the Buddha lived. I feel a great proximity to Tibetan culture and the incarnate, and my guru His Holiness the Karmapa who is a living Buddha to my mind. People's lives are changed just by meeting the great gurus. We say that anyone who has been seen or touched by His Holiness, his foot is on the path to liberation.

The intuitive recognition that the guru is a buddha is an advanced stage of the spiritual path. It requires not just lip service but a voluntary and entirely natural surrender of body, speech, and mind to the guru who embodies the primordial buddha, Vajradhara.[11] In the pro-

---

11 In the Dzogchen tradition the primordial buddha is called Samantabhadra.

cess, spiritual evolution happens naturally. Sister Palmo moved within the divine play of universal energies that arise spontaneously in an intimate relationship with the guru. Sufis speak of the beloved; Hindus describe it as a dance, the only dance there is. In the Vajrayana, it is described as guru devotion, the precarious but fast track to enlightenment.

> The Kagyu sect is based completely on devotion to the guru. That's the way to get through the forest. The individual aspiration has to be there before the guru can bless the arising of individual effort. Devotion to the guru is the heart of the practice, especially in the Kagyu. I am not a person, though an intellectual, who can learn out of books. I learn through precept. I need a guru to teach me.
>
> The path is made more human, warmer, more effective by having somebody to guide you. We believe not only in teaching but also in blessing; they are perfect celibate monks, and they shower a rain of blessing on their pupils. You can feel it as an electrical current and your depth is increased by this. The wave of energy comes in the presence of the guru. The guru's hand resting on the head, we believe in that. With a guru it's much easier and quicker to feel the all-permeating, all-merciful, all-illuminating effect of the great ones. So I believe in gurus.
>
> The inner guru is a stage when you know his blessing is within you. He sits in the lotus in your heart. I do feel his presence even more when I am away. We are within the mind of the guru even when they are not present.

The Sixteenth Karmapa manifested a buddhafield wherever he went. Being at Rumtek, the foremost physical center of his mandala, enabled the Tantric practitioner to transform worldly view into pure

CHAPTER EIGHT ❖ WHEN THE IRON BIRD FLIES

perception in which all sounds are mantra, all forms are divine beings, all thoughts are transcendental wisdom.

> When one becomes a disciple of Tantra everything is pure because we have been empowered by the initiation of the lama: our body becomes like a buddha body, our voice like a buddha voice, our mind like a buddha mind. It's not things that change but it is the mind that changes. The mind is the forerunner of all creative things. This path is so full of beauty that it purifies the body, speech, and mind to the ultimate purity.

In this state of submersion, Palmo entered retreat, encircled by the radiance of nature.

> The rainy season retreat that I am spending in Sikkim is so beautiful and restful. It's a drama of the clouds. Every morning I wake up and see whether they are rising like incense from the valleys or are piled like whipped cream in the depressions of the hills and sailing in space or ringing the hills like a hoop.
> It is a rest badly needed after all that travelling and the great blessing of my Guru-Lama, His Holiness the Karmapa. We all fast after midday in the Buddhist way and this is the specially sacred season of the Varsha when the lamas wear the yellow upper robe every day... and the ghoom ghoom gatang of the wooden gongs wakes us all up before dawn. (1969)

Said Goodie Oberoi,

> She was almost always in retreat, very close to God, to Buddha, to the Twenty-One Taras, and she was closest to Karmapa. There was total spiritual unanimity between them. If she

suggested something, it happened. They just clicked spiritually. He was spiritually above her, she was a little below.

Whenever I needed her she just arrived like that. One time she came from Rumtek. I had been crying and she came and said, "I'll see to it that this doesn't happen again." And she saw to it and it never happened again. It dissolved. Once I slipped on the floor when somebody spilled a cocktail and I broke my arm. It set badly. Again I was missing her. I could almost hear her saying 'You need a mother.' I replied in my mind, "I wish you would come." And the next day she came. I wouldn't dream of disturbing her. Whenever I was in trouble she was always there the next day or even the same day. She said I was not to speak about it, not to tell anyone.

When Sister Palmo was not in retreat, she would keep in close contact with her family, appearing suddenly at a moment's notice. Shortly after she was ordained as a Gelongma, she visited Ranga and his wife Umi in the Assam tea estate where he worked as a plantation manager.

It was there that Jim Robinson, the fifteen-year-old-son of a neighboring tea planter, dropped into Ranga's villa one day in 1972 and saw a nun nicknamed Oogi by her family with shaven head and maroon robes flicking through the pages of Vogue. It made an indelible impression.

My father was also a tea planter working for the Jokai Tea Company. When we met Oogi he had been posted to a tea estate, Borpatra, in Upper Assam close to the Naga hills, not far from the Himalayas. We lived alongside tigers and leopards, elephants, snakes, wild porpoises. Long-snouted gharial crocodiles cruised the rivers. Borpatra was close to the Naga hill tribes whom we

CHAPTER EIGHT ❖ WHEN THE IRON BIRD FLIES

saw regularly and I kept in the back of my mind that they had once been fierce headhunters. The closer you came to the borders of Sikkim and Bhutan, the more Buddhist the villages were, such as the Man Mow Mukh village where a colony of Burmese had a small temple. They would send their young boys across the border to Burma to train as novice monks.

My first meeting with Oogi was in the comfortably furnished lounge of her son's bungalow on the tea estate. The room was pleasantly air-conditioned, a luxury in the humid heat of Assam. I had been told to go in to see her by my mother and realized I was being invited into her presence. I walked into the room and saw a woman with a shaven head sitting in maroon robes flicking through Vogue magazine. Oogi, it seems, was not only a nun, but a Gelongma having recently received the highest ordination. I was somewhat shocked. It seemed a strange mix of religious tradition and modern culture.

She peered over her lunette spectacles and invited me to come and sit beside her. She asked if I was interested in religion and I said "Yes, Hinduism." She suggested I focus on Buddhism and gave me a copy of Jonathan Livingstone Seagull by Richard Bach. It was, in her opinion, the best introduction to Buddhist beliefs. It remains my favorite book to this day and lives on my bedside table. I found it a source of inspiration, a reminder of the importance of belief in the self and the value of focusing to attain any goal you put your mind on, a valuable teaching in being true to oneself and not following conventional belief systems.

Freda seemed very jolly and cheerful but was also quite determined and had a very definite presence. She had an air of otherworldliness, what I would call holiness. I would put her on the same level as Brother Roger, the Swiss Christian monk who founded the ecumenical Taize community in the Burgundy region of France, whom I met as a teenager.

Oogi could be bossy and insistent but, I believe, with the best of intentions. At the time I knew nothing of Tibetan Buddhism other than the thangkas that Ranga and Umi had in their homes in Assam and Calcutta. As far as I was concerned, Oogi was a family friend and I accepted her religious background and practices.

I also heard about Oogi's husband Baba Bedi who had special abilities after what seems to have been a mystical experience. I knew he helped children with emotional difficulties in Milan by analyzing their artwork. My mother showed him some paintings I had done and he wrote about them. I still have these on my desk.

Some days later I saw her again but this time she was chanting with some monks upstairs in the tea bungalow at Borhat. We met her just before we left India in 1976 when she came to stay with us in the company house in Calcutta. She was accompanied by a nun, her attendant Pema Zangmo, and we had several conversations about the merits of going to either Oxford or Lancaster University to study Comparative Religions. She insisted that I study Buddhism and go to Oxford. She gave me a list of people who were her friends and acquaintances and told me that I should meet them in Oxford.

As it happened, I went to Lancaster and while there learned Samatha meditation, joined the group in Manchester, and went on retreats. I gave up meditation some years later but these were definitely formative times and even now in stressful situations I feel myself instinctively slowing down and going into slow motion because of the Samatha practice.

CHAPTER EIGHT ✤ When The Iron Bird Flies

When my family decided to travel from Calcutta to Delhi on the Rajdhani Express before going to Kashmir for a final holiday in India, Oogi tied sacred threads around our wrists for protection and safekeeping. She told us that if we were to take them off we should place them somewhere high up like on the top of a cupboard. I remember mine just fell off as I stepped onto the platform at Delhi at the end of our journey.

Years later I moved to Oxford purely by chance at the invitation of some friends and did a DPhil at the Oriental Institute in Hindu studies. However, I reestablished the Oxford University Buddhist Society with Shenpen Hookham who also knew Oogi or Sister Kechog Palmo, as she was known. We ran meditation classes with invited teachers, including many Tibetan lamas. I also met all the people on Oogi's list including Michael Aris and his wife Aung San Suu Kyi who once served me lunch. Oogi sent me several publications which I passed on to Shenpen.

There have been many ways in which these links and friendships have continued to this day. Wolfson College has become linked with the Oxford Center for Buddhist Studies under Professor Richard Gombrich, my supervisor and the Boden Professor of Sanskrit with a particular interest in Buddhism and Pali studies. He was delighted when we offered to set up The Buddhist Society again even though we had to ignore the University requirement to "promote an interest in God."

The seed of this Buddhist legacy in Oxford was planted in that room where I first met Oogi in Assam all those years ago. Only now do I understand that the nun in robes flicking through Vogue was living the message of Jonathan Livingstone Seagull. She had no fear of flying high above the crowd nor of swooping down to touch a young life on the seashore below.

• • •

By the early 1970s Sikkim, the ancient kingdom with its old world maharajah, was in crisis. When Tamara Hill, an American graduate of the elite liberal arts college Sarah Lawrence was researching Tantric paintings in India in 1972, she was invited by Queen Hope to stay at the Royal Palace in Gangtok. Not until she was followed by the police did she realize that her friendship with the Queen put her under suspicion. Hope Cooke, an American by birth, was being targeted as a spy in a plot to remove the King and annex the Buddhist kingdom.

Hill reported,

> An unruly mob of disenfranchised Sherpas and Nepalese tribesmen had apparently been stirred up (and secretly fomented) by the government of India to look as if they were objecting to the Chogyal's rule and to topple his administration.

The hidden land of Padmasambhava was officially invaded by India in 1974, its spiritual identity truncated.

Rumtek was protected from the politics surrounding the monarchy. While the Karmapa was alive, it remained a kingdom with its own Dharma King and as long as she lived, Palmo had a place in it. He sent serious Western Dharma practitioners to her for instruction in advanced Buddhist practices, a measure of both the realization she had attained in meditation and the esteem in which she was held.

Tamara Hill recalled the sequence of events.

> I was accompanied out of the Chogyal's Palace to the walled compound of Rumtek in an official Jeep with an escort from the Palace and was thus granted a special private audience with His Holiness the Karmapa. This took place at his own house

CHAPTER EIGHT ✦ When The Iron Bird Flies

and aviary on the hillside above the monastic temple. Tea was served in gold-glazed porcelain cups while a translator helped us to converse in a rudimentary manner. He was the most impressive and austere spiritual presence I had ever encountered. His gaze simply penetrated to one's core, and one felt that he could truly read one's mind and heart without a word.

I was able to ask him how I could learn more about Tantra and Buddhism while I was travelling around India and Nepal. To my utter surprise, he told me that I should go to meet one of his own great teachers, the Venerable Lama Kalu Rinpoche who had just been at Rumtek and who was in the course of returning to Sonada, India at that time. I could hardly believe that this was the only guru's name I had noted in all of India and that I was now being directed to go study with him! His Holiness wrote and signed a letter of introduction for me to give to Kalu Rinpoche to deliver in a valuable personal referral.

In early April, she returned to Rumtek with a parcel from Kalu Rinpoche for the Karmapa. She learned later that the heavy parcel she had transported contained a valuable gilded Buddha statue. This time the Karmapa guided her to Sister Palmo.

He spontaneously granted me a confidential personal yidam or tutelary deity, related to the spiritual Dharma name that I told him Kalu Rinpoche had already assigned to me. When I asked him how I could learn about its meaning and the associated advanced meditation practices, he said that I could learn this with Sister Palmo, an educated British woman who was also presently the most elevated rank of ordained Tibetan Buddhist nun (Gelongma), resident at Rumtek. She had her own small cottage near his house. Obviously, he had great respect for her in delegating this responsibility for teaching a neophyte and foreign Dharma student such as myself.

I was eager to spend as much time as she had available to instruct me in these practices. This took place from April 2 to 3, 1973. Apparently it was rare that women would be allowed inside the temple areas that were not open to the public; but due to her position, we were permitted to enter and walk around rather freely.

During our time together Sister Palmo carefully told me about the yidam deity, outlining the meaning of this figure (which I was instructed to never reveal to anyone else), the prayers, chants, meditations, yantra diagrams, and visionary mandalas that represent its secret inner meanings and the practices associated with it. This was a very profound teaching and although she could never have known just how much I was actually able to absorb or what I did comprehend at the time, it has resonated intuitively with me over the years with an ever-deepening understanding.

I feel very honored to have received such meaningful teachings from this learned lady. It also created a bond of friendship and gave me an exemplary role model who embodied female wisdom, generosity, and scholarly-based insight.

Nonetheless, she still retained the characteristics of her previous life as Freda Bedi, said Hill, "an expatriate memsahib, manager of an Indian family household in an unusual interracial marriage, with a professional life as a journalist. She could be imperious, somewhat self-entitled, and at times rather bossy, probably without recognizing that she was commanding someone to do her bidding."

More head prefect than prototype of a perfect saint, "Mummy made a very pithy statement," recalled Barbara Pettee who became her

CHAPTER EIGHT ❖ When The Iron Bird Flies

spiritual companion: "The lamas are not teachers; they are beings, just beings." In other words, being human is a flawed condition.

Sierra Zephyr, an American disciple of the Hindu guru Yogi Chen, met Freda before she became Gelongma Palmo and observed the different aspects of her personality, first as a mother and wife in Delhi, then as a travel companion on the train to Bodhgaya, and finally a dragon lady in San Francisco when the Karmapa's spontaneity disrupted her timetable.

> Freda Bedi and her husband were literally the first people I met in India in 1969. I'd just stepped off the train and a dakini, obviously, met my boyfriend and me and said "Would you like to meet my friend, a remarkable woman?" She told us nothing about her.
>
> We had travelled overland on the Orient Express, Switzerland to Istanbul, steerage boat from the Bosphorus to Trabzon, bus to Tabriz, Iran, train to Teheran, train to Mashad, bus to Herat, Kandahar, and Kabul, hitching atop lorries through the Khyber Pass, down to Peshawar, then Islamabad, Lahore by bus, across the border to India by oxcart, buses and trains to Delhi.
>
> Freda who had short greying hair, greeted us at the door of her Delhi apartment in her shentab and blouse, and went to her kitchen, to prepare tea. The house was a cool haven from the long dusty noisy journey. She was getting ready for a big family gathering so she didn't have time to chat much or be her gracious self. She introduced us briefly to her husband who I was surprised to see, was a large dark Indian man dressed traditionally. One of her children drifted through. It wasn't a good time to linger but I remember the meeting as being light-filled and pleasant. She treated us as if she'd known us, as if we'd just stepped out into the garden, come back in, and we'd have to scoot off until

another time when she was less busy. It felt like a dream that I'd finally arrived in India.

I had that feeling of familiarity with Yogi Chen when I met him a couple of years later in his hermitage in Darjeeling as if we just picked up a conversation we'd left off recently. Likewise with other Kagyu lamas and practitioners.

I next saw Freda when I was leaving Delhi for the States for my brother's wedding in California. Freda needed someone to travel with her to Bodhgaya. We boarded the train with more luggage of every size, extra blankets rolled up, bags, suitcases, than I had ever seen one person travel with. "You travel like a Tibetan!" I said. She wasn't amused, in fact I think she hated travelling by then. She'd had an amazing life. She needed a sharp eye to keep track of all her luggage and getting her on and off the trains successfully was some relief. In those days the train went to Patna, another one to Gaya, and then horse carts, each blighted beast more decrepit than its driver, trotted us down to Bodhgaya. The heat, noise, chaos of the trip was a given, but she seemed to have a direction as true as a large ship plying through turbulent waters.

She told me on that trip and when I saw her later in Bodhgaya about her time at the Young Lamas' School in Dalhousie. She spoke of them fondly, obviously proud and delighted with her time there and what she contributed. She said Trungpa Rinpoche was so brilliant that she had only to walk with him, pointing out things in the surroundings and mentioning them only once, and he memorized them forever and could repeat back to her perfectly any time later. He was the fastest learner of all those she taught, a pleasure to teach and be with. His mind was extraordinary. I've since thought, after interacting with him and having teaching dreams from him, that he was a mahasiddha.

She talked about going to South Africa and looked forward to so many projects, happy to have an outpost there, always looking to the future. Her speech was pure Oxford. She was as refined as a thoroughbred, as tough as the jungle weeds that grew between Old and New Delhi. Her heart was so accommodating, so kind, and her eye so keen, that it was a delight to travel with her despite the rough journey, her discomfort, and the loss of my sleeping bag in one of our train changes.

The next I saw her was the first time Karmapa came to San Francisco. I was cooking for the lamas in the kitchen and underfoot in the mansion, and thus able to pop into his room frequently. Trungpa Rinpoche had ordered a golden Cadillac to whisk him around in, and Freda was marshalling the itinerary, herding everyone around the agenda on time. She was a marvel and a bit of a dragon as I recall.

One day I went in when Kalu Rinpoche and Karmapa (my root lamas) were talking and I mentioned that Yogi Chen wanted to see him but I couldn't get him to come to the mansion. He stubbornly refused saying that he didn't want to waste Karmapa's time. Karmapa said 'Is he here?' I said, 'No, he's across the Bay in Berkeley' (in a little rented studio apartment downtown piled high with his trunks full of texts and books). Karmapa's face lit up and he said, "Well then I'll go see him."

Freda Bedi couldn't believe her ears and put her foot down immediately, saying adamantly that he was scheduled to go out (shopping and sightseeing it turns out) and that he could not go. Karmapa kept saying, 'Where is he?' and finally I said, 'Well, I have his phone number, maybe you could talk to him.' So he did, and to my surprise, he got on the phone and chanted mantras, dozens of them, nonstop, for what seemed like ten minutes. She just looked at her watch annoyed, but I couldn't have been more ecstatic.

By the time my boyfriend and I got to Kathmandu (trains, buses, a boat over the Ganges under the full moon, more buses up into the Himalayas) and we met Karmapa at Rumtek after a long trek through the Annapurna Range to Jamsom by the Tibetan border, I felt like Karmapa had been reeling us in on a kite string. The peripatetic travel with fortuitous meetings and sudden partings was just to get there to sit in his presence.

♦ ♦ ♦

Rumtek was on the hippie trail. Spiritual seekers were arriving hungry for the Dharma, searching for cosmic consciousness, a new generation whose doors of perception had been opened chemically. They

His Holiness the Sixteenth Karmapa greeting Surya Das   *Courtesy of Lama Surya Das*

CHAPTER EIGHT ✤ When The Iron Bird Flies

listened with intuitive understanding and were receptive to blessing and meditation.

When the long-haired pilgrims arrived, the young monks brought them to Palmo's door. She was the bridge from East to West, the doorway to the Dharma, although she never forgot who the spiritual master was.

The Karmapa has lived sixteen lives as the head of a sect and reached the illumination of a buddha. He has chosen to come back time and again to teach his students and liberate all beings from the suffering of this world.

Surya Das, an American whose name means "servant of the sun" given him by the great Hindu yogi Neem Karoli Baba, spent several months at Rumtek in the early '70s as a young devotee. He was uniquely privileged to observe the relationship between the Karmapa and the extraordinary British woman he called Mummy.

His Holiness Gyalwa Karmapa seemed to me the greatest lama of his time. His prodigious powers and ability to see through us all, high and low, intimidated most everyone, even the khenpos, abbots, and other Rinpoches, or so it seemed. He also could show a wrathful demeanor when needed.

I remember once in the early '70s when I was a sprite, I had the fortunate opportunity to be in the presence of His Holiness the Sixteenth Karmapa and his translator Achi in His Holiness's room upstairs in Rumtek. That's where I met Freda Bedi (Gelongma Palmo), his attendant and secretary for some time, as well as the caretaker of many orphan boys and little monks. Once when a lama came in who had displeased or disappointed His Holiness he pinched that lama so hard he got a black and blue mark on his side and pushed a chair at him, something I'd never seen him do before. The lama bowed, apologized profusely, and scuttled away. Then His Holiness laughed. He called "Mummy" and her very presence seemed to ease things up a bit, which impressed me immensely. The woman he called Mummy was remarkable. She was ordained by His Holiness the Karmapa as Karma Khechok Palmo, a Brit who became his beloved disciple and right-hand nun. It was unprecedented to see a Western woman among all the monks alongside the Grand Lama Karmapa in such a traditional setting as Rumtek Monastery in the remote kingdom of Sikkim.

"What?" I thought in my naïve, youthful way. How could a living Buddha and grand bodhisattva, incarnation of the Buddha of Compassion Chenrezig be angry?" It shook my faith.

The next day I asked Gelongma Palmo about it and she reminded me of Jesus's wrathful action in driving the moneylenders from Solomon's holy temple. 'We take refuge in the Buddha's enlightened teaching and not the teacher-person, not the words but in their meaning, not the mere forms but in the essence.' Though she herself was totally devoted to the Karmapa and served him in every way possible, her patient, gracious, and kind explanation to a young pilgrim on the path helped me go deeper into the true refuge and eventually find and realize the essence of Dharma.

Austere, rigorous, and disciplined as the monastic training was, the gentility, gentleness, patience, and sweetness evinced by the Karmapa toward his Mummy and hers toward him was quite unique in Buddhism at the time. It was a period before Westerners had really discovered and inhabited Tibetan Buddhism for its meditation, yoga, and compassionate life practices.

Chapter Eight ❖ When The Iron Bird Flies

Mummy's unstinting devotion and selfless service was unparalleled, and His Holiness responded in kind.

In the Karma Kagyu school, we belong to the lineage of devotion, as Milarepa said. Devotion helps transport us beyond egocentric emotionality into other dimensions, including oneness with the object of devotion—which is the purpose of Guru Yoga. If anyone has left this world and been reborn at the right hand of her guru, it would be Gelongma Palmo, the pioneering nun.

Another pilgrim whom Palmo guided was an American, Ward Holmes who was in India following the hippie trail in 1970. By 1971 he reached Rumtek Monastery, walking all the way from the bottom to Rumtek at the top of the mountain to find the Karmapa.

I knew Freda Bedi only as Sister Palmo. I first met her in April 1971 at Rumtek Monastery in Sikkim. I was longing to meet the great Sixteenth Karmapa, Rangjung Rigpe Dorje, but by the time I reached the main entrance and walked into the courtyard of Rumtek, I was completely exhausted.

Suddenly four young monks appeared on the top floor and as I bowed to them, I burst into tears overcome by the feeling that I had finally come home. They came running down and took me by the hand pulling me up the stairs to meet whom I thought would be Karmapa, but instead they took me to Sister Palmo's room. She was actually living in the monastery on one of the upper floors. I was very surprised to see a Western woman in such an exotic, awesome setting. She greeted me very cordially and as we talked about my trip to Rumtek, I explained that I had to meet the Karmapa. She said, 'That will not be a problem, I will arrange it myself. You may come tomorrow morning.' She made me comfortable in the very strange setting I found

Kabir Bedi as Sandokan giving the order, "Attack ship!" *Courtesy of Kabir Bedi*

myself in. I was only twenty years old at the time and it was my first trip to India.

She took me under her wing, and under her guidance, I took the refuge ceremony alone with Karmapa. She translated every time I met His Holiness and taught me the fundamental principles of Buddhism. She introduced me to Grace McLeod who was living in Seattle, Washington with whom she was working to publish English translations of the various meditations and teachings of the Karma Kagyu Lineage. These were so helpful at a time when I knew not a word of Tibetan. Later, on the Karmapa's first trip to the US, I met Grace McCleod in Seattle and received a copy of the works she had completed with Sister Palmo. It helped me begin my practice of the Dharma in the early years. I have fond memories of Sister Palmo guiding my

CHAPTER EIGHT ❖ When The Iron Bird Flies

first study and practice of Tibetan Buddhism. Truly a "Lady of Realization."

Anderson Bakewell was living in India and acting in the popular Italian TV series Sandokan when he visited Rumtek to escape from the heat of the plains.

> I was living in Madras in 1973 studying music, and it was there that a chance encounter occurred that changed my life. I was walking along a crowded street one day when two Italian gentlemen approached me and one of them blurted out something like 'Perfetto tutto, ha la barba!' He explained that he was a casting director for a film that was being shot just across the Adyar River and asked if I wanted a job working on a film set. I apparently fit the image of a British officer in colonial India and was needed among other things to ride elephants and shoot tigers. As I was short of cash, I leaped at the opportunity.
>
> For the next few months he was occupied by the filming of Sandokan, a joint Italian/German production about James Brooke, the "white raja" of Sarawak and an eponymous pirate/hero. The pirate hero was played by Freda's son Kabir who was by now a famously charismatic Bollywood superstar.
>
> When the filming was nearing its end and the hot season was coming on, I remember mentioning to Kabir that a trip to the Himalayas might offer a welcome change of climate. He mentioned that his mother lived in Sikkim and suggested that I go there. He gave me an address that I pocketed.
> A few weeks later in Gangtok, the capital of Sikkim, I handed the address to a taxi driver and asked him to take me there.

Sister Palmo   *Courtesy of the Bedi Family Archives*

CHAPTER EIGHT ✤ WHEN THE IRON BIRD FLIES

We drove for some time outside the town and finally arrived at what, to my surprise, was a Buddhist Monastery. I was greeted by a monk and ushered up to a small room on the highest level. When I knocked and a voice inside responded in what sounded like Tibetan, the monk opened the door and I was amazed to find, sitting on the floor amongst books stacked to the ceiling, a shaven English woman in robes. She looked at me with the most remarkable eyes I have ever beheld, hugely clear and radiant, almost vertically oblong, and said, 'Do come in. How is Kabir?' I felt I had known her all my life. I spent as much precious time in her presence over the next few days as I could, and it was a wrench to leave.

Over the next few months we exchanged letters, and in one she announced that she would be resident for several months in San Mateo, California, where she would be giving teachings. I joined her there and my devotion became even more intense. Rather miraculous things seemed to happen around her: spontaneous combustion, appearance of water in the air, collective swoonings, all evidence of her effect on her pupils and the power of the transmission.

I was with her only twice after that, but she is still held in my heart. I remember her absolute equanimity and the way she saw through to each person's core, never distinguishing between the outward forms of rich, poor, important, or lowly, young or old. Her only concern was for the Dharma and the liberation of all sentient beings.

◆ ◆ ◆

Behind the scenes, the Karmapa's tour to the USA and Europe was gathering momentum. He had already received an invitation from Namgyal Rinpoche in Canada who first visited Rumtek in 1968 and

His Holiness the Sixteenth Karmapa and Namgyal Rinpoche at the Dharma Center of Canada   *(copyright Peter Deutsch)*

again in 1971 with over one hundred students. His group, the Dharma Center of Canada, issued an invitation in November 1973 for His Holiness to visit Canada and "consecrate the land in full Kagyu tradition." Namgyal offered to pay for round-the-world tickets for His Holiness and a full complement of attendants.

Finally, the Karmapa consented. Anila Pema Zangmo filled in the rest of the story. One day two years later, Yeshi Norbu called Palmo to his room and said, "Now I am going to America. You tell Chögyam Trungpa and arrange. Send letters to everybody and say now I am going." The invitations came quickly. She had needed to get his consent first.

CHAPTER EIGHT ✤ When The Iron Bird Flies

According to Mary Jane Bennett who was working for the Kagyu International Office, His Holiness was reassured by the more stable presence of Namgyal Rinpoche in Canada. Like Palmo, he was an Oxford graduate.

Namgyal Rinpoche had the same British upper class demeanor as Sister Palmo. Karmapa had a feeling of trust in both of them. Namgyal had been instrumental in the gift of Johnstone House in Scotland to the Tibetans and his desire to help them was clear. He was also a meditation master in the Burmese tradition. Because of these auspicious conditions, Karmapa accepted the invitation to the West.

In early 1974, Sister Palmo replied to Namgyal Rinpoche in a letter signed by the Karmapa with a proposed itinerary for Europe and North America. In the airmail letter was a reminder to contact Chögyam Trungpa in America.

When Chögyam Trungpa was informed of the proposed tour, he contacted the Dharma Center of Canada and with characteristic aplomb offered to sponsor four first class tickets, one for His Holiness and his attendant, one for Sister Palmo, and one for the sacred Black Crown.

It was a remarkable coup. "Sister Palmo in the USA!" she cheered. The Karmapa knew when the time was right. The two Rinpoches, Akong and Trungpa, the first Kagyu tulkus in the West, were separated by an ocean of hostility. That Yeshi Norbu shower his blessings and heal the division would be good. Palmo was overjoyed.

I am happy that he will meet many people all over the country and they will have the wonderful experience of coming within the shower of blessings of the gurus. It's like the light radiating from the sun. He's always very cheerful, very dignified, extremely warm and understanding. It's like saying what is a mango like? Only when you taste it can you know.

Before the tour, the Karmapa sent Palmo to the USA to take the temperature and check the lay of the land. "She was his emissary to other countries," said Goodie Oberoi. "She popularized the Tibetan Dharma."

Her mission was to go to Boulder, Colorado to liaise with Vajradhatu and its centers. The brilliant and bold Chögyam Trungpa was creating waves with his style of teaching in the unorthodox crazy wisdom tradition.

On February 25, 1974 Sister Palmo set off on her fact-finding mission prior to His Holiness's first tour, scheduled for September. The plan was to return to Bombay in mid- May. Joanna Macy was her hostess in Syracuse where she recovered for a week from a twisted ankle before flying to New York. There she was scheduled to give lectures and meet Chögyam Trungpa whom she had not seen since 1963 when he left Delhi for Oxford on a Spalding Scholarship to study comparative religion. She was excited at the prospect of meeting the "lama brother of our family."

> The great interest of this tour is to meet Trungpa Rinpoche again. We've had many happy days with Akong and Trungpa in Moti Bagh. Trungpa is now a truly famous Dharma teacher with an enormous network of organizations and projects. It's astounding when you think he's been here for only four years.

In Trungpa's first four years in the USA he had created Vajradhatu, an organization that controlled fourteen small groups across the country, as well as Naropa Institute, the first accredited university in

CHAPTER EIGHT ❖ WHEN THE IRON BIRD FLIES

America offering a modern Buddhist approach to the arts, literature, and politics, and talks on the Mahayana. He established two large centers, one in Boulder and one in Vermont, while in New York State he started a therapeutic community using Buddhist exercises and modern interpretations of Buddhist psychology.

Palmo landed at midnight in New York where Tamara Hill, the only available person who knew her, was delegated to greet her on arrival. Communication about the exact time was imprecise and Hill ended up waiting eighteen hours before she found Palmo exiting serenely from customs.

> She was weary but completely unfazed, assuming that I would certainly be right there and that I would somehow know that she would be appearing at that very time. We did not have mobile phones in those days, so any such connections were something of a fortuitous mystery, especially with Sister Palmo.

Hill chauffeured her to Chögyam Trungpa's Dharmadhatu Center in Manhattan. Even at that hour, Trungpa's students welcomed her warmly. "Rinpoche has a large number of Jews in his sangha," she noted. "His shrines have a Japanese feel, not Tibetan." Chögyam Trungpa came into town to meet with her and at his request she prepared a delicious home-cooked Indian meal for him. The iconoclastic guru was homesick for the family life he had shared with the Bedis in Delhi.

Palmo was accorded the status of a lama. While in India she had taught when instructed to do so by the Karmapa. A young relative Monisha whom she guided in Buddhist philosophy and introduced to the Karmapa said,

> She was central to my life. From '71 onward she would instruct me in meditation, in visualization, in some belief system. Once

she gave me a piece of bark from the bodhi tree in Bodhgaya so I set up a shrine and I would do some meditation.

"She could guide," said Goodie Oberoi. "She had a photographic memory of past, present, and future. Very few people have that."

On this tour she taught Buddhism publicly to groups, giving meditation instruction at the Theosophical Society and a talk on Arya Tara the Divine Mother at the Asian society. At Trungpa's Dharmadhatu Center, she offered the Green Tara initiation to twenty-one people, oddly enough, one for each of the Twenty-One Taras.

Ani Pema Zangmo confirmed that she had received His Holiness's seal of approval. "She gave initiations. Anything His Holiness the Karmapa ordered, she gave. Karmapa said she was a bodhisattva, a White Tara emanation."

Tamara Hill arranged a weekend seminar on the Goddess Tara at the Bowery Street loft of John Giorno, a famous poet and Buddhist practitioner who had offered his work space for the gathering. About forty people attended. She also organized a teaching at the Sharon Springs Zen Center near Albany: "Sister Palmo's presence and her meditation teachings delighted the Zen Center's resident-students and director."

She was introduced to Allan Ginsberg and various other Beat poets and artists. The interest of Americans in world religions impressed her. One of her teachings was elaborated with audiovisual aids, music, and film and at another lecture, a beautiful film on the Buddha families accompanied her talk. At the Mongolian Center in New Jersey she lectured on bodhichitta, the aspiration to benefit all beings, and tathagatagarbha, the innate pure mind.

She was open to New Age spirituality.

CHAPTER EIGHT ❖ When The Iron Bird Flies

We went to a Cosmic mass, a New Age prayer meeting organized by the Sufis along with a New Age group. Pir Vilayat Khan read a commentary on the creation, and five groups representing Christians, Hindus, Jews, Muslims, and Buddhists performed a purification ceremony around a central figure sitting high on a big pulpit representing a creator God. The audience sang devotional songs in chorus, ending with songs of Hallelujah, all of which had a liberating, happy effect.

At Tail of the Tiger in Vermont, Trungpa's first center, she observed students in a month-long retreat, sitting twelve hours a day. "I had time to do my own meditation and write letters, and I showed them slides of Rumtek." By mid-April she reached Boulder, Colorado where an astonishing eighteen inches of snow had fallen. Finally she had a chance to have long talks with Chögyam Trungpa.

I went to Rinpoche's home and met Diana who is now barely twenty-one, a lovely healthy English girl. Their two children, Taggi who is a tulku of about three with soft skin and almond eyes and the young one who is dark and chubby like a well-made momo. His home in the Rocky Mountains provides a quiet setting for Rinpoche. After the accident in England he has a slight impediment in walking but has overcome all the other side effects that were there in the beginning. He looks well, a little heavier now that he is thirty-three, dressed like an American, neat, modern, not at all a hippie type, a businessman variety. Retains his great feeling for color and texture. We had very long talks. At the public meeting Rinpoche reminisced about the old days, remembering Babaji and the friends in Delhi.

Chögyam Trungpa and Sister Palmo at Dharmadhatu Center   *Courtesy of Shambhala Archives*

On the whole, she was deeply impressed by Trungpa's activity and his teaching.

> It was an unforgettable tour. Trungpa Rinpoche has given me a great welcome and his Dharma influence is so vast that one cannot believe that in four years so much could have been done: five big projects, hundreds of acres of land, and the human center in Boulder, Colorado where over two hundred pupils live all over the city, working, sometimes deep in the Dharma work, and "sit" and attend seminars. Trungpa in his suit and tie is different from the tulku floating about in his robes, but in essence is the same, with a rather stronger aspect, both smiling and semi-wrathful. He is beginning a Naropa Seminar Institute this year with nearly nine hundred registrations already and a magnificent faculty. E Ma Ho, wondrous is that!

CHAPTER EIGHT ❖ When The Iron Bird Flies

He has a great sense of humor and a great fund of modern American idioms. He teaches the deeper truths of Buddhism and meditation. He is teaching the Mahayana path of the bodhisattva.

Privately, she had certain reservations which she expressed in her letter to Babaji.

Trungpa is doing a vast and highly significant kind of "mind training" Dharma work. Putting things right at the grassroots. His methods are tough and sometimes cutting (perhaps a shade too much so) and perhaps too that was why my visit and mother touch was needed at that point.

I taught a great deal on Mantra, the Divine Mother, and deeper Buddhist philosophy of the naturally pure mind (Gyud Lama or Mahayana Uttara Tantra Shastra). Created the climate for the coming of Chenrezig in his earthly form of His Holiness Karmapa who has pledged himself to leave India in September. There is such a vital new life movement in the States that old religions in their Christian form have no meaning... There is a great deal of interreligious fellowship among the discerning. Looking at it from the Buddhist point of view, it is fertile for the perennially new Dharma, grounded in the Reality and not too tied to the Tibetan, Japanese, or any national idiom.

The next stage of her journey would take her to the heart of Hopi Indian country where Barbara Pettee had arranged a meeting with the native Americans and their leader, White Bear. The prospect filled her with joyful anticipation. The two women had met at a yoga conference in Delhi in 1970 and at the first initiation given at Tilokpur

Nunnery. Barbara, initially a disciple of Baba-ji, now entered Palmo's life as a significant spiritual companion.

Unlike Sister Palmo, Barbara Pettee was an heiress. Born into a family with considerable wealth, she chose to dedicate her energy and funds to the furthering of the Dharma in the West.

Ani Gilda Taylor who shared Barbara's home in the Los Altos hills, said

> I was amazed at Barbara's energy. She could put together a delicious dinner in a flash, eat it in a flash, and leave the dishes for 'them' to clean up. This always amused me as the 'them' was me.'

Her driving reflected her restlessness. On one occasion when traffic was clogging the narrow undulating highway to Santa Cruz, she drove a Tibetan Buddhist lama at top speed along the narrow shoulder, dust flying as she sped her way on the nonexistent road to get him to a Dharma center on time. The lama appeared unperturbed. Coming from India, he found such driving commonplace.

In the '70s the exploitation of the land and spiritual culture of Native Americans by the white man made the privileged feel shame and guilt. Barbara 's comfortable residence only forty minutes from San Francisco placed her at the very hub of New Age trends. With Karmapa's tour in mind,[12] she had contacted White Bear of the Hopi tribe to make a date for Palmo to meet the American Indians and get an historical overview of the continent. Tibetans and Native Americans

---

12   The Karmapa was already familiar with a plan to meet the Hopi. In 1973 he had been approached by a psychedelic seeker called Michael Hollingshead who asked the great Guru "to open a dialogue with the Chiefs and Elders of the North American Indian Tribe called the Hopi." Their holy lands were about to be taken over by the US Government and then by builders. "Yet potentially they could provide a spiritual backbone for a future, more spiritualized America."

CHAPTER EIGHT ✤ When The Iron Bird Flies

Sister Palmo and Barbara Pettee (the third from the left) with Senator Percy and his wife
Courtesy of Ani Gilda Taylor

resembled each other physically and there was a belief that they shared similar social values and spiritual lives.

Together, the two women drove to Arizona. They soon fell into a relationship similar to guru and disciple with a focus on Dharma activity. Like Barbara Pettee, Palmo moved quickly, fueled by a similar high-powered energy, but she also had a rare visionary quality which gifted her with the power to manifest. Her success was due to the vast scope of her life, said Kabir. "She had the British upbringing, Oxford, family situations, the Indians, Tibetans, so she was living in a multicultural, multinational world which was also multi- dimensional."

When they arrived, White Bear welcomed them and showed them around some ancient ruins. Palmo engaged him in a discussion of moon ceremonies and masked dances. They then drove to the edge of the Grand Canyon where Palmo sat in meditation.

During her time with Barbara in San Mateo, Palmo gave newspaper and TV interviews to introduce the Karmapa to Americans, lectured on incarnate lamas, Tibetan Buddhism, and the suffering of samsara at several impromptu locations – Alan Watts's houseboat in Sausalito, the Seed Center in Palo Alto, and a small house in Berkeley, the only Dharmadhatu affiliate in the area.

Barbara described one memorable gathering.

She began to intone the Tara mantra in a melody and with an intensity which riveted everyone present. In a very restless crowd which included babies, dogs, potheads, and so forth, every activity ceased and people became quiet and motionless, forgetting what they had been doing. Jolted by this loving energy and complete command that this sweet feminine voice produced, this vast group on the lawn became totally absorbed. It was like

Grace McLeod, Seattle, Washington, August 1996   *(photo by Tamara Hill)*

CHAPTER EIGHT ✤ When The Iron Bird Flies

a loving mother keening for all her children lost or in pain. It was Tara. High Rinpoches called her Jetsun Dolma. Karmapa and all the monks she knew and helped called her Mummy-la, as she had played that role for scores of them.

Barbara's whirlwind schedule for Palmo included a meeting with Senator Percy and his wife in Washington to sound him out on the Karmapa's tour later in the year. Palmo was delighted with the visit.

> We had a wonderful two days in Washington with Senator and Mrs. Percy and they gave His Holiness and party an open-door invitation. I do so like the Percy's: they are human beings primarily, knowledgeable about the earth and people around, but yet conscious of the Higher Man, the Bodhichitta. Meditators. Quite rare.

She remembered Goodie Oberoi's request to visit her husband Bikki who was at the St Regis Hotel in Washington and she appeared quite unexpectedly, holding the Karmapa's red blessing cords.

> My husband playing polo had fallen about eight feet off a horse flat onto his back on the snow. He broke his back and he was wearing a steel brace. Four nuns came to visit him and no one had seen the likes of it. She tied a blessing cord onto him. She said, 'You will have no more pain.' That night he went to sleep without the brace and had no pain in his back. He never had to wear the brace again.

Palmo then visited the home of Grace McLeod who lived in a prosperous suburb of Seattle. "Grace worked tirelessly[13] in her windowless basement office organizing and printing Mummy's

---

13   McLeod typed seventy translations of the teachings accompanied by thirty original black-and-white line drawings drawn by lama artists.

translations of Buddhist teachings and prayers," said Frank Miller who set up a whole-food restaurant and bakery on Vashon Island after leaving the Peace Corps.

His last encounter with his iconic mentor was when he picked her up at McLeod's respectable middle-class home to ferry her to his hippie hangout in the alternative culture of Vashon Island. "I remember thinking at the time how appropriate it was to be on a ferry boat to Vashon, as a ferry is symbolically connected to progress on the Dharma path."

> I picked up Mummy in my old beater truck. I felt no reluctance in exposing her to the rough, dusty interior of my vehicle because Mummy had no pretensions of class or caste. She was completely at home wherever she ventured. She was as saintly as Mother Theresa, but with a humorous, light touch and a beguiling warmth. What kind of a vehicle she travelled in was of little importance to her; there was, after all, the Greater Vehicle.

∴

Three months after Palmo's voyage of discovery to the USA, Barbara received a message from Sikkim: "Please prepare for four days and nights for the Karmapa and ten of his monks who are coming to the West for the first time so that they can meet the Hopi Indian chiefs and see their villages."

It was the result of their visit with White Bear and of Palmo's meditation at the Grand Canyon. With their combined force, the Iron Bird was destined to land. Karmapa and his monks would be with the Hopi chiefs in three weeks. Barbara was stunned. "The news was startling and awesome."

CHAPTER NINE
Karmapa and the Gelongma

And as we walked through the streets of Arklow
Oh the colour of the day wore on
And our heads were filled with poetry
And the morning a-comin' on to dawn.[14]

The iron bird landed in New York on September 18, 1974 a few weeks before the release of Van Morrison's greatest album, Veedon Fleece, a synchronistic but seemingly unrelated event, were it not that its joyful lyricism set the tone for the tour. On board were His Holiness Karmapa and an entourage of twelve including Tenga Rinpoche, Sister

His Holiness the Sixteenth Karmapa arriving in a gold Cadillac on his visit to North America greeted by Sister Palmo and David Rome, 1974 *Courtesy of Shambhala Archives (photographer unknown)*

---

14   Van Morrison, Veedon Fleece, released October 1974

Palmo, and as translator Achi Tsepal. They were chauffeured to Bodhi House, the lavish Long Island estate of C.T. Shen, the principal patron of Buddhism in America. After years of requests and feverish last minute preparations, the Dharma King had arrived.

Chögyam Trungpa's Vajradhatu organization, then based in Boulder, Colorado, had worked uninterruptedly under the watchful guidance of their guru, even covering the walls of the Karmapa's private apartment in satin to create a palace befitting a universal monarch.[15]

The first Black Crown ceremony was presented three days later to three thousand people in a stunningly transformed dockyard warehouse. From New York State, the plan was to visit Tail of the Tiger in Vermont which His Holiness renamed Karma Choling, the Dharma Place of the Karma Kagyu, then on to Boston and Ann Arbor, Michigan. After that, it became a pilgrimage in the Southwest to Hopiland, stopping first at Boulder and the six hundred acre Rocky Mountain Dharma Center at Red Feather Lakes in Northern Colorado.

The magnitude of the Karmapa's personal blessing and the role of his Gelongma becomes clear with the experience of those whose lives were suddenly transformed. Without these inner journeys, we have only a program of places visited, important people met, and ceremonies bestowed. As Palmo said, "The journey isn't from here to there but from this to that."

Dale Brozosky was on the Hindu path with the great yogins Neem Karoli Baba and Swami Muktananda. Later he met Chögyam Trungpa and was magnetized by his teaching. When his close Dharma friend Ram Dass (Richard Alpert) invited him to become his assistant at the newly-established Naropa Institute, he acquiesced and joined the Boulder community. Ram Dass's tenure ended and the two friends exchanged gifts. Ram Dass presented him with a beautiful statue of

---

15   The Miraculous 16th Karmapa, edited by Norma Levine, p. 151

CHAPTER NINE ❖ KARMAPA AND THE GELONGMA

a female deity and in return accepted a dancing Shiva. It was the first link in a chain of auspicious coincidences that led him to Karmapa with Gelongma Palmo in the role she would perfect on this tour, that of eminence grise, the luminary behind the throne. He was in Boulder when the Karmapa arrived with Sister Palmo.

Sister Palmo had a powerful role in forging my relationship with the Sixteenth Karmapa. For several years I had studied primarily with Hindu teachers like Swami Muktananda whom I respected greatly. In the summer of 1974 I went to visit Baba Muktananda in Denver. We discussed Chögyam Trungpa and he gave me his candid opinion of him and then added, "Trungpa's guru, the Karmapa, is a supreme mahasiddha." I knew then and there I would meet him soon.

Months later in Boulder I joined the line awaiting the arrival of the Sixteenth Karmapa. Accompanying the Karmapa and his entourage of Tibetan monks was a British nun, Sister Palmo. She was striking with her smile, energy, and large bald head. She was at the center of the activities surrounding the Karmapa, accompanied by several young Europeans. I experienced Karmapa as a great king -- powerful, radiant, smiling, and often laughing. Sister Palmo and the monks of the entourage were like the moon reflecting the powerful sun of the Dharma King. After many days of teachings, initiations, and blessings, I had not yet spoken directly to him nor to Sister Palmo.

When the Karmapa travelled to bless the land at the Rocky Mountain Dharma Center, I was invited to join the procession and brought the statue that Ram Dass had given me. During the drive I placed the statue on my lap and closed my eyes. At that moment I had a vision of a friend named Dolma, another name for Tara. I knew the vision had a relationship with the statue.

His Holiness the Sixteenth Karmapa performs Chenrezig empowerment for Hopi tribe at Second Mesa, Arizona, 1974, here blessing Sister Palmo   *Courtesy of Shambhala Archives*

After the hours of prayers and ceremonies dedicating the land, all of us stood in line to greet the Karmapa. Sister Palmo was standing by the Karmapa's side. I offered the statue to His Holiness. Upon receiving it, he exclaimed to Sister Palmo how auspicious the offering of Tara was at that moment. His success in establishing Dharma in America, my success as a Dharma practitioner, the success of the Mountain Center, and Trungpa's work were all assured. He instructed that the statue be ceremoniously installed at the center of the foundation of the land. It was only then that I realized the statue was Tara.

Sister Palmo approached me. She said that I had created "quite a sensation" by presenting the Tara statue. She asked me to join the entourage of the Karmapa for the remainder of his tour. Back in Boulder, she invited me to visit her. I knew that she had studied the Theravadin, the Vajrayana, and the Hindu paths so

CHAPTER NINE ✤ Karmapa and the Gelongma

I asked her what was in common and what was different about the Buddhist and Hindu paths and shared an experience I had years earlier. She told me that she was uncertain if the experience had been a jnana state from concentration or a vipassana insight of "entering the stream." From her reply, I understood that she had deep understanding through experiential knowledge.

She told me that I had an inner connection with the Buddhist tradition and the Karmapa lineage in particular. She said that when I practiced the refuge vows and the deity practices that I had received from the Karmapa I could be certain that the connection was not intellectual or conceptual but an inner spiritual connection that would protect and nourish me. I should honor this connection and know it was a profound link with the great lineage of the Karmapas, the Karma Kagyus, and the lineage of the Buddha. That was how I began my relationship with the Karmapa and my friendship with Sister Palmo.

From Colorado, the Karmapa led a pilgrimage to Hopiland via the Great Kiva and Canyon de Chelly in New Mexico, passing other sacred American Indian sites. The many hindrances, planning trips, and hundreds of miles driving to and from Arizona climaxed in a finale as dramatic as a protector puja with the clash of cymbals and throb of drums. The Berkeley Barb reported the scene: a burgundy-robed Karmapa with a golden parasol held over his head was introduced to Chief Ned Netanaya, "a tiny, withered, snuggle-toothed old Hopi in a grey-peaked cap." Achi, "a hip and handsome Tibetan, a prototype right out of central casting" provided the translation.

Barbara Pettee described the moment of meeting.

The Karmapa presented the chiefs with beautiful Bhutanese weaving and was given permission to go into the kiva

His Holiness the Sixteenth Karmapa at the Grand Canyon, 1974 *Courtesy of KTD Archives*

(ceremonial room). When told that the winter had brought little snow and the summer no rain and the crops were drying up, he replied, "I will keep it in my prayers," and from a clear blue sky on that bright October day, a tiny edge of grey smog seemed to appear on the horizon. Of course in the middle of a vast desert this was not possible, but the greyness became more so, then billowy, then true cloud formations, ever darker, then storm-dark. Torrents of rain fell all within an hour or so. The bringing of the rain made the Hopi know intuitively that a "Great Spirit" was among them.

CHAPTER NINE ❖ Karmapa and the Gelongma

I had asked the chiefs for permission for his people to meet the Karmapa, bring our cars into the villages, and take photographs, all of which are generally forbidden on the mesas to give the Hopis the privacy they desire and deserve. I had to formulate a simple concise statement. intended for those who didn't know where Tibet was or who a Karmapa was. I had found myself saying, 'A great chief with ten of his men are coming from halfway around the world to meet your chiefs. They are people of peace as you are; they are red men as you are; they live in very

"Karmapa Brings Rain to Hopiland" in Qur' Toqti, Oraibi, Arizona, October 10, 1974: foreground His Holiness the Sixteenth Karmapa, Chief Ned Nayatewa, Tenga Rinpoche with Joel Willey behind; back left is Achi Tsepal, Diana Duncan, and Dale Brozosky   *Courtesy of Dale Brozosky (photo by Lawrence Hamana)*

"Tibetans Fulfill Prophecy In Hopiland," article by Arn Passman in the Berkeley Barb, October 18-24, 1974   *Courtesy of Allen Penny*

CHAPTER NINE ❖ Karmapa and the Gelongma

Arrival at the San Francisco Tarmac. His Holiness the Sixteenth Karmapa descends stairway with his entourage, Ani Palmo behind him. Vidyadhara Chögyam Trungpa in orange chuba greeting him with Western students   *Courtesy of Shambhala Archives (photographer unknown)*

cold winters and hot summers as you do; they have coral and turquoise as you do. The chief is a man of great vision, of great heart, and is a healer. He would be honored to meet your leaders.

The Karmapa and Chief White Bear exchanged rings, each exquisitely wrought in turquoise, silver, and coral. Those present were not in the least surprised to see that the rings were identical.[16]

That night after dinner with no announcement, the young and the old and babies in arms appeared in an empty room where lamas had set up a cushion on a table and a shrine on another table so the Karmapa could give a Chenrezig blessing. The room was filled and faces looked in at the windows while everyone else stood in file for a blessing. This spontaneous event

---

16   The Dance of 17 Lives, Mick Brown, p. 71

His Holiness the Sixteenth Karmapa visit to America in 1974 accompanied by Achi Tsepal and Sister Palmo   *Courtesy of Shambhala Archives*

fulfilled the Padmasambhava prophecy of the eighth century: "When the iron bird flies and horses run on wheels, the Tibetans will be scattered like ants over the earth and the Dharma will come to the land of the red man."
This was 1974.[17]

The procession returned via the Grand Canyon and Phoenix where the Karmapa boarded a flight to San Francisco. There he gave a Karma Pakshi initiation at the request of Trungpa Rinpoche and a Medicine Buddha empowerment at Barbara's request. When His Holiness bestowed the Vajra Crown ceremony at the Fort Mason Center for Arts and Culture over 2500 people gathered to receive the blessing. Among those attending this extraordinary spiritual occasion were

---

17   KTL Newsletter 1983

CHAPTER NINE ✤ Karmapa and the Gelongma

"the beautiful people" dressed in gorgeous Eastern-style garments – flowing robes, Indian shirts, exquisite saris, flowers, and beads.

Ward Holmes had come to San Francisco to reconnect with the Karmapa whom he had met at Rumtek. Once again Sister Palmo guided him and he became the Karmapa's driver, a coveted position in close proximity to his guru.

> At our meeting in Rumtek, Sister Palmo had encouraged me to try to see Karmapa on his trip to the West. I felt very blessed to be able to go, but when I arrived at the address of a private house in San Francisco and knocked on the door, the Vajra Guards would not open it. Then suddenly someone in his party recognized me and invited me in. What a joy it was to see the Karmapa's beaming face! He was so happy to see me that he showered me with gifts, many of which were Sister Palmo's translations, as well as various presents he had received.
>
> With Sister Palmo's encouragement I went on to become His Holiness Karmapa's personal assistant and driver on the next two trips he made to the US. In 1980 for over three months I travelled extensively throughout the East Coast with him and his party and had powerful experiences with my Guru and Jamgon Kongtrul Rinpoche who was always by his side as translator.

Sister Palmo was also by the Karmapa's side in a unique role. She was his eyes and ears among Westerners, his adviser and consultant, and at times, his voice. She had the ability to communicate the Dharma and provide commentaries and instructions where needed.

To New Age authors Jose and Miriam Arguelles she gave impromptu teachings on the innate clarity of mind, and after the Karmapa bestowed the five precepts Freda gave a brief commentary on the reason for taking precepts. In the garden of the Nyingma Center in San Francisco she elaborated on the suffering of samsara.

> We are all old warriors who have lived many lifetimes. We have inhabited the world of animals, fighting and quarrelling, living only for the moment. We have passed into the state of hell being, and that of the hungry ghosts suffering unremitting pangs of remorse. We have lived in the higher states of the gods suffused in happiness, but this joy has been impermanent. Always we have been forced to take rebirth again and again. In this life, we have found a precious human body and a mind capable of receiving the Buddha's teachings. Precepts held create wholesome karma. They are the foundation of holistic living. They create a unity within the personality. We are no longer in conflict with the self. A calm mind naturally arises.[18]

By October 1974, the Karmapa and his entourage were in Vancouver, welcomed by the Venerable Kalu Rinpoche. He was received by the Lieutenant Governor of British Columbia officially at Government House in Victoria. In Canada the time was ripe for the visit of a great spiritual leader. Prime Minister Trudeau was more aligned with Plato's philosopher kings than with politicians and was convinced of the importance of meditation to live life well. Canada was among the first countries to open its door to Tibetan refugees.

In Toronto the Karmapa gave the Vajra Yogini empowerment, an advanced deity practice said to grant the attainment of siddhis or power. Diana Duncan followed the Dharma trail from Hopiland to San Francisco and onward to Toronto. At the empowerment of Vajra Yogini, Duncan came into contact with Palmo, who had completed

---

18   Sheila Fugard, Lady of Realization, section 28

CHAPTER NINE ✤ KARMAPA AND THE GELONGMA

the practice of this deity in a six-month retreat at Rumtek, and her almost invisible, gentle loving presence.

It was in Canada that I came close to Sister Palmo. After I received the abhisheka of Vajra Yogini from Karmapa, she came up behind me and taking me by the arm said, 'Come with me, you have to have the oral transmission for the Vajra Yogini practice.' At the time I was swept along with the energy of the monks and their rituals. I had never noticed her before because I was so glued to Karmapa.

She introduced me to Kalu Rinpche and he gave the oral transmission. She guided me through the sadhana and explained how to do it, giving me the teaching. She had a soft sweetness about her, not authoritarian, but very gentle and with unconditional giving. I felt her blessing. She was a quiet person, in the background. She didn't come on at all. She came to me because I was there for the abhisheka and she knew it would not mean anything unless I got the oral transmission. So she pushed me forward. She also showed me the lineage tree which I had never seen before. I was the only one she took in hand like that.

The enlightenment of Karmapa was so overwhelming that's all I saw until she came along and took me under her wing. She was almost like a ghost, a shadow. In her loving way she was a spiritual guide without saying she was. She took me gently into what I needed, not intrusively. You felt 'Yes, absolutely' and you listened to her. She had the power of making people listen to her. She was like a mother, a gentle mother, not like a guru.

Although I didn't know anything about her, she entered me to take me through this. She was so silent, so quiet. We made a heart connection and she remained in my mind. I will always remember that beautiful lady. It would fit that she was an emanation of Tara. Heavenly, she had beautiful eyes, clear shining eyes. Maybe she was an enlightened being herself.

The Karmapa then spent three weeks in the Canadian countryside at Namgyal Rinpoche's Dharma Center of Canada. During that time he conferred the Black Crown ceremony, gave refuge, bodhisattva vows, Kagyu lineage empowerments, and monastic ordination. He consecrated a temple, a stupa, and a small Mahakala shrine in the forest, conferring the empowerment of the Kagyu Lineage protector at twilight to a few select students who had prepared for the transmission in retreat.[19]

Mary Jane Bennett was one of them.

In the spring of 1974, we Dharma people sold our communal farm in the Yukon with the intention to travel to Mexico to attend a month-long teaching retreat lead by the Venerable Namgyal Rinpoche. However, at the last minute that retreat was postponed and we found ourselves with no home and no immediate plans. We decided to head to Ontario and made the long cross-country drive arriving at the Dharma Center of Canada, 400 acres of retreat land northeast of Toronto. At that time there was only the original one hundred fifty-year-old farmhouse, a temple, and a few somewhat rundown buildings.

We arrived toward the first of May in a freak snowstorm that I now know was considered an auspicious Tibetan portent. When the night of our arrival Namgyal Rinpoche announced his next course would begin in a few weeks, the caretakers decided they wished to attend, and Bob - my partner- and I agreed

---

19   The Miraculous 16th Karmapa edited Norma Levine, p 161

CHAPTER NINE ❈ KARMAPA AND THE GELONGMA

to take their place. These were the fortuitous circumstances that led to our being in charge of preparing the Dharma Center of Canada for the first visit of His Holiness the Sixteenth Karmapa to the West with an entourage that included Sister Palmo.

Only a few weeks after the invitation was accepted, our quiet job of caretaking a remote property turned into a full-scale renovation and building project. We now had to house the Karmapa and his entourage as well as prepare the temple for the empowerments of the Karma Kagyu lineage to a group of approximately fifty of Namgyal Rinpoche's disciples.

The arrival that autumn of the Karmapa accompanied by Sister Palmo and his entourage became the defining point in my life. There were about forty students in retreat nearby and since it was off-season a summer lodge had been rented just north of the Center. Each day the group travelled back and forth from the lodge to the Center to receive the empowerments of all the main yidams and deities of the Karma Kagyu Lineage. Namgyal Rinpoche had requested this from the Karmapa for himself and his senior students. Although I was quite new to the Dharma, having taken refuge in 1972, I was among the few fortunate ones included outside this group.

The first day's experience of meeting His Holiness and receiving empowerment was so powerful that I wanted to immerse myself in it. That night in my retreat cabin I decided to remain at the Center after the empowerments the next day and volunteer in the kitchen. There were only a few women staying at the Dharma Center and Sister Palmo immediately made herself available to us, sharing her life and imparting teachings about the Kagyu lineage.

She was staying in the Tara retreat cabin usually reserved for women, close to the main temple. From the main house, you went down a path past a slight ravine and a small woods, then up the other side to the temple where the Tara cabin perched beside it in an open space. It was an idyllic spot, close enough to the main building to feel safe, and yet far enough to truly experience the quiet Canadian wilderness. That particular spot felt empowered and blessed by the dakinis.

My lasting impression was how powerful and utterly exotic these ten days were: His Holiness, his monks, Sister Palmo and her nightly discussions with a few women, and all of it in the Canadian wilderness. His Holiness was bestowing two or three empowerments each day for about ten days. The temple was quite small and very basic. Taking empowerment after empowerment in the forest with the group who left afterward and then spending several hours each evening in the Tara Cabin discussing Dharma and the Kagyu lineage with Sister Palmo was a glimpse of what it must have been like in old Tibet.

Every evening an intimate group of women gathered in the Tara Cabin with Sister Palmo. Many of the women who felt a connection with her were feminist types, interested in advancing the cause of women in Tibetan Buddhism. It was Sister Palmo who began to change the emphasis from only monks to include nuns. She was preparing Mrs. Raff, a close student of Namgyal Rinpoche, and another older woman for ordination. Our discussions were mostly about taking ordination and the future of women in the Karma Kagyu lineage. I was enthralled and also considered taking nun's vows.

Those evenings in the cabin were magical. She was ephemeral but warm and personal and had a translucent look with dark circles under her eyes, yet her eyes shone with an unmistakable spiritual light. She spoke often of Rumtek, the monastery wreathed in a thousand rays of rainbow light.

CHAPTER NINE ❖ KARMAPA AND THE GELONGMA

Sister Palmo   *Courtesy of the Bedi Family Archives*

She gave us each a copy of her booklet A Garland of Morning Prayers, the first translation of the Karma Kagyu Tibetan prayers, poetic in style rather than literal. It was produced with the help of Karma Thinley Rinpoche who had also worked with her to establish Tilokpur Nunnery and printed by Grace McLeod from Seattle. It was the most exotic book I had ever seen, printed on rice paper with an even more beautiful thick slightly beige rice paper cover and bound with golden thread. It was my favorite possession for years until it was lost in a fire.

That little booklet of prayers presented in a gem-like way was a treasure.

We did not get things in Canada from India easily in those days, not in experience or actuality. Each evening we gathered around her, sitting on the floor cross-legged in a cabin in the woods. The exotic feeling of the East and Eastern wisdom was embodied in Sister Palmo and that small booklet.

She had a little pointy hat which she wore all the time, the same hat that Lama Govinda used to wear. She was otherworldly, but then they all seemed otherworldly. I even thought that perhaps the monks flew at night! They were imbued with the atmosphere of a spiritual period in North America before the psychedelic spirituality of the '60s, earlier than that of the '50s: It had an Alexandra David Neel feeling of the magic and mystery of Tibet.

Her guru was the Sixteenth Karmapa and he lived in another realm. She was his disciple and also his English secretary. Her whole being was filled with devotion. She left her life behind completely and gave up the world of her family, her life of privilege, her status. She gave it up to live in another reality with a shaved head and that quaint little hat. You either shifted into that realm or you didn't connect. Sister Palmo was living that reality.

Her presence was like a nun's should be, standing erect, quiet, not intimidating. I remember clearly how much Karmapa loved her. He was always calling "Mummy, Mummy." Later he would call for Jamgon Kongtrul in the same way, 'Rinpoche, Rinpoche.' They were like family. He absolutely adored her. I can still hear him calling 'Mummy,' while sitting on his throne. 'Mummy, where's Mummy?' he would ask, like 'What's going on here?' He was in a foreign environment and he lived

CHAPTER NINE ❖ Karmapa and the Gelongma

in another dimension. She was family. There is a concept of royalty in the Karmapa's lineage. Sister Palmo would never have been called Mummy if she had not fitted the image of an aristocrat.

At times Sister Palmo looked a bit frail. Maybe she was not so well. In 1977 I was in the house in the Yukon Territory of Canada when Karmapa heard the shocking news that she had had a heart attack. In 1981 when I was in Rumtek, I used to look up at her meditation house halfway up the mountain just below the three-year retreat center, gazing in wonder at the time she spent there in strict meditation.

After the Karmapa gave ordination to the nuns, Palmo offered guidance to the newly ordained Westerners.

The requisite for a Buddhist nun is not necessarily a mastery of meditation. It is rather an ability to live a special kind of life. A woman who wishes to become a nun should examine her motive carefully. She should be able to live alone, no longer desire men, and abstain from alcohol. The vocation of a nun is more dependent upon a lifestyle than control of the mind.

At the same time she was reading Carlos Castaneda to keep pace with questions coming from the psychedelic members of the new generation, people who wanted to understand how Don Juan's astral travel compared to esoteric Tibetan yogas. She even had an answer. Don Juan's power was similar to the Tibetan adepts' power to create tulpas, a projected thought form which takes a human shape, in Western terminology, a doppelganger or replica of the real person.[20]

---

20   Lady of Realization, Sheila Fugard

❖ ❖ ❖

"His Holiness has had a triumphal procession through the West," proclaimed Palmo when they returned to Europe. "Chenrezig in his earthly form," as she described the Karmapa," caused a virtual meltdown of the heart with his sphere of radiation manifesting the energy of unconditional love and compassion of the thousand-armed Chenrezig."[21]

She was enjoying the company of Barbara Pettee, her cheerful friend and assistant on the tour. It had also been a homecoming for her. When they arrived in London, Chime Rinpoche and a few of his students formed a welcome party at Heathrow. The record producer Tony Visconti observed the Karmapa in dark sunglasses "whisked through with entourage in tow, one lama carrying the Black Hat in an elaborately decorated box."[22] At the Friends Meeting House in London over one thousand people gathered to see the first Black Crown ceremony in the UK with Sister Palmo in attendance and Kabir in the audience. She introduced the meaning of the Black Crown to the assembly and told them how she had met the Karmapa. The long since transcended working class girl from Derby had become a bridge to the transcendent.

While in London Palmo contacted Barbara Castle, her old friend from Oxford who was now a member of the Labour Cabinet. Castle invited her to lunch at Westminster. In her memoirs Castle noted, "She sailed into the House of Commons dining room in her flowing Buddhist robe, serenely indifferent to the covert stares at her shaven head. What her prim widowed mother made of all this, I never knew."

When she accompanied the Karmapa to Westminster Abbey escorted by Dean Edward Carpenter and his wife, Palmo's observations

---

21 The Miraculous 16th Karmapa, edited Norma Levine, p. 156
22 The Dance of 17 Lives, Mick Brown, p. 65

Chapter Nine ❖ Karmapa and the Gelongma

showed how unused she was to being in a cathedral. She seemed to have forgotten that historically, cathedrals were places where important people were buried.

> In London the Dean of Westminster and his wife gave a great welcome to His Holiness, and Mrs Carpenter gave us a tour of Westminster Abbey. She is charming and knowledgeable, a great asset to the Dean. We wandered around the Abbey, amazed to find how many burials there had been, almost like an enclosed cemetery, with many stories. It gave me a heavy feeling. The lofty roof was protected with sandbags by volunteers who sat on the roof during the whole of the German blitz.

It was November and London was buzzing with the Christmas spirit, she reported excitedly in her family letter. She was still a Mummy, a grand Mummy and mother-in-law who loved giving presents. She began to think of all the children wanting something for Christmas "so I began to send off little things to everyone from London." She bought *Wind in the Willows* and Tolkien for the grandchildren. "In Cambridge I got the most beautiful disc of Christmas carols and I want you to hear them because the voices are out of this world." She made a note about bringing back joy into Buddhist festivals.

> I am very keen on the ecumenical approach generally and on enjoying festivals. Have been putting some thought to the fusion of Buddhist festivals and approaches with those at present in the West.... with a strong vote for enjoying oneself with the children and picnics on Buddhist New Year. Western Buddhists tend to be too earnest and too gloomy. Buddhists are a cheery race internationally.

They arrived in Birmingham a few weeks after the IRA (Irish Republican Army) pub bombings in which 21 people had died and 182 injured. In the wake of the attack, the city was locked in a state of terror. His Holiness bestowed the Crown Ceremony in the hall of a Catholic school. With the population turning against the local Irish, the Catholic nuns were staunchly upholding unanimity between the faiths.

At Samye Ling in Scotland, the visit that year of the great yogin Kalu Rinpoche had stirred the spirit of Dharma after a dormant four-year period from 1970 when the wild and exotic Trungpa had departed for America. The hostility between Akong and Trungpa left a divorce-like wound in the family. Through the gaping hole came the mentally ill, the bruised casualties of the psychedelic generation, magnetized by the lack of boundaries to their socially disruptive behavior.

The 1974 visit of the Karmapa was crucial to furthering the progress of the traditional Dharma in what would become the most impressive and important Tibetan Buddhist monastic establishment in Britain. Palmo reported they spent a peaceful three weeks in the gently rolling lowlands. People thronged to see His Holiness; and many came to talk to her, finding it comforting to speak to somebody in their own language.

Angie Ball was at Samye Ling for the '74 visit of His Holiness. It was an unforgettable three weeks in her life.

> The Karmapa was amazing. I never met a being like that. He showed something that was so familiar that you had forgotten, Buddha nature so tangible that you could touch it, feel it; you knew it, then you forgot it. He was giving initiations in that small shrine room at Samye Ling, with its bright-colored carpet, giving powerful initiations – Hevajra, Red Tara, Karma Pakshi.

CHAPTER NINE ✤ KARMAPA AND THE GELONGMA

I went to all the initiations, mesmerized by him. Akong Rinpoche pulled me to one side and said, "Be careful, don't take all these initiations." Many of us didn't know anything. A lot of the initiations had commitments and we didn't know about them.

The energy was so high and exciting. It was like a party – you just wanted to be there. The Karmapa was so radiant that all the focus was on him. I wasn't facing the direction of Sister Palmo; I was facing the Karmapa.

Basement shrine room in Copenhagen   *Courtesy of Benny Friis Gunno*

I saw this woman around and people calling her Mummy. She was tall and quite striking in her appearance, the first Western woman I had seen in robes. I didn't grasp who she was. She was always there with him in the background, but with a strong presence. She and Karmapa were companions. They had a mutual respect, a closeness, a friendship. I didn't feel that she was subservient at all.

I was thinking about moving to Samye Ling at that time, planning to give up everything. I went in to see Karmapa and took off my rings and wanted to renounce everything, but Sister Palmo took me to one side and said, "You would do best to go back to London and finish your studies, not to give up everything." I felt indignant because I thought, "Can't you see I'm devoted to the Karmapa?" On reflection I saw that she was right. A lot of people gave everything away to the lamas and left nothing for themselves. We didn't know anything. She was a smart woman. She was very wise, so when she said that, I was only slightly put out.

We were mostly hippies at that time. We were into Lobsang Rampa, and thought all the Tibetans were able to astral travel and had powers. We were so naïve. We were ready to give it all away.

Akong, said Palmo, had acquired a yak with a companion dri from the Whipsnade Zoo and "there is speculation among farmers as to whether there will be any yak calves." He generously exchanged her screechy old tape recorder for a smart new one. The center was making quiet but steady progress.

When she visited her brother's family in nearby Stirling, she uncovered her English roots. Edna, her brother Jack's widow, had a daughter who would be the link between her family in England and India. She was irresistible, "rather like my brother, real charm and poise, fair,

CHAPTER NINE ❖ Karmapa and the Gelongma

Sister Palmo in Copenhagen *Courtesy of Benny Friis Gunno*

curly hair, a thoughtful little meditator." They received a blessing from His Holiness who was delighted to meet them.

◆ ◆ ◆

Copenhagen, December 28, 1975. Palmo began to record her memoirs in Copenhagen of the tour where, the year before, she had visited a basement space converted into a shrine room, preparing the ground for His Holiness the Karmapa to give the oral transmission of Manjushri on his '74 tour.

As the first qualified teacher ever to visit, she had given basic Buddhist teachings and introduced the Danish sangha to the practice of Manjushri on the Lion Throne (Jampal Maseng). "We received the Jampal Maseng initiation from her, my first initiation ever," said Benny Friis Gunno, whose girlfriend owned the apartment. "Personally I felt a deep connection with Sister Palmo who was a wise and compassionate person." She also introduced the ritual of the Sixteen Arhats. Later in the year the Dalai Lama visited Denmark and consecrated the basement room.

All of Scandinavia was pulsing with Dharma from the activity of two enthusiastic organizers, Ole Nydahl, a former prizefighter, and his wife, Hannah.

> Ole has dedicated his life to bringing the young people out of the drug scene. The work he is doing is exceptional. The whole group is so loving, more so than in any of the other Western countries. They are not extremely learned like Trungpa's group is,[23] but they make up for it by this truly beautiful atmosphere of metta and helpful cooperation.

---

23   According to Benny Friis Gunno, she did criticize Ole's anti-intellectual style. "You keep people with an education away. Don't you think these people long for liberation as much as other people?"

CHAPTER NINE ❖ Karmapa and the Gelongma

His Holiness the Sixteenth Karmapa and Pope Paul VI at the Vatican, Rome, 1975
Courtesy of N. Levine, The Miraculous 16th Karmapa

They made magnificent arrangements for His Holiness everywhere. Thousands have seen His Holiness and the Crown Ceremony in the state museum and other places. Now we have to start organizing this in India. I think the Bengalis and Punjabis would love it. It is something extraordinary, huge stages with backdrop curtains and lighting. It had the most extraordinary vibes and a liberating effect on the mind.

His Holiness was slightly ill in Copenhagen, continuing the tour but finding it somewhat stressful after his usual calm life in Rumtek. "The enthusiasm is terrific and the program is heavy. He's the main figure in this drama, seeing people, giving interviews constantly." His idea of relaxing was to go into a bird shop and make friends with all the birds. "He has finches and super canaries larger than you've ever seen with beautiful voices." By this time he was travelling with eight huge birdcages and three dogs, including a white Pekinese puppy.

Sister Palmo and B.P.L Bedi in Milan, 1975   *Courtesy of the Bedi Family Archives*

It was a nonstop itinerary: Denmark, Norway, and Sweden to Hamburg and the House of Stillness, one of the oldest centers in Germany; then to Amsterdam and the international headquarters of the Theosophical Society; on to Paris for a week before going to the Dordogne to meet Bernard Benson, a British millionaire/inventor who had offered his castle the Chateau de Chaban to the Karmapa with its 500 acres of land; and from there to Switzerland.

The major event on the European tour was the Karmapa's visit to Pope Paul VI organized by Chögyal Namkhai Norbu, a Dzogchen

CHAPTER NINE ❖ Karmapa and the Gelongma

Barbara Pettee, Sister Palmo, and B.P.L Bedi in Milan   *Courtesy of the Bedi Family Archives*

master living in Italy. The two Holinesses were scheduled to meet by papal appointment in Rome on February 17, 1975.

> I went straight to Rome and met His Holiness there for the interview with the Pope on the seventeenth. The Vatican was most impressive with enormous corridors. The Pope's bodyguards were like those in Sikkim at the Royal Palace. We were taken care of in every way. While in Rome, the monks were put up in a very beautiful monastery and we got rooms in a nunnery.

His Holiness the Pope invited His Holiness the Karmapa to return to Rome and stay longer there and made arrangements for a Cardinal to take us around the basilica of St Peter. We had a guided tour around that temple with its priceless paintings and sculptures of Michaelangelo. It was a very memorable day. The Pope gave us all inscribed medals to show we had received his blessing.

That evening the Karmapa and entourage left for Milan where Babaji Bedi, now a guru, and his followers met them at the airport. He left for France promising to return. Palmo had the opportunity to visit with her husband, rest for three days in a quiet place, and see his Aquarian Center. She could hardly speak without coughing.

Alas, the leaden grey skies of Paris and polluted air hid the germs of La Grippe and it hit me straight. I must have been a little tired from the journey and I got it with a hacking cough, so I was quite out for the French visit. Things went on well and were very successful for His Holiness and Barbara nursed me carefully.

She was scheduled to rejoin the Karmapa at Rikong where Tibetans were coming from different parts of Switzerland. The sight of Swiss Tibetans, well-dressed and cheerful, coming in with their children in good boots and windbreakers filled her with delight. "They were so happy to meet His Holiness and hear the *pujas*."
Just before His Holiness was due to fly back to Delhi, they all celebrated her birthday on February 5. "It's been an extraordinary tour. His Holiness will be glad to get on the Air India plane and reach Delhi on February 9."

I keep on thinking how much better the conditions everyone here lives in rather than that of the middle classes in India but it

CHAPTER NINE ❖ Karmapa and the Gelongma

pains me to realize we have things they haven't got. There's a certain atmosphere in India that makes you feel happy all the time. I really always remember India and want to go back. It's really coming home when I return.

In closing Palmo shared the merit of the tour, dedicating it to the attainment of inner peace, while reminding her family to celebrate Losar and enjoy life.

New Year is Feb 12. You know to light lamps and make offerings on the shrine. Have good food and make presents to each other. Guli and Shakti, your visit to Europe this past summer gives me a lot of satisfaction, knowing that you've seen something of your Western background.

I pray the New Year on Feb 12 will bring all peace and plenty, development in Dharma, and good and fruitful things. I share the merit of all this travelling with all of you that you may attain realization and reach inner peace without which material prosperity doesn't mean anything. May the blessing of the Buddhas, the Divine Mother, and the transcendent Triple Gem follow you.

My dearest love to you all.

The recording of Palmo's travels ends with Van Morrison singing "Streets of Arklow." The joyful experience of Chenrezig in his earthly form with his thousand arms of compassion embracing the world was as moving for her as the moment the Buddha at his enlightenment touched the earth which shook until the sound became song. In spite of the intensity of the tour and the demands it made on her health, Palmo was in God's green land, roaming the mythical streets of Arklow.

Sister Palmo and Barbara Pettee in Milan   *Courtesy of the Bedi Family Archives*

CHAPTER NINE ✤ Karmapa and the Gelongma

And as we walked
Through the streets of Arklow
And gay profusion
In God's green land
And the gypsy's rode
With their hearts on fire
They say "We love to wander,"
"Lord we love,"
Lord we love to roam..."
And as we walked
Through the streets of Arklow
In a drenching beauty
Rolling back 'til the day
And I saw your eyes
They was shining, sparkling crystal clear
And our souls were clean
And the grass did grow

It heralded a finale to the glorious '74 spiritual road trip, the only tour Palmo would make in her lifetime with the great Sixteenth Karmapa. The festive spirit she so wanted to bring into Western Buddhism sparkles through, lighting up the diamond path of Dharma. At 65, she was back in her English childhood, skipping along the lanes and hedgerows, her heart filled with joy.

CHAPTER TEN
Transmission of Dharma

You have to think that the path to death is the path to enlightenment. It's a good feeling to know the art of how to pass at the time of death like people teach natural childbirth. It's an inspiring practice because it takes away the fear of death.

After the '74-'75 tour, it became increasingly clear to Palmo, as well as to her closest friends and devotees, that her life force was quickly diminishing. Death was approaching and she wanted to make full use of her time, not just by entering retreat, but by transmitting the precious Dharma she had received from her masters.

She was in her sixty-sixth year, the inexhaustible energy of a twenty-five-year-old girl long since spent. On the tour with the Karmapa she had been introducing the Crown ceremony, explaining pujas, teaching, and translating texts. People came to her to arrange interviews with His Holiness or to seek her advice. On her return to India, she stayed with Kabir in Bombay and Ranga in Calcutta to assist the process of recovery. "Really it is the blessing of the Guru and Triple Gem that this loving attitude surrounds us in these later years," she wrote to Bedi on February 8, 1976. The healing vibrations from His Holiness the Karmapa and of Rumtek completed the process: "I am ninety percent back to normal."

Her travel plans for '76 were somewhat reduced although her activity had the same intensity. First she planned to attend a special cycle of initiations, the Kagyu Ngadzo, to be given by the Karmapa in Nepal where he was consecrating a new temple Ka Nying Shedrup Ling. Then she would fly from Calcutta to California with Anila in attendance to teach for several months at the impromptu center at 501 Edgwood Road in San Mateo

Concern for Palmo's health was uppermost in Barbara's mind when she next had an audience with the Karmapa. With one stroke of a red pen he wrote a few characters on a piece of paper and signed it: 501 Edgwood Road, Jane Taylor's residence in San Mateo that she shared with Barbara, became Karma Tengay Ling or Place for Increasing Buddha Activity. Thus was created the first Dharma Center born in the USA directly under the supervision of Rumtek (KTD).[24] "What does all this mean?" Barbara asked Palmo. "You now have a new center," she replied. "Don't worry, I will come and teach."[25]

Vajrayana is based on transmission, the very lifeblood of the Dharma, without which all the Diamond Vehicle teachings of the Buddha remain a lifeless body. Transmission is more than verbal teaching; it is the deep experience of knowing. The quality of experiential realization has to be conveyed from the original source through master to disciple in an unbroken lineage. Transmission has to be given person to person: heard, seen, felt, tasted, and experienced.

Said Palmo,

> Transmission is more fully realized by people who have a special intuitive type of mind. The aspirant must have the higher, deeper, intuitive intelligence of a truly spiritual person. Everybody gets something but not all; then there is the mind that slowly stage by stage can get it; and the mind that cannot get it. There are different grades of intellect among humans and animals. We can see it in pets. His Holiness selects the birds to find out which

---

24 In later years the name was changed to Karma Theksum Choling (KTC) and it became an affiliate of the main seat of His Holiness the Karmapa in America, Karma Triyana Dharmachakra.
25 KTC Newsletter June 27, 1983.

CHAPTER TEN ✤ Transmission of Dharma

birds have the finer intelligence so they can benefit from what they receive. Those birds die in samadhi in Rumtek.

From May until August 1976, Palmo gave an extensive series of teachings, initiations of Green and White Tara, public talks on Feminine Aspects – Vajra Yogini, the Divine Mother, and Arya Tara, individual and group interviews, with two weeks reserved for her personal retreat on Mount Shasta. There were celebrations of Buddhist festivals, chanting sessions, all-night vigils with walking meditation, and mantra recitation. She gave refuge accompanied by the precepts to be observed on full moon days and the bodhisattva vow. Special teachings were planned for initiates only on advanced tantric practices, Vajra Yogini and the Phowa or consciousness transference, one of the six yogas of Naropa.

It was a nonstop Dharma marathon. The program for May and June alone numbered forty-three events. People flew in from London, South Africa, Texas, the Northwest, crowding the new KTL center at Edgwood Road like a youth hostel. Some were sleeping on the floor and even shared rooms with sheet dividers to separate men and women.

Barbara said,

> The transmission quality of Tara and the Great Transmission from His Holiness were evident. Students from all over the Bay area came as both scholarly knowledge and compassionate insight combined with the clearest English made this emanation of Tara a deep personal experience for disciples.

Palmo claimed in a down-to-earth way that she had come to meditate and teach meditation, give lectures, and help people who needed somebody on the spot. "I came to establish the center in San Mateo dedicated to my own guru," she explained in a radio interview. Her nonsectarian tone appealed to the prevailing New Age trends, Transcendental Meditation, and self-appointed gurus.

I know there is great beauty in many schools of meditation, among the Hindus, the Sufis, the Christian mystics in the desert. The inner world of the meditator has no national flags attached to it. Everybody has a karmic direction, a tendency to go to one guru or another, devotion to one line or another. It doesn't matter where you start as long as you start. Keep a little time apart in the morning, not changing the time and just look within, be quiet, consciously quiet. Just being so simple really is the thing that starts the inner search. Many people harassed by the strains of daily life take to meditation. I don't know what TM is because I haven't practiced it. Anything that takes the person out of ordinary mind and into a transcendental mind state helps that person. They may not end up in TM but they may be forever grateful to TM. The same thing with Buddhist meditation. To me Buddhism is the full moon, the total aspect of the meditative enlightenment of the Buddha.

Allan Penny and his wife Kathy were present at the San Mateo cycle of teachings. They first met Palmo on her previous visit to San Mateo in '74. At that time they were working in a gift shop in Palo Alto, Ca. owned by a Tibetan.

One morning while going through a new shipment of tingshak or cymbals, the postman arrived with a parcel. Inside the package we saw a picture of an English Buddhist nun with a beguiling smile like that of Mona Lisa. The brief description in the article resonated immediately in us. She was a visiting nun who

CHAPTER TEN ✤ Transmission of Dharma

was giving a public talk at a home in San Mateo, California. We were fans of Tibetan culture but knew little of Buddhism. On the spot, we decided to go.

We met Sister Palmo at Jane Taylor's house in San Mateo a close friend of a well-connected Buddhist, Barbara Pettee. The two were similarly affluent and influential. Barbara would later become a friend and Dharma sister to Kathy and me. Our meeting with Sister Palmo triggered an instant connection. She exuded a deep compassionate familiarity not unlike that of a favorite aunt or one's mother. In fact she was also known as Mummy-la.

A few years later in 1976, we had regular meetings with Sister Palmo over a period of a few months. We attended weekly talks along with a small group of Westerners who gathered in Jane's garage. In this unlikely setting, Sister Palmo gently and eloquently introduced us to the Buddhadharma, its view and practices. She generated a booklet, The Garland of Morning Prayers in 1976 and I still have it in its original binding. It was dedicated to the Fourteenth Dalai Lama followed by a short prayer dedicated to Karmapa. It contained prayers and short sadhanas for daily recitation. These were all written in English, along with her handwritten notes clarifying certain visualizations and their meanings in the appropriate colors of the Tibetan pantheon of deities. She wanted us to learn the Tibetan language so we chanted in Tibetan, but we recited the Tibetan and English together so we could know what we were saying. It was a unique method of practice for its time.

Mummy was considered an emanation of Green Tara; I believe Karmapa himself said this. She taught us the sadhana of Green Tara and we practiced intensively. We associated her deeply with the deity and that connection still carries now for me, making it a significant practice. I wasn't sure at first what this meant but later on it became clear.

Indeed her compassion and loving kindness were deeply apparent. We learned the significance of the Karmapa Black Pills. She taught us things like how to observe aspects of the Dharma with mindfulness. There were red strings called blessing cords and Mummy always reminded us to pick up any red string we found and keep it to remember the significance of a Buddhist blessing. This was one of our first lessons in Buddhist mindfulness.

It didn't take us long to realize how incredibly fortunate we all were to have access to these teachings in our native language. Her gift as a translator was like a golden key, but beyond the words was the meaning she would impart to the teachings. She introduced us to the concepts of refuge and ngondro. We took our refuge with Mummy and received a Dharma name on a beautiful handwritten card, a black and white portrait of her and underneath it a refuge name. In her wonderfully patient manner she would lead us into our own heart center so that the meaning broke through the words. Her translations were at the core of the dissemination of Dharma in the West.

She told us wonderful stories, but we never had intimate conversations about her private life. Her son Kabir visited our tiny center in Jane's garage and brought along Persis Khambatta, a beautiful woman with a shaved head, best known for her role as Ilia in the 1979 Star Trek adventure. We were awestruck when she turned up with Kabir and marveled at the colorful spectrum of Mummy's life and her presence with us.

In 1977 this small garage in San Mateo also hosted at her request the Sixteenth Karmapa who bestowed upon our group the Karma Pakshi empowerment, a yidam associated with the energy of the Second Karmapa. By practicing the deity associated

CHAPTER TEN ✤ Transmission of Dharma

with this manifestation of enlightened mind, one could develop the enlightened attributes of the Karmapa.

Thus our small sangha became the first Karmapa center in the US. Named Karma Tengay Ling and later Karma Thegsum Choling, this center continued to flourish for the next few decades relocating itself in different areas around the San Francisco Bay Area, all the while expanding to smaller localized groups in Santa Cruz, Palo Alto, and San Francisco.

I remember Mummy telling a small group of her students about her first glimpse of enlightened mind. She said it occurred while walking down a sunny street through the market in Burma alongside a teacher. She was holding a small parasol. She recounted suddenly how she perceived the scene around her in amazing clarity and expanse, seeing the interconnectedness of everything. She became intricately and visually aware of interdependence. This left an indelible memory as the gift of a brief insight into the view of emptiness. It reinforced the possibility for us as new practitioners that we could also develop such a level of awareness. Our path was marked out by Mummy-la.

Years later, Allan and his wife Kathy made a pilgrimage with Barbara Pettee to retrace the steps of the Sixteenth Karmapa's legendary trip to Hopiland under the auspices of White Bear, holder of the Hopi Prophecies, revisiting all the sites, including the restricted kivas and private spiritual locations and communities such as Old Oraibi, usually forbidden to outsiders. Thus the meeting of the Hopi Elders and the Tibetan Chief passed into sacred history.

The truth of Dharma was audible in Palmo's voice, reaching also those unfamiliar with the teaching of the Buddha. On her way back to India via New York she spoke with Lex Hixon, esoteric scholar and host of a radio show on WBAI-FM. The phone kept ringing from unknown listeners to the program who asked, "Who is this person? I must see her" and "I don't know anything of what that lady was talking about but I want to come and learn more." Barbara wrote,[26] "All of this shows the transmission power of pure humans like Sister Palmo who through her devotion to the Karmapa offered body, speech, and mind to the Dharma."

Palmo kept a low profile throughout.

> From the time I met HHGK in 1959 and entered the mandala in 1961, I have not only taken initiations from the gurus but have also tried to practice in whatever way I could. Not to boast of this, since the more one gets into Tantra the more one realizes how little one knows. It is a vast ocean. I say it because the teacher who teaches Tantra has to say what he has done. If I give an initiation it is because my guru His Holiness the Karmapa has allowed me to give it, not because I have decided to do it.

In a talk titled "Introduction to Tantra" she made the esoteric and obscure accessible to Westerners. Tantrayana, she explained, was the way to reach the ultimate goal of enlightenment quickly in this very life. "In Tantrayana realization is more immediate. In fact it is the inner side of the Mahayana. It is the fruit; Mahayana is the seed from which the fruit is produced."

> The vehicle of the Vajra or Diamond Vehicle means indestructible, essence of the eternal, not bound by ordinary laws of the world. Tantra can be described by great scholars but Tantra is not to be understood in theory. It is to be taken step-by-step in the here and now, hour by hour, entering into a new world

---

26   KTL newsletter, June 27, 1983

CHAPTER TEN ✤ Transmission of Dharma

life. The key of this path is the great devotion to the guru. It is a sacred bond to take an initiation with the lama. The link is to a large extent with the lama in this life and in lives to come. It is a very deep pledge.

Charged with a sense of her own approaching death, she spoke the stark truth of impermanence.

Where should we learn Tantra? People in ancient times went to the cemeteries, on the banks of the Ganges. Those places are sacred, lonely, in the presence of death, reminding us that life does not last long and we had better do what we can as quickly as we can. One day we have to reach this place. That's the feeling. A place of death is where we feel impermanence, a clean, pure, and lonely place: a place near the ocean, in the mountains, or near a high guru.

But death did not have to be a lonely, haunted landscape or a cliff edge with a dark shadow in pursuit. In the Phowa or consciousness transference teachings, she painted an inspiring picture of the pure land of the radiant Amitabha Buddha of Limitless Light.

The reading transmission and general introduction to Phowa that Palmo gave was part of the practice[27] she had received from Ayang Rinpoche, a Drigung Kagyu Phowa master. In Tibet, the Drigung Kagyu lineage was renowned for Phowa or the yoga of consciousness transference for use specifically at the time of death. As many as ten thousand people have been known to gather to receive the empowerment.

Ayang Rinpoche had given the Phowa empowerment, transmission, and instructions privately to a small group including Sister

---

27 To be complete, a Vajrayana practice has to include the initiation, the reading transmission, and the teaching instruction (wong, lung, and tri).

Sister Palmo, studio portrait *Courtesy of the Bedi Family Archives*

CHAPTER TEN ✣ Transmission of Dharma

Palmo on his visit to Rumtek to meet with the Sixteenth Karmapa. "The methods taught by the Drigung lamas are extremely powerful. I pray you may have a Drigung lama here to get the blessing from that lineage," she said to her students. She offered a lengthy explanation and reading transmission of the secret practice to a select group of close initiates, all of whom she knew personally.

> I'm going to give you the transmission, the precious essence, in English. Just listen to it and after that I will explain it. Just put your head down and listen with complete faith. You can get various signs during the reading. Just have complete faith and take it like that. Spontaneous faith is a necessity for a practitioner if he is to succeed.

Some excerpts from that private teaching indicate that she was turning her mind toward Amitabha's Pure Land of Dewachen in the West, the direction of the sun setting in a blaze of splendor.

> We don't know the time of death; it is in the hands of karma. We have made good, bad, and neutral karma. The state of our mind is important at the time of passing. We could go into a lower state or a higher state. If we have complete faith we could go into the land of the Buddha of Limitless Light, Amitabha.

Palmo's South African devotee Sheila Fugard saw the many faces of the Divine Mother in the last stage of Palmo's life.

> Sister Palmo as a woman teacher brings in elements of the Great Mother which make the journey into the diamond quality of Dharma a unique blessing. I saw the radiance of the mother energies and the subtle power of the yogini. I was to see through

Sister Palmo's eyes, the Dharma on the enlightenment day of the Buddha when she gave the eight precepts to be kept for that day only. The precepts were no longer rules but the natural way to be. The thought of enlightenment as it arose for Sakyamuni Buddha was of itself the natural order of things, as sunlight or the tide relentlessly coming in.

Knowing intuitively she would never see her guru again, Fugard prepared a tribute commemorating Palmo's three aspects: her outer form as a nun, her inner form as the Divine Mother or Green Tara, and her secret form as a siddha with miraculous powers, analogous to a renowned eighth century nun also called Gelongma Palmo. Born a beautiful princess, her evil karma resulted in leprosy so contaminating that her limbs began to fall off. She cured herself by dwelling hermit-like in a forest performing a rigorous cycle of fasting purification until she reached the tenth bodhisattva level.

At the end of the text that the Rinpoches use in the fasting practice of Chenrezig is a little note that refers to Gelongma Palmo citing her outer, inner, and secret aspects, and then they give credit to Sister Palmo. Barbara and I read this account to her at the end of the Tara empowerment and we played music. 'You Sister Palmo,' we said, 'you are the ancient siddha who dwelled in the forest of India.' After that tribute I said goodbye to her. Her health and energy had declined. I sensed I would not see her again.

During Palmo's visit, Chögyam Trungpa came to bless the shrine room at San Mateo. He turned to the mother of his extraordinarily successful activity and remarked: "I shall not see you again, but after the passing of time, we shall be reunited." It was their last meeting.

CHAPTER TEN ✤ Transmission of Dharma

In the last pause before these omens came to pass, a great celebration occurred. Word of mouth spread of Palmo's tenth anniversary as a nun bringing one hundred people spontaneously, bearing offerings of food, music, and dance. Karma Thinley Rinpoche flew in from Boulder as special guest for the weekend. A fire puja was performed to eradicate obstacles, and sandalwood incense hanging from tree branches perfumed the air.

In the final scene of her spiritual odyssey, Palmo went into solitary retreat on Mount Shasta in Northern California. The vision of the sacred mountain as a retreat place had come to her in India.

Dale Brozosky who often did retreats on the mountain offered to arrange a place on land belonging to his friends. They received her joyfully, offering the smaller of their two domes. After a brief visit with her hosts on the evening of arrival in July, she went into seclusion, facing the crown of the snow-capped mountains. On Sunday she sat in a meadow while questions were handed to her and she wrote the answers, remaining in strict silence. Anila brought her food every day but no other communication or conversation took place.

Brozosky said,

> We would often hear the sound of ritual bells and damaru coming from the retreat dome. When her retreat ended, we said farewell. It was the last time I saw her. Travelling with His Holiness in 1977 in Canada, I learned that Sister Palmo had passed away.

Ani Gilda Paldrön Taylor who had lived in "501" with Barbara before taking robes had the clearest indication of the imminence of Palmo's death:

> It was a circuitous route through an upper-class neighborhood to Karma Tengay Ling that was located in a large double garage

of Jane Taylor's home in San Mateo, California. I had flown down from Portland, Oregon, an hour-and-half flight, to see a Tibetan Buddhist nun who, thankfully, spoke English. I had taken refuge in Tibetan Buddhism the January before, but felt frustrated as there was no Tibetan Buddhist teacher, very few books on the subject, and no internet. I knew next to nothing of lineages, sects, and subsects as this was before the plethora of information now available.

Barbara took me up the long stairway with a landing midway, and down a hallway leading to what was her bedroom, now being used by Sister Palmo. It was a large room, filled with light and sweet-smelling air gently blowing in through a bank of open windows. An extended desk occupying one wall was generously covered with stacks of papers, booklets, a typewriter, and the paraphernalia of a well-used area. A single bed was against another wall. The entire floor was covered in a beige carpet with small Tibetan-style rugs overlaying various parts of the carpet.

Seated in the middle of the room in an Eames-style chair was Sister Palmo. She was a large woman seated cross-legged, clothed in the maroon and yellow robes of ordained sangha and her head showed only a stubble of white hair. She welcomed me with a wide smile and I immediately relaxed. Her voice was pleasant, strong, rather high and sing-songy, with an English accent. I noted the mild malocclusion of her teeth, providing an interesting aspect to her oval-shaped face.

It was forty years ago that the meeting took place and what remains in my mind is that we shared an early spiritual nature and both sought a path that allowed it to grow. She had been raised and grew up in the Church of England and, although I had been baptized a Lutheran, as time passed I had become a High Church Episcopalian. She had three children as did I,

CHAPTER TEN ✺ Transmission of Dharma

and we both had problems with a prolapsing heart valve. There were a number of other less significant similarities that we shared. I was in my mid-forties and she in her mid-sixties.

While I was there at "501," Sister Palmo gave some short talks in what had become the shrine room. On the following day, a Sakya lama from the East Bay gave the Bodhisattva Vow. In between, we spent time with locals and those coming from various parts of the world. Some had met Sister Palmo before, but most of us had not. Afterward we gathered in various settings across the large yard behind the house

Later the afternoon of the second day when the majority of people attending were gone, I noticed Sister Palmo sitting alone on the long couch that looked out over the extended lawn and trees indigenous to California. I startled myself by asking if I could massage her feet. It was out of character for me as I was rather reserved in this new spiritual environment, but she quickly agreed and extended her legs so her bare feet appeared from under the maroon robes. When I asked, she said her feet were tender and I took her advice and began with just gentle stroking while getting a sense of her energy. Then, as I moved on to a bit of light massage I immediately noted her feet were like glass, firm without elasticity. I was taken aback, but gently continued in the quiet environment. Having been in nursing for over twenty years, I had given massages to many patients, as well as friends and family. The immobilized tissue and muscles of her feet were alarming. I had noted it only with patients who were nearing death.

I continued with the massage for a few more minutes, then rose and started to do prostrations before leaving her presence. Sister Palmo quickly brought up her hand, "Oh, don't do prostrations when leaving, otherwise we won't meet again."

Sister Palmo *Courtesy of the Bedi Family Archives*

We never did. Sister Palmo died a few months later, early in the next year.

Palmo returned to India in the autumn and put plans in place for the year ahead. She ordered a "yellow Gelongma ceremonial coat" in Hong Kong and added a postscript to Jane Taylor on November 15 asking her to keep it until her return the next year.

On December 5 she wrote to Olive,

CHAPTER TEN ✤ Transmission of Dharma

Sitting on the verandah of Ranga's flat surrounded by our indoor garden of bougainvilleas, poinsettias, and money plants... bright sun, but a hint of cold in the air... My bronchial heart complaint seems very much better with good Californian medicine . ... I'm ashamed to say I'm not strong enough to dash around in the old carefree way, although my increase in energy is considerable following the treatment.

She was preparing her retreat house at Rumtek, "The Hermitage on the Hill," on land His Holiness had consecrated and Anila was in her element "supervising and feeding the village workers."

A few weeks later on Dec 21, 1976 she wrote to Sheila Fugard:

I had to be in Sikkim, but the family felt that I was somewhat weak after my sally into the Nursing Home, eleven days. Want to catch His Holiness before he goes to Nepal. Want to discuss all my '77 plans with him in the light of this health setback.

According to Didi Contractor, the Karmapa had said, "We all know you have a big heart. You stay here this year and build your house." So she stayed in Rumtek and did not accompany him on the '77 tour. She confided to Didi, "I don't know which house he meant, whether I am building the house of my incarnation or my physical house." Perhaps the Karmapa was saying to build the house of her incarnation, Didi commented.

In her letter to Fugard, Freda looked on the positive side of her health check:

One can of course say it has strengthened me, since the all-out antibiotic attack on the bronchial congestion has relieved the pressure on the heart (which I was not formerly conscious of).

I am looking slimmer and some puffiness gone – all to the good. (This is a private report as between friends.)

I'm going through a thorough health check up in Bombay so you can see I'm being careful. Feeling good but keeping up all the rules. And then, doctors willing, fly to Delhi by 26 March for the World Buddhist Jayanti 2600 Seminar before surfacing in Calcutta about the end of March.

The cardiologist in Bombay found no cause for alarm; she had an enlarged heart but it was not life-threatening. On March 26, 1977 she reached Delhi on time for the World Buddhist Conference scheduled to commence on March 27. She checked into the Oberoi Hotel and went to room 146, reserved by Goodie. Before her evening prayers, she asked Anila to put on the recording of Karmapa singing the deeply devotional chant, Lama Chenno. Palmo went into meditation. Anila left but she could not sleep. She heard heavy breathing. Immediately she went to Palmo, only to find she was gone, still sitting in meditation.

After her cremation in Delhi her ashes were brought in an urn by her devoted son Kabir to Rumtek, the fabled monastery of the Sixteenth Karmapa, wreathed in a thousand rays of rainbow light. Her body which had shown signs of life four days after death did not make it.

◆ ◆ ◆

In a letter of condolence to Gilda Taylor, Gyaltsap Rinpoche, the Karmapa's heart son and regent, expressed his shock at her untimely death: "Her expiration caused us immense and deep sadness."

Ayang Rinpoche, a close friend of the Bedi family as well as a teacher of Palmo, sent a letter of condolence to Kabir.

CHAPTER TEN ✤ Transmission of Dharma

The sad news of dear Mummy's death has brought a quivering shock to all of us who have been, in the past and I am sure still, very close to her noble heart. I sat down in a deep thought, as our dear Mummy would have in times of grave situations, and I have decided she has fulfilled her life's goal - first as a freedom fighter, then as a selfless social worker, and finally as a Mahayana Buddhist. She was like a mother to the cause of Tibetan Buddhists in particular.

The loss of Mummy, therefore, is not only a great deprivation to you and me or the Tibetans alone, but it is a great loss to the whole of mankind. However, at a time like this, sorrow cannot bring back the loss and the best mankind can do is to follow her noble steps. This applies to all our friends who loved her and truly appreciated her deeds.

Sheila Fugard wrote an accolade:

One knew instinctively that Sister Palmo was a realized being. As a Dharma teacher she was patient yet illuminating, with a quality of Manjushri, the bodhisattva of wisdom, seeing the essence of the path. As a yogi, she was subtle, powerful, and a possessor of siddhis contained behind the quiet exterior of the bhiksuni.

Sister Palmo came to Africa in 1972 and touched many in an extraordinary way. It was auspicious that she was the first Buddhist sangha member to reach our shores. She brought the awakened consciousness of buddhahood. She taught profusely by example, her own radiance being enough to encourage the inward turning of the mind... Her way was transcendental, and in life she put into practice the great simplicity of the Buddhist

FREDA MARIE BEDI (*née* HOULSTON), GELONGMA KARMA KHECHOG PALMO

FREDA came up as an Exhibitioner to St. Hugh's in 1929 from Parkfield Cedars School, Derby, and graduated in the Honours School of P.P.E. in 1933. Shortly before her death on 26 March 1977, she wrote that the National Committee of Indian Women had given her an award for 'outstanding service to India', adding: 'Well, the honour also goes to St. Hugh's.'

In 1933 Freda married Baba Bedi, an Indian and an Oxford graduate and from then on her life was bound up with India: 'It had never been our fate since our marriage to live a particularly safe life in the political conditions then obtaining in India, and we had hoped that with the dawn of independence we should have a chance to settle down to solid constructive work to build up free India.... But there was a stretch of danger and difficulty still to be crossed, and we landed in Kashmir at the end of November 1947 to contribute what we could to the resistance.... We camped out in our first house in Srinagar, along with Ranga, then fourteen and Kabir, then two.... Along with the brave Kashmiri girls and women ... I took up the organisation of women's work in the different refugee camps, all of us acting as older sisters to the thousands of children and women suffering not only physical hardship in the desperate cold, but often mental torture when relations and children had been killed, abducted, or lost on the miserable trek to safety.... January 1st, 1949, saw the Cease-fire. In September 1949 little Gulhima (Guli) was born. Her name means "Rose of the Snows", a fitting one for a child born in this valley of the Himalayas, famed through the centuries for its natural beauties, snows and flowers and lakes and gardens....'

The year 1950 saw Freda back at work again, at a pioneer college for women in Srinagar, University of Kashmir. In 1959 she was invited to report on Tibetan refugee camps and threw herself unreservedly into the work of rehabilitation; she was especially concerned about the young Tibetan incarnate Lamas upon whom much responsibility for the future leadership of their country rested. In 1961 she became Hon. Director of the Young Lamas' Home School and in 1965, alive to the danger of having so many of the future leaders of Tibet together, she wrote: 'Due to the China-India war emergency I am leaving with three nuns and about twenty-three lamas for Andretta.' In 1963 she founded a Buddhist nunnery, became a Buddhist nun in 1966, and was subsequently ordained Gelongma, the highest ordination available to a Buddhist nun, and one not awarded in India for many centuries previously. By 1970 she was a valued speaker on the world stage in her chosen sphere and travelled extensively. A letter written last December, among the bourgainvillias and poinsettias on the verandah of her elder son's flat outside Calcutta, was full of news of her children and grandchildren and of Baba Bedi—gay and full of spirit, but recognizing at last that a modicum of rest was needed. 'Some there are who have left a name behind them to be commemorated in story.'

O. C.

38

Copy of obituary from St Hugh's College magazine *Courtesy of St Hugh's archivist, Amanda Ingram*

CHAPTER TEN ❖ Transmission of Dharma

nun. All things of the world of glamor and material knowledge had fallen away. She had penetrated deep into the nature of suffering and understood impermanence ... She was free of her own clingings and viewed all with a deep compassion born of the knowledge of the void. Like a good teacher she taught that all must find their own truth and that the Buddha himself was only a finger pointing the way.

Sister Palmo travelled the world on the instructions of His Holiness the Karmapa to lead those with little dust on their eyes to the wonder and knowledge of the Buddha. She was preparing in old age to withdraw from teaching. HIs Holiness had granted her some land at Rumtek Monastery, Sikkim. A small hermitage was being built there.... But something other, the need for rebirth for higher work or a place in the Paradise of Great Bliss, came sooner than was expected. She has gone, and rainbows cracked the sky and the earth was flooded with light.

❖ ❖ ❖

The manner of Palmo's death was like a puzzle with a few missing pieces. Was she practicing the Phowa in her evening meditation although warned by His Holiness not to practice it at night? Had she projected her consciousness into Amitabha's Pure Land and left her body before her time? Surely she wanted a long life. She was making plans for the future. Perhaps she was not doing Phowa but a Guru Yoga practice. She had asked Ani Zangmo to play a recording of a Guru Yoga supplication. Perhaps she simply died of a heart attack and passed away while sitting up.

With these thoughts circling like the three animals locked inside the hub of samsara's wheel, I delayed my departure from Delhi in December 2016 to keep an appointment with Ayang Rinpoche who was arriving from Japan after giving a Phowa transmission. Over tea and cakes in the privacy of my hotel room, we had an intense conversation about Freda Bedi – her life and sudden death.

They had met when he was very young, he said, at the refugee camp in Assam and at that time did not make a personal connection.

When we reached India we didn't know the Indian language or culture. We Tibetans were just like the dumb; I saw people talking to this English lady and saw her helping. She was not a nun, she was Freda Bedi, the only Western person in the camp, so she stood out, tall with fair skin and blue eyes. She was very kind, very peaceful with everyone.

Our personal connection developed through the Sixteenth Karmapa, my root master. I visited Rumtek Monastery often to see him and then we got to know each other. I didn't know English, I knew only a bit of Hindi. Sometimes when she met with the Sixteenth Karmapa she asked me to translate for her from Tibetan to Hindi. When she asked Karmapa to open centers in the West, I was her translator. By that time, 1967, she was a nun.

I visited Rumtek briefly to take an empowerment from His Holiness the Karmapa. There, a few older monks and Sister Palmo asked me to give Phowa teaching. We did the ceremonies and teaching over a few days inbetween receiving His Holiness's empowerment. It was not for the public; no other Westerners were there.

She was an advanced practitioner, mainly interested in meditation, not Buddhist knowledge in general. Karmapa treated her in a very special way; he gave her a nice apartment in the monastery and she lived there. She was the only woman Karmapa accepted as resident in the monastery.

Her life history, her connection to the Dharma shows that in her previous life she must have had a strong connection to

CHAPTER TEN ❖ Transmission of Dharma

Tibetan Buddhism and Tibetan people. She had devotion to buddhadharma at a time when there were no other Westerners in Tibetan Buddhism. Of course she must have been a master in a previous life but who she was, I don't know. I'm not qualified to recognize previous lives, but just her activity, how she did everything shows it. When she died I was not there.

I described how she had passed away in meditation and the signs of life in her clinically dead body.

He responded:

There are five different levels of Phowa. I teach on all levels, but who can do which level depends on the practitioner. I teach all five levels together. In the Phowa teaching it is mentioned that those who have clearly recognized buddha nature, the true nature of mind, in this lifetime and have realization of the practice at the time of death, that level of practitioner can do dharmakaya Phowa. The result of dharmakaya Phowa will show in the body which will have life-like characteristics, not like a dead body. The corpse of the dead will not rot. This indicates a recognition of the ground clear light.

There is the path clear light and the ground clear light. Path clear light is the very clear recognition in this lifetime of the nature of mind and the experience of realization. Ground clear light is like the mother. At the moment of death every being will experience the nature of mind (ground clear light) naturally. In The Tibetan Book of the Dead it is mentioned that the first intermediate stage after death is the clear light state, meaning the nature of mind, buddha nature. Whoever can recognize and meditate on this until complete realization will attain the dharmakaya Phowa. In dharmakaya Phowa there is no need for consciousness to pass through the crown chakra. It doesn't depend on projection. Only those practitioners who have great realization can do this. So I think she passed away through dharmakaya Phowa.

It doesn't matter even if she had a heart attack. Good practitioners will recognize when they will die. In dharmakaya Phowa breathing has already stopped. After the outer breathing has stopped, then the inner breathing stops. At that time they can do dharmakaya Phowa. A heart attack would not make any difference.

Tukdam is the name for a corpse in which some characteristics of a live body are present. The body is malleable, not stiff; the body does not rot, does not smell. The white sweat that occasionally appears on the brow is nectar, dutsi. The yogi who does dharmakaya Phowa sometimes remains sitting as she did. In the teaching these special signs are mentioned. All the signs are that she attained perfect dharmakaya Phowa, the highest level.

I asked, "Then she would have had the capacity to choose her reincarnation?"[28]

Reincarnation depends on what wish or dedication prayers were made in that lifetime. If one has prayed, "Until the end of samsara, I want to help all sentient beings," if done with strong determination, then that person can reincarnate. If one wishes not to come back anymore to samsara and wants to go to the Pure Land, then it will happen. It depends on what is wished in that lifetime. We don't know what she wished, whether she wished to come back or not.

---

28   All sentient beings reincarnate. Those with little spiritual accomplishment are swept by the winds of their karma without any control over a next life.

CHAPTER TEN ✣ Transmission of Dharma

Sister Palmo was like the bridge between Tibetan Buddhists and Westerners. Everything she did was successful. If she reincarnated, her work will have continued. If she has reincarnated, it will have shown and people will know. But nobody requested it. She is already born, already grown up. Who knows? Freda Bedi was first a worldly lady, finally she became a great spiritual lady. She was very great, not an ordinary lady. She was definitely a tulku or emanation. I believe she was a dakini.

◆ ◆ ◆

Two years after her mother had passed away, Guli, her daughter, moved to the US. In the summer of 1980 she had "a most remarkable experience" while driving in New Hampshire. "By a series of bizarre coincidences, the Sixteenth Karmapa came to my house."

We had decided to go on a picnic to the Rhododendron State Park in New Hampshire to look at the rhododendrons, but it turned out to be too early for the shrubs so we decided to go back to a place we saw on the way called Cathedral of the Pines. We were curious and decided to go back and check it out. There was only one other car in the parking lot. We parked the car near it and saw a lama walking with a white American man.

I had heard that the Karmapa was coming to the United States so I thought I would ask the lama. I said, "Rinpoche, I would like to ask you if you know about the visit of His Holiness the Karmapa." He looked straight at me and said, "Guli! That is the reason I am here. I have just set up a date for the Black Hat Ceremony." I got goose bumps. I said, "How did you know my name is Guli?" He said, "I just know." I think it was Lama Tenzin from the Woodstock Monastery. He said he knew my mother. He couldn't have known that I had moved to the US.

Then he told me that the Black Hat Ceremony was taking place in August at the Cathedral of the Pines. He said, "Be here and I'll make sure you meet His Holiness."

We went on the given date. There were huge crowds. I told somebody who I was and they told somebody else. I was taken into the hall where His Holiness was seated with other monks and a Chinese monk in grey. As I approached, His Holiness exclaimed, "Guli, Guli, Guli." My mother always said to do prostrations when I met His Holiness, so I did prostrations. He said, "Do not prostrate before me. You should be prostrating to this man. He's the man who ordained your mother." He was a Chinese monk from Hong Kong who had ordained her as a Gelongma. So I met him too.

His Holiness said, "Come here. How are you?" and he was so loving. I said, "If you're in Massachusetts, please come and visit me." He replied immediately, "I will definitely come." He was a guest of Governor King of Massachusetts. He said, "When I come back I will come and see you. Leave your name and address." So I did. I gave my name and address to one of the Buddhists who was organizing it, who said, "There is no way he will have time to visit. He has a chock-a-block schedule." Then I saw the Black Hat Ceremony at the Cathedral of the Pines. My mother had wanted me to attend the Black Hat Ceremony but I never had until then.

About three weeks later I got a call, "Would it be alright for His Holiness and a party of twenty-five to come and visit on this date?" We had just got into the country. I galvanized my friends, borrowed furniture, trained one friend to make tea in the Tibetan way, and cooked up a storm. About three hours before His Holiness arrived, the limousines drove in. The secret service came to check it out. His Holiness came, and we had a lovely

CHAPTER TEN ❖ Transmission of Dharma

Ranga Bedi *far right behind;* his daughter Ami *front* with her two daughters; daughter Sohni Bedi *far left*; Ranga's wife Umi Bedi holding arm of His Holiness the Dalai Lama *center,* c. 2000   *Courtesy of the Bedi Family Archives*

lunch. This happened in 1980. He looked very pale and he was spitting a lot into a spittoon. He didn't look well to me. The following year he died.

It was amazing to happen to run into the only car in a parking lot in New Hampshire. They were just about to leave when we drove in. They had seen pictures of me when I was very young, but at that time I was about thirty years old!

In 2011 the members of the Bedi family in the Bombay area heard that His Holiness the Dalai Lama was coming to a location near Bangalore. They requested an interview to ask for his blessing and received a date and time. The whole family came to Bangalore to meet him, spending the night in Mysore. In the morning they went to the address given. Before entering, they met his secretary who confirmed their appointment and gave them instructions – not to spend more than ten minutes and not to take photos.

315

Ranga said, "When we entered His Holiness was sitting on a settee. He recognized me and rose to greet me. We just talked about Mummy. I kept a close watch on the time. When we had reached ten minutes I thanked His Holiness for spending the time and got up. He said, "Sit down" and summoned someone to bring tea and biscuits. We continued to chat. Then His Holiness inscribed a book to the family and gave it to us as a gift. Just after that, he summoned someone who brought a camera. His Holiness stood in the center with the family on either side and had pictures taken with us.

"As we were leaving, I bent down to touch his feet. The Dalai Lama lifted me up and held me by the shoulders. He said, "Thank you for coming. You brought Mummy's picture before my eyes." The tears were streaming down our faces. Every one of us was wiping our eyes. He sent us a copy of the picture and we all still have it."

Ranga's eyes were moist with emotion as he spoke of Mummy.

ACKNOWLEDGMENTS

This spiritual biography of Freda Bedi was compiled with the full cooperation of the Bedi family who allowed access to their mother's archives. Their generosity, hospitality, and contacts were invaluable in re-creating her story.

Ranga, Kabir, and Gulhima Bedi gave me interviews, tapes, photos, and answers to my questions. Umi Bedi prepared delicious healthy food and Ami Bedi gave me a wonderful room. Parveen Dusanj-Bedi provided organizational skills and computer competence.

Many great beings accompanied me on Freda's spiritual odyssey:

His Holiness the Seventeenth Karmapa advised me with wisdom and skillful means.

His Eminence Goshir Gyaltsab Rinpoche, the Venerable Chime Tulku Rinpoche, the Venerable Ringu Tulku Rinpoche, and His Eminence Choeje Ayang Rinpoche showed their trust and belief in the worth of this adventure. His Holiness Sakya Trizin gave me one precious sentence about Freda.

Some contributors were friends but many, whom I did not know, also became friends:

Ngodup Burkhar was my guiding light and encouraged me to write her story.

Mick Brown, offered professional editing skills, support and encouragement. The fluency of the book is due to the time he took to read each chapter and discuss the edits.

Anila Pema Zangmo met me at the Institute in Delhi after thirty years.

Mrs Goodie Oberoi (now deceased) consented to an interview while lying ill in bed.

Lama Shenpen Hookham explored the state of tukdam.

Michele Martin translated the history of Tilokpur Nunnery.

Ani Damcho (Diana Finnegan) arranged the use of photos from the KTD Archives.

Stories from Lama Surya Das, Allen Penny, Sheila Fugard, Frank Miller, Ward Holmes, Mary Jane Bennett, Dale Brozosky, Sierra Zephyr, Ani Gilda Taylor, Jim Robinson, Benny Friis Gunno, Didi Contractor, Monisha Mukandan, Ani Wankchuk Palmo, Anderson

Bakewell, Diana Duncan, Angie Ball, and Seerat Rajendra make the book unique and personal.

The venerable scholar Professor Lokesh Chandra gave an overview of Freda's life and her place in the political and cultural movements of her time.

Tamara Hill sent scans, recordings, and a story and helped in contacting Achi Tsepal. Chester Wood responded immediately with invaluable scans.

Jeanne Riordan of Shambhala Archives was patient and skillful in finding photos.

Amanda Ingram, archivist at St Hugh's College Oxford provided a significant group photo with Freda, and invaluable scans. She also arranged for a guide, David Hodges, on my visit to St Hugh's. I am deeply grateful to both for their generosity of spirit.

Pat Murphy kindly put me in touch with Nick Salt and accompanied me to Derby, Wales, and Oxford.

Nick Salt let me copy his invaluable tape recordings of Freda when she was interviewed by his mother, Olive; and Marion Partington, his partner, kindly hosted us at their home.

Katia Holmes gave huge encouragement and loyalty.

Gita Pandit introduced me to Ranga Bedi.

Louise Marchant and the Buddhist Society gave their photos and encouragement.

Inbal Levi's tarot readings were insightful and accurate.

Artur Skura, the project manager of Shang Shung Publications, was impeccable throughout, and Nancy Simmons, the Senior English Editor, was dedicated and thorough. My thanks to the entire production team at Shang Shung.

I would like to offer heartfelt gratitude to the Dzogchen master Chögyal Namkhai Norbu who willingly agreed to the publication of Freda's story.